The Encyclopaedia Of Scottish Cricket

Written & Compiled by

David W. Potter

Manchester
EMPIRE PUBLICATIONS

EMPIRE PUBLICATIONS LTD
62 Charles Street, Manchester M1 7DF

© David W. Potter 1999

ISBN 1-901746-07-0

Typeset by
Michael Hubbard
Printed in Great Britain
by MFP Design & Print
Longford Trading Estate
Thomas Street
Stretford
Manchester M32 0JT

"Nobody will deny that cricket is the most boring of all games. I am that nobody"

R.H.E. Chisholm

Acknowledgements

I would like to acknowledge my gratitude to the following:

Strathmore C.C. – for whom I scored (in the scorebox rather than in the middle) as a boy

Kirkcaldy C.C. – (sadly no more) for whose 2nd XI I played briefly and badly

Glenrothes High School pupils of many years who responded so well to the rudiments of the game imparted by their imperfect coach

The Umpires with whom I have shared so many Saturdays and Sundays and with none of whom do I remember having an angry word

Scottish Cricket Union for all the help they have freely offered me in preparing this book

The Secretaries of all the Clubs and Institutions who have been so kind to give me all their details

Andy Searle and the team at Empire Publications for seeing the manuscript through to book form

Foreword

It is often said, to my annoyance, that cricket is not a Scottish game. This book is an attempt to prove that statement wrong. It is true that we sometimes suffer from our climate, our lack of population, our class structure and our national obsession with football, but this is to do less than justice to the many of us for whom cricket is our first love.

This book, by its very nature, is idiosyncratic and eclectic. Grave injustices will have been done to people who have been omitted. No doubt errors will have been made and not spotted. Great achievements will have been minimised or eschewed, and trivial ones magnified and sanctified. For all this I apologise, and hope that no lasting offence has been caused.

It is certainly true that intelligence is required to understand and appreciate this most subtle and intricate of games. Cricket requires depth of character as well - it needs people who can accept reverses and come back, people who have to work at ironing out faults, people who are able to share laughter and tears. Fortunately this country is blessed with loads of such people.

To those who have only a passing interest in the game, I say "Pass no more". Go to your local club – there is bound to be one within a reasonable distance – make yourself known. Like me, you may well find that sheer lack of ability and now advancing years makes playing the game a less than desirable idea. Worry not. A job will be found for you as an Umpire, perhaps, or a Scorer. Even if it is to be your lot in life to do little more than prop up the bar, you will be welcome at a cricket club. Enjoy the game.

A

ABBOT ALE CUP – a British based trophy – one of only two competed for by Scottish teams, the Village Cup being the other. It is a 45 Over a Side tournament played for on a Sunday. The Scottish section has been played for since 1977. No Scottish side has ever done particularly well in the British context, although Grange reached the Quarter Finals in 1998. Aberdeenshire in three successive years, 1979, 1980 and 1981 reached the Quarter Finals of this trophy (then sponsored by John Haig), and each time they lost to Scarborough, twice at the lovely North Marine Road in Scarborough and once at Mannofield. Sadly, with so many other competitions on the go on a Sunday, the Abbot Ale Cup has tended to assume less importance.

An example of the sort of thing that can happen can be detailed in the adventures of Dumfries, who in 1997 won the Scottish section. Round One saw them against Selkirk who called off and conceded the tie. Grange were next due down to Nunholm on a Sunday when the weather was clearly better in Edinburgh than in Dumfries. Grange did not accept Dumfries's assessment of how bad conditions were and travelled south-westward to discover that conditions were indeed very wet and that a bowl out was the only solution. Prolonged discussions took place about whether it was one stump or three stumps, etc, but at the end of it all Dumfries won 1-0, a score that sounds more like one registered by their football equivalents, Queen of the South.

The mighty Grange thus conquered, Dumfries then travelled to Edinburgh to play the equally mighty Heriots. Except Heriots were not all that mighty that day, for they were also committed to the Scottish Cup and had to split forces. Dumfries triumphed 238-5 to 147-7.

Thus, with two mighty Edinburgh scalps dangling from their belts, the Doonhammers found themselves in the Semi Final of the Scottish section against a third Edinburgh giant, this time Watsonians. This Sunday, however, Myreside did indeed resemble a myre and Dumfries accepted Watsonians' postponement. Events now took a bizarre turn, for the toss of the coin rule was invoked. Only problem was that the coin to be tossed was at Lord's, Dumfries were in Dumfries and Watsonians were in Edinburgh. It could only be done by telephone. Quite what happened on the three way phone link we do not know, but Dumfries called correctly and were now in the Scottish Final.

Could anyone now stop these mighty men? Well, next stop was Greenock. The Glenpark men were struggling at 52-4 when the rain came on (well, it always does at Greenock, they say, don't they?) and the game had to be abandoned in favour of a bowl out. Dumfries had previously shown a great deal of expertise in this respect, and this time the score read Morton 1 Queen of the South 3, as it were.

Dumfries had now won the Scottish section of the Abbot Ale, and hopes were extremely high that the British section could be won, and possibly after that they could go on to beat the Australian and West Indian champs. Sadly, it was not to be. Dumfries made the comparatively short (for them) trip to Newcastle to play Benwell Hill, the winners of the North East Division. The Geordies made 271 for 9, and then the rain came down. A revised target of 201 in 32 Overs was set, and Dumfries could only make 139 for 6.

Thus ended one of the oddest stories in Dumfries's history. But the record books will say that they were the winners of the Scottish section of the Abbot Ale Cup for 1997, and no-one can take that away from them.

ABERDEENSHIRE – 19 times winners of the Scottish Counties Championship, Aberdeenshire are quite clearly one of the consistently best Scottish cricketing teams. Their success has been owed to their ability to choose a good professional e.g. Schofield Haigh, Alma Hunt, Nigel Hazel and also the strength of the Aberdeenshire Grades Leagues, which has ensured a constant supply of local talent. They have now played at Mannofield for over 100 years. Their glory days were in the immediate aftermath of the Second World War when they won four Championships in a row, and many a veteran will testify to the large crowds and enthusiasm for the game in these days. 10,000 people for example were reputed to have attended Bradman's last game on British soil in September 1948.

Aberdeenshire – the second winners of the Scotish County Championship in 1903

Cricket had been played in Aberdeen in the 1840s and 1850s, and on a famous occasion in July 1849, an Aberdeen team played Arbroath at Montrose, providing great custom for the railway company who could offer special excursions on the still fairly new method of transport. The game was ruined by rain, but so successful was the venture in Montrose that nearby Brechin felt moved to start a cricket team!

A team of Aberdonian cricketers made many such trips, including in 1852 a venture to the North Inch in Perth where they were so heavily defeated that the scribe in a local newspaper was moved to write

"We trust our players will profit by the lesson and advice here given them, and at once adopt the overhand style of bowling, so that they might have a chance at no distant date of getting into the right direction for their opponents' wickets"

It is not clear however to what extent these intrepid, if occasionally ill-advised. Aberdonians saw themselves as a club. The foundation of the club, as we know it, is dated from the time that a team called Aberdeen Cricket Club was formed in April 1857 and played their first game in July of that year. Some might argue however that the real foundation of the club came ten years later when they changed their name to Aberdeenshire and moved to a new home called the Holburn Ground. But this was quite clearly a continuation of the team founded ten years earlier by James Forbes Lumsden, and the change of name was merely an attempt to identify itself with the North Eastern hinterland.

Highlights of the club's stay at Holburn included a visit by W.G. Grace in 1873, and a remarkable game against Arbroath in 1868 in which Aberdeenshire were dismissed for 19, and then skittled Arbroath for 2! It was however a two-innings game, and Arbroath managed to hold out for a draw!

In the late 1880s Holburn was given up and Mannofield opened on May 9th 1890. Shortly afterwards the arrival of a Yorkshire professional called Schofield Haigh saw great progress being made by the club. In 1902 they were one of the five founder members of the Scottish Counties Championship (along with Fifeshire, Forfarshire, Stirling County and Perthshire). Aberdeenshire played the inaugural match at Bonvil Park, Cupar against Fifeshire. Because Aberdeenshire had fine players like W. Webster and R.G. Tait (both of whom were capped for Scotland) the Championship was won three times before the First World War.

Twice in the immediate aftermath of the First World War the Championship was won (1921 and 1922) but not again until the 1940s, apart from 1931 when they shared the title with Fifeshire. In the early 1920s they employed the famous South African googly bowler A.E.E. Vogler as their professional, although for a spell they were not allowed to play him in County Championship matches. In 1934 however they broke new ground for a Scottish club by employing a Bermudan called Alma Hunt as their professional. Hunt scored 7948 runs and took 590 wickets. He endeared himself to the Aberdeen public until 1947, particularly in the first post War season of 1946 when, under veteran captain Sandy Catto,

Professional and Captain of Aberdeenshire in 1947 – Alma Hunt & A S (Sandy) Catto

Aberdeenshire won the Championship to the delight of the cricket starved Aberdonians.

The success continued until 1949, and it was hardly surprising with fine players like George Youngson, Ronnie Chisholm and Hunt's successor Nigel Hazel in the team. But when Hazel left to go to Strathmore, the team went into a decline and the Championship was not regained until 1975. This was done under the guidance of David Brown who was also a Scottish cap, and from 1975 until the end of the Scottish Counties Championship in 1995, Aberdeenshire won it another 8 times including three in a row from 1986-1988, during which time the left arm spin of Dallas Moir was very effective before he went to Derbyshire. They also won the Scottish Cup in 1986 and 1996.

In 1998 Aberdeenshire did well to qualify for Division One of the Scottish National Cricket League, but tarnished their reputation somewhat by their antics on the last Saturday of the season. Having themselves already qualified for 1999's Division One, they gave the impression of not trying too hard against Greenock by doing strange things like reversing their batting order. Greenock duly took full advantage of this light-hearted approach and defeated the "Dons" very heavily. This allowed Greenock to qualify for Division One, but teams like Prestwick and Freuchie were unhappy about this, and Prestwick in particular lodged an appeal. Aberdeenshire were censured for this, and given a suspended sentence of 15 points, not enough to lose them their First Division status.

Clearly, Aberdeenshire are one of the most successful teams in Scottish cricket, and attempts are now being made to update the facilities at Mannofield and develop more youngsters for the game.

ABERDEENSHIRE CRICKET ASSOCIATION – founded in 1884 to provide competitive cricket for the many teams which played the game in the area. There is an excellent history of their activities published on their centenary in 1984 written by D.A.C. Miller of the St. Ronald Club, one of the original members. In this excellent and well-researched booklet, one of the fascinating things to emerge is the amount of teams who are sadly now defunct. For example, there were teams called Kittybrewster Mechanics, the Royal Lunatic Asylum and Telegraphists, although my favourite would have to be Trawlers and Traders.

This Association continues to do sterling work in this part of Scotland where it is claimed that more people per head of population are involved in cricket than are in places like Yorkshire, Sussex and Kent. In recent years, some of their teams have "defected" to other competitions, notably Stoneywood-Dyce who are in the First Division of the Scottish National Cricket League for 1999 and Inverurie who now play in the Strathmore Union, but the Leagues continue in strength.

ACADEMY C.C. – an Aberdeenshire Grade team who won the Bon Accord Cup in 1980, 13 years after their founding in 1967.

ADVERTISING – it is a sad fact that Scottish cricket does not advertise itself very well. Very seldom, so seldom in fact that one could almost say "never" does one see in a pub or a public library a poster advertising a forthcoming cricket match in a particular town or village. Similarly, in local newspapers one often has to look very hard to see who the local team is playing on Saturday.

A particular example of a missed opportunity is often found in the various midweek limited over games that are played throughout the country. These games are often very exciting and are "consumer-friendly" in the sense that one does not have to be a connoisseur of cricket to enjoy a close finish. Very often those of the "cricket is boring" persuasion have had to swallow their pride on such occasions if they happen to be passing as the game reaches a climax. Yet these games often pass without a whimper of advertising, and one only knows of their existence after they have gone.

In the 1950s, cricket advertised itself far better. Clearly it is now the received wisdom that such putting up of posters would not attract a large harvest of spectators and interest. Yet we should remember the principle of the bathyscope in marine archaeology. We will only get a beam back if we send one down first.

AITCHISON, Rev. James (1920-1994) – generally regarded as the finest Scottish batsman since the Second World War. He played 50 first class matches for Scotland between 1946 (his debut being against the touring Indians at Myreside in May 1946 when he scored 59 and was the only Scottish batsman to show any resistance to some brilliant Indian spin bowling) and 1963. He scored 3,669 runs at an average of 32.77 and 7 centuries. His best innings is generally considered to be his 100 against the likes of Lindwall and Miller at the end of the 1956 tour at Hamilton Crescent, Glasgow. He might well have turned professional with an English County but opted instead to stay in the pulpit. He was a minister in both Edinburgh and Glasgow, and retired in 1986. Being a man of fine Christian spirit he was able to cope with the comments that opponents made about him being "blessed" after seeing him dropped in the slips, or after a confident lbw appeal was turned down.

Ronnie Chisholm tells the story of how one day Aitchison was getting the better of Worcestershire's fine spinner Roly Jenkins. The Reverend was indeed batting well, but also enjoying more than a little good luck when some of his drives fell just out of reach of Jenkins' boundary fielders. At the end of one over, Jenkins approached Aitchison and said "They tell me you're a minister". Aitchie nodded. "Well, with your bloody luck you will soon be the Archbishop of Canterbury". Aitchie forbore to tell him that Archbishops and the Church of Scotland did not really go well together!

At club level, he excelled for Kilmarnock, Grange and Carlton.

ALLAN GLEN'S – team who play in North Glasgow and are now an amalgamation of the School F.P. team, Bishopbriggs and Hyndland. They play at the Allan Glen's Sports club in Bishopbriggs and participate in Division One of the Western Union.

ALLINGHAM, Mike – (Heriot's F.P. and Scotland), a tall fair-haired all-rounder. Mike has played for Scotland 42 times since 1991, his best score being 64 not out against Transvaal Under 23s in 1992. With the ball, he bowls fast medium, and he also plays rugby, golf and squash. He is a teacher at Fettes College.

ALMOND VALLEY – a team who play at Druid's Park, Murthly, Perthshire. They play mainly friendlies, but the day may not be too far away when they re-join the Perthshire League. They already play in a midweek League and they have many young players, including one who is sufficiently committed to the club to travel every week from the south side of Glasgow.

They are an excellent example of a resurrection. They were the first winners of the Perthshire League in 1963 and won it again in 1965 playing at the "Cricket Pitch" at Almondbank on the west side of Perth. But they fell on bad times and went out of business some time in the mid 1970s.

This seemed to be the end of the matter, but a few dedicated men like Sandy Fyfe, Adam Christie, Alan Wright and John Taylor brought the club back in 1989, even though it was only for a limited amount of friendlies. They also had to move ground and now play at Druid's Park within the grounds of the former mental hospital called the Murthly Institution. The highlight of the season is the Annual Invitational Tournament with four teams playing each other in Semi Finals and a Final in a 15 Over thrash.

The emphasis in this club is on the social side and tours have been organized to places like Innellan and Campbeltown. It is gratifying to hear that the closure of a club doesn't always have to be a permanent one, and we hope that Almond Valley will soon once again become a permanent feature of the Perthshire League.

ALVA – a now defunct team who used to play in the East of Scotland League. They played on a public park in Alva with a lovely view of the Hill.

ANCHOR – a Paisley team, sadly now defunct since the late 70s. They were a team composed of employees of J. and P. Coats, which derived its name from "Anchor" thread. They played their games at Blackhall in Paisley and were very strong in the 1960s, being able to maintain a position in the First Division of the Glasgow and District League with the help of talented cricketers like Kenny Ferguson, Douglas Muir, David Orr and Barrie Walters. Sadly, as is the way of the world, the team all aged simultaneously. A lack of adequate youngsters to replace them meant that the team began to drop through the divisions of the Glasgow and District League in the late 1970s, and to the regret of many in the Paisley area, the team folded.

ANCHORIANS – an Aberdeenshire Grades side made up of ex-members of the Boys Brigade, as their name might suggest. They were founded in 1933 and have no great record of success. They play at a ground called North Seaton, which does indeed have a lovely view of the North Sea.

ANDERSON, W. – a famous Fifeshire bowler who played 25 times for Scotland between 1922 and 1937, and was one of the mainstays of Fifeshire's success in the 1930s. On one famous occasion in 1932, he took all ten Clackmannan wickets for 27 runs, and that included two hat-tricks!

APPLECROSS ALLSTARS

APPLECROSS ALLSTARS – this team play the very occasional game of cricket. They are based on the mainland opposite Skye, so their opportunities to play are somewhat limited. In 1997, when according to their own reckoning they had won only one game in eight years and were quite happy to list themselves as the worst team in Britain, they invited Mike Atherton to play a game for them. Atherton had just come back from leading England on a fairly disastrous tour of South Africa and Zimbabwe, and the thinking presumably was that if the Allstars were the worst team in Britain, England could reasonably be described as the second worst. No record exists of whether Atherton saw the funny side of this, but certainly his debut for Applecross has yet to take place.

ARBROATH – have been called Arbroath United, although at one point they ludicrously called themselves Arbroath County when they played in the Scottish County Championship. They have played at their ground Lochlands since May 14th 1887 when they drew with Perthshire, but have been in existence since 1840 and possibly as early as the mid 1820s. If they were indeed around in the 1820s they were the first of the extant teams in the Angus area to be founded, and their very presence was a stimulus to the rest. Indeed they were only one of three teams in the town of Arbroath itself, the other two being called Arbroath Albert and Arbroath Albion. On one famous occasion in 1868 at Holburn, Aberdeen, they managed to get themselves dismissed for 2!

Their ground on the west side of Arbroath is well appointed with a large pavilion. They are a pleasant, friendly club who now play in the Scottish National Cricket League Division 2 in 1999. Previously they had been in the Scottish County Championship, which they won in 1989 and 1993. Before that they had been founder members since 1929 of the Strathmore Union which they first won in 1934. Since the War they have won it in 1959, 1973, 1978 and 1979 and four times in the 1980s. In 1995 they became the first winners of the SCU Cup, a trophy for teams who did not quite qualify for the Scottish Cup. In 1998, Arbroath XI who play in the Strathmore Union had a guest player on one occasion – one Derek Randall, the famous England Test player of the late 1970s and early 1980s. This was apparently Derek's way of saying sorry for letting the club down over an invitation to speak at their Dinner.

Arbroath also have a team in the Second Division of the Strathmore Union, and participate in the Under 17, 15 and 13 leagues. There is also a Kwik Cricket section, so the future of cricket in the town of the Red Lichties looks bright. Their scorer is the polymath Ian Chisholm, doing a job that he has now done for many decades. Another attraction of Arbroath is the teas, which are lavish and plentiful.

Famous players in the past include M.R. Dickson (opening bat and capped ten times for Scotland between the years 1909 and 1913) Davie Storrier (who also played full back for Celtic at the turn of last century), Neil Burnett, Chris Plomer, George Salmond, Omar Henry and Clarence Parfitt of more recent vintage and of course the great R.W. Sievwright (q.v.) founder of the family dynasty.

AREA CHAMPIONSHIP – a tournament last played for in 1997 and discontinued without any great amount of tears being shed. It began life in 1975 as the Inter-District Championship and the idea was it would be a good testing ground for potential Scottish "caps", given the fact that in the mid-1970s League cricket was regionalised and there was little opportunity for the best of the West to play the best of the East and North. The games were played on a Sunday.

The tournament enjoyed a certain amount of status and prestige for a while, but one of the problems was that the West always seemed to win. In 1988, the tournament was re-vamped with the West being split into Strathclyde West and Strathclyde East and an extra team called Central being introduced. From the early 1990s onward, it became increasingly clear that the tournament was struggling, as fewer and fewer players seemed willing to play a competitive game on a Saturday, then a glorified friendly on a Sunday for a vague geographical concept like Strathclyde East with which it was not easy to identify. "Injuries" and "family commitments" lead to call-offs with on several occasions one of the Districts having to declare themselves unable to field a team.

In any case, by the mid 1990s, the now vibrant Scottish Cup (supplemented by the Scottish Cricket Union Cup for those who did not qualify for the Scottish Cup) and the advent of the Scottish League obviated the need for this tournament in that there now was a clearly defined national standard of attainment for clubs and players. For the record the last winners in 1997 were Edinburgh.

On the plus side there are still excellent Under 19, Under 17 and Under 16 Tournaments organised on a District Level.

ARTISANS – now play at Harlaw in Aberdeen, although they have played at a variety of grounds. They owe their name to the fact that they were founded in 1948 by craftsmen employed in Aberdeen Town Council's Works Department. They play in the Aberdeenshire Grades. In 1969 they won Grade 1. Among many loyal servants, Henry Rennie and Ian Cumming deserve a mention for commitment and service to the club. Henry won the Grades wicket-keeping award in 1955, 1966 and 1975, and Ian has played regularly for over 40 years, many of them as skipper.

ASIM BUTT – (Heriot's and Scotland) Asim was born in Lahore but is qualified to play for Scotland (and has done so 15 times) after years of playing for Corstorphine, R.H.S.M and Heriot's. He is a left arm bowler with an ability to bring the ball back prodigiously. He won the Man of the Match Award in the Benson and Hedges Cup game against Yorkshire in 1998.

AUSTRALIA

AUSTRALIA – Most Australian tours to the British Isles have included a game against Scotland, usually played at Hamilton Crescent, or Grange or (famously in 1948) Mannofield. Although Australia have tended to play their fringe players, they have usually been good enough to outclass Scotland in the 30 games they have played, unless rain has intervened. Once, only once, can a Scottish side claim to have beaten Australia and even then there were extenuating circumstances. It happened in 1882 at the Grange. There had been a three day game scheduled, but Australia won it easily in two days. The Australians then agreed to play a one day game on the third day. Scotland batted first and scored a respectable 167 for 7, with captain Leslie Balfour-Melville scoring 73. Australia then reversed their normal batting order, giving every impression of desiring to entertain the public rather than win the game, and collapsed to 122 all out. It would be nice to think that they danced in the streets of Stockbridge that night to celebrate a famous victory, but there is no evidence of such revelry.

A couple of years previously in 1880 Scotland had availed themselves of the services of two England Test players Ivo Bligh and A.G. Steel, but still lost. These two aristocratic dilettantes were actually on a hunting and fishing holiday in Perthshire when they heard that there was to be a game between "18 of Scotland" and Australia. They offered their services. Their offer was gratefully accepted, but when it was discovered that it was a "real" match of 11 v. 11, discretion became the better part of valour and they tried to withdraw. But the Scottish authorities held them to their promise, and they played. Not entirely unpredictably, the hammering duly occurred in spite of the presence of the two Englishmen.

Further evidence of the "Mickey Mouse" nature of such contests comes almost a hundred years later on 23rd July 1981 at Titwood when Scotland needed 11 runs off the last over to beat an Australian side, apparently demoralised after their Botham mauling at Headingley a few days previously. Rod Marsh, the wicket keeper and acting captain came on to bowl and bowled three men for a duck!

Yet there was one occasion in 1912 at the North Inch, Perth when Scotland declared before lunch on the third day and set the Australians 264 to win. To the intense disappointment of the large Scottish crowd, the Aussies, who included Warren Bardsley and Charles Macartney in their line up, decided to put up the shutters and finished at 200 for 3.

AYR – a progressive team who in 1996 won the Western Union Championship and then promptly withdrew unilaterally and joined the Scottish Cricket League, probably compelling the other Western teams to enter negotiations for entry a year later. At about the same time they decided to move across the road from Cambusdoon to a fine new ground called Robertson's Field, symbolizing the desire to move forwards, and credit is due to President Norman Simpson, whose sons carry on the family tradition of playing for the club. A current Internationalist is Bruce Patterson, a fine opening batsman and off spin bowler and their most famous "old boy" is of course Mike Denness, to date the only Scotsman to become captain of England.

Their new ground is about half a mile away from Burns' Cottage, and they were founded in 1859, some hundred years after the great man's birth. Their first recorded game was on June 18th 1859, a match confidently predicted by the Ayr Advertiser the previous week: "We believe that a match at (sic) cricket will come off next Saturday". The match took place on the Low Green against the exotically named Kilmarnock Morning, whom Ayr dismissed for 20 and 17 (and a lot of them were extras!), and scored 175 themselves with their captain de Lacey scoring Ayr's first half century.

A month later, when Ayr were due to play Glasgow Caledonian at Low Green, a farmer whose cows grazed there arrived, damaged the wicket and threatened to cut the ropes of the marquee that had been erected. The farmer was bribed to go home and the game proceeded. Another of their early problems was finding opposition, although there were some rival local teams including one calling itself Ayr Burns.

Like many clubs, they struggled in the early days to find a home for themselves. Their grounds have included Low Green, Beresford Park, Northfield Park, Dam Park before they moved to Cambusdoon in 1936, where they stayed for 60 years. They joined the Western Union in 1909, and under a fine captain called T.C. Dunlop and, with good players like W.R. Drinnen and a professional called Harry Turner, won the Championship in seasons 1912 and 1913. Ayr then went on a tour of Belgium (the highlight being one occasion when they actually had lunch on the battlefield of Waterloo!). In 1914 they unluckily lost out in the Western Union to Uddingston late in the season when the First World War was already under way.

Ayr Cricket Club 1st XI – Western District Cricket Union Champions 1912

AYRSHIRE

The 1920s and 1930s were comparatively lean years for Ayr, although they did have some good players like I.G. Collins, A.F.M. Morton, I.T. Parker and W.R. Drinnen who won caps for Scotland. Never again was the Western Union won until well after the Second World War when, with Mike Denness on board, they won it in 1960 and 1961. More barren years intervened until they were once more successful in 1994 (with professional Marty Haywood outstanding) and 1996.

Arguably their greatest ever player was Hunter Cosh, who was almost an ever-present in the Scottish International team in the 1950s, winning 42 caps in all and becoming captain of Scotland in 1956. Cosh never scored a century for Scotland, and must surely be one of the most unlucky players in Scottish history in this regard, for at Buxton on 2nd June 1954, in a game against Derbyshire after what Wisden records as "forceful hitting" and "two 6s and ten 4s in a stay of 109 minutes", the luckless Cosh was run out for 99! In the second innings he was bowled for a duck.

It was Cosh's determined captaincy of Ayr, allied to his fine batting along with that of the young Mike Denness, that was to a large extent responsible for the re-building of Ayr's fortunes towards the end of the 1950s.

AYRSHIRE – a team who competed in the Scottish Counties Championship, albeit with no great success until 1990 and 1991. They are now called Prestwick (q.v.) and compete in the Scottish National Cricket League.

B

BALFOUR – MELVILLE, L.M (1854-1937) the first President of the revised Scottish Cricket Union in 1909. In his playing career he had won 16 Caps for Scotland (latterly as captain) between 1874 and 1893 and was a fine batsman and wicket-keeper for Grange. His most famous innings was in 1882 when he scored 73 for Scotland against the "Demon" Australian F.R. Spofforth. Incredibly in 1909 and 1910 he was recalled to play for Scotland when he was well into his 50s.

He also had been invited to play for I Zingari and M.C.C. and, in addition to cricket, he played for Scotland at Rugby, and won the Scottish Championships at Golf, Tennis and Billiards. Somewhat of an all rounder! His son James, also a Scottish Cap, was killed in the First World War in 1915.

L M Balfour-Melville

BALL – most Leagues specify a particular type of ball to be used in their competition. An innings is begun with a new ball. The newer a ball the lighter it is and therefore the more easily it moves in the air and off the pitch in the hands of a fast bowler. When the ball becomes older and heavier and more worn, the spinners can use it to more advantage. So at least goes the theory. In fact, the determining factor is the intelligence and skill of the player.

Youngsters (and their mothers) often express concern about the hardness of the cricket ball, and the potential dangers involved. There is a point in all this, but accidents and injuries on the field with a cricket ball are mercifully rare, and often the direct result of some irresponsible or reckless behaviour. Nowadays in junior games there are restrictions on the positioning of fielders close to the bat.

Understandably however some boys are reluctant to play with a real ball, preferring to stick with a soft ball. They must be gently led away from this, for it is only with a hard ball that a bowler can "do things".

BALMORAL

BALMORAL – no connection with Royal Deeside, other than in their name, Balmoral play in the city of Aberdeen in the Aberdeenshire Grades. They were founded in 1900 and won Grade One in 1940 but, apart from that, there has been no great sustained success on the field.

BANCHORY – founded in 1860 and began playing at Burnett Park in 1889. They played in the Deeside and District League until the Second World War. In 1956 they joined the Aberdeenshire Grades and have been members ever since. They built a new pavilion in 1985.

BANFF – a young team founded in 1980 who entered the Aberdeenshire Grades the following year.

BAR – an indispensable part of some clubs' finances. It is usually the takings from the bar that pay for the professional and, as a general rule (although there are many exceptions), a team with a bar also has a professional. Licensing laws normally demand "signing in" of non-members etc., but these are frequently and blatantly flouted. At one point, those with a moral conscience in this nation used to worry about the effect on youngsters of what they see in the bar, but in the past two or three decades there has been a general easing of the traditional Scottish Presbyterian attitude towards alcohol.

BARCLAY, Bert – Honorary Secretary of the Scottish Cricket Union for over 20 years, Bert has been an able administrator of the game.

BARNES, S.F. – (1873 -1967) famous spin bowler for Warwickshire, Lancashire and England who, through his friendship with Dr. N.L. Stevenson of Carlton, used to play a few games for Carlton in the early 1920s. Although Barnes was about 50 and well past his prime, huge crowds used to flock to Grange Loan to see him play.

BARRIE, J.M. – (1860 – 1937) otherwise known as "the dreamer of Thrums", the creator of Peter Pan was an avid cricket fan. Born in Kirriemuir in 1860, he soon developed an affiliation for the local team, for whom he became a "marker" as the job of scorer was then known. When he made his name as a playwright, he went to London and there met the 1902 Australian touring team including the famous Joe Darling who had just won the Old Trafford Test. It is believed that the heroine of "Peter Pan" was called Wendy Darling after the famous Australian.

How ironic it is that the following beautiful description of an English rural cricket match was written by this prolific Scotsman;

> *A rural cricket match in buttercup time, seen and heard through the trees; it is surely the loveliest scene in England and the most disarming sound. From the ranks of the unseen dead for ever passing along our country lanes on their eternal journey, the*

Photo courtesy of Tom King of Dundee

Sir J M Barrie tossing the coin at Kirriemuir June 7th 1930. The game is between Barrie's Select XI The "Allahakbarries" and West of Scotland.

Englishmen fall out for a moment to look over the gate of the cricket field and smile.

It was Barrie who donated the pavilion on the Hill at Kirriemuir, and this was officially opened on June 7th 1930 before a game between West of Scotland and Barrie's own team called the Allahakbarries, which included two Australian Test players in C.G. Macartney and A.A.Mailey. This occasion was attended by almost all of Angus and the Glens including loads of unemployed jute workers who walked from Forfar, Brechin and Dundee to see the great Macartney.

Yet Barrie was not universally popular in Kirriemuir. Some of his "Kailyard" writings about Scottish towns were ill-disguised attacks on the small minded people of Kirriemuir and Forfar and, although he donated the pavilion, he gave very little for its upkeep. In addition, his attitude towards children was misinterpreted in an age which was far less tolerant than this one towards matters of sexuality. Never was there a better example of the Biblical tag "A prophet is without honour in his home town".

But he was a great fan and friend of cricket. His team, the Allahakbarries went round both Scotland and England playing charity matches and were financed entirely out of J.M. Barrie's pocket.

BAT – the necessary piece of equipment, often sadly and ridiculously overpriced. Most players aspire to use their own, but a good club will have a large collection. Probably no make of bat is better than any other and, in any case, it is the use to which it is put that determines its real value. A common misapprehension by youngsters is that the bat must be wielded vigorously. Not so! The important aspect is timing.

BEHAVIOUR

BEHAVIOUR – it is often regretted that the behaviour of present day Scottish cricketers leaves a lot to be desired. Often this is said in a spirit of nostalgia, prefixed or suffixed by statements like "In my day..." One suspects that there is a certain amount of wilful self-delusion among those who talk like this, for cricketers of long ago no doubt had their weaknesses as well.

All this does not of course excuse or justify some of the excesses that are currently seen on a Scottish field. Foul language, dissent, verbal intimidation of batsmen are sadly all present. The Umpires, of course, are empowered to report perpetrators of such boorish conduct, and the authorities can take action in the form of warnings and suspensions against those found guilty.

What is harder to pin down however is the bad behaviour that does not reach those blatant levels. I refer to the comments from one member of a fielding team to another but loud enough for the batsman to hear like "He doesn't want to be here" or "He simply doesn't have the talent", or for the Umpire's benefit, an encouragement to a bowler along the lines of "Hit the stumps. It's the only way you're going to get a wicket".

There is also the sullen refusal to shake hands at the end of a game, the ignoring of the opposition in the bar and the deliberate delay in paying the Umpire. Such conduct is to be pitied and laughed at rather than umbrage to be taken at it, but it is extremely hurtful and unnecessary. The simple fact is that some people simply should not play cricket because they do not have the necessary strength of character to cope with disappointments. Cricket of course mirrors life in that any player will from time to time receive a blow, an unfair blow, an unjust blow. A man can take it on the chin and carry on. A child will throw the rattle out of the pram. And the painful part of it all is that sometimes the finger of accusation must be pointed at men who have worn or are currently wearing a Scotland jersey.

The question must be asked of some people, "Why do you play a game that you obviously hate?" Clearly in many cases it is to make up for some personality defect or some problem, perhaps financial, perhaps marital, perhaps relating to one's job. One of the great things about cricket is that it does, for a few hours at least, take you away from such problems. But for a game of cricket to take place, you need an opposition and you need Umpires. Bad behaviour can only antagonise both.

It would be nice to dream of a world in which good play by an opponent could be appreciated, the Umpire's decision would be unquestionably accepted and everyone could have a nice drink with the opposition afterwards. This would not mean that the game would be in any way less competitive. All it would mean is that it would be recognized as a game, and the greatest and most loved game of them all.

BENAUD, R. (1930 –) doyen of B.B.C. commentators and of course a fine Test player in his own right. His best tour of Britain was in 1961, and the Scottish crowd saw him at his best at Grange's ground at Raeburn Place on September

12th and 13th. The game was drawn, but Benaud's leg spin took 7 for 53, then he scored 77 before being run out, perhaps a casualty of Grange's undulating outfield which often makes it impossible to follow the ball all the way to the boundary.

BERWICK – play at Pier Field, Berwick and current Champions of the Border League. They are technically in England but, like their footballing counterparts, associate themselves with Scotland. They were founded in 1844 and compete in the Border League. They had never won this competition until 1998 but several times have been good enough to win a place in the Scottish Cup.

Their best season in the Scottish Cup was 1994, the year of their 150th anniversary, when they amazed quite a few people by winning their group which contained Ayr, Ferguslie and Edinburgh Accies and then going down in spite of a century by Tim McCreath to the eventual winners Forfarshire in a high scoring quarter final at Forthill.

They were formed on 28th June 1844, and a few weeks later the Berwickshire Advertiser announces that:

> Cricket – A club has been formed in the town for pursuing this popular amusement. There are, we understand, fifty members entered, and they have secured for their purpose that piece of ground near the Cowport-gate used as a tank during winter, upon which some improvements are being made for their convenience.

If the word "tank" in Victorian English means a reservoir (and it is difficult to see what else it could mean) we must hope that the pitch was a wheen drier in the summer! The earliest recorded game is a two innings game at Newcastle against Northumberland 2nd XI in 1852. In 1856 there is an account of Berwick v. Kelso, which must be one of the longest lasting continuous fixtures in Scottish cricket history, and it is from one of these fixtures that a story comes about disgraceful aristocratic behaviour. Kelso's Lord Haddington was being accused by spectators of illegal bowling because "his arm was higher than his shoulder". Berwick's batsman W. Mather dissociated himself from this because the bowling was easy, but Lord Haddington took umbrage and walked off. On came the Marquis of Bowmont, who had been one of the objectors to Haddington's action, and immediately he decided to bowl. This is contrary to all laws of cricket, but nobody could object to people with money!

From the 1880s onwards, the ranks of Berwick cricketers were swelled by soldiers of the King's Own Scottish Borderers who were stationed in the town, but it is difficult to gauge how good Berwick were because they did not play in any League until 1985. It is clear that the 1990s have seen great advances for the club who have been blessed with some fine professionals. In 1994, they celebrated their sesquicentenary, and produced a fine brochure of their club's interesting history, which included a short-lived Ladies' section in the 1970s.

BIRD, H.D.

BIRD, H.D. (1933 –) the famous Test Match Umpire has stood several times in Scotland. On one occasion, in a Benson and Hedges Cup game at the North Inch, Perth in May 1984, he and John Holder managed to have two tea intervals! Previously the regulations for this tournament were that tea was to be had after 25 Overs of the team batting second, but for 1984 it was after 35 Overs. Dickie forgot about the change in rules and took the teams off after 25 Overs. While having tea, he was reminded of the change in the rule. He accepted this and apologized. Then in attempt to right the wrong, he took them out for another 10 Overs, then brought them off again! The players and the crowd were bemused by all this, as was the loudspeaker operator who said "Aye, they sure do like their tea, these English lads." The serious side was that the Scotland team chasing Yorkshire's 231 lost momentum twice and lost by 45 runs. It is difficult to avoid the conclusion that a less flamboyant and more careful Umpire, although capable of the original error, would not have compounded the felony.

BISHOPBRIGGS – a Glasgow team, founded in 1884 who have now amalgamated with Allan Glens.

BIZARRE – Scottish cricket is full of unusual occurrences, some of them mentioned in other entries on these pages. Some almost defy belief, like the time a batsman came out in a East of Scotland League game with headphones on, all prepared to bat and listen to how his favourite football team were doing at the same time. Fortunately, his colleague was also his captain and told him sternly to give his headset to the Umpire but not before finding out that Hearts were a goal up.

Once at Carlton in 1997, the Umpires were grateful for the rain for saving cricket from national ridicule. The opponents were Arbroath. At 1.00 p.m. the Angus men had only three members, the others (as it later transpired) held up in a horrendous traffic jam on the Edinburgh By-pass. None of the remaining eight had a mobile phone to inform Carlton of what had happened, so the toss took place, Arbroath's acting captain won it, and after a consultation with his other two men, decided to field! This astonished those present, but the thinking was that if they batted, the team could be all out by the time the others arrived.

Presumably, Carlton would have given them some substitutes, but in any case the rain arrived preventing a start of play. By this time, although there was genuine concern for the other 8 Arbroath players, Carlton made it quite clear that whenever the rain stopped, they would, quite rightly, insist on the start of play. Fortunately for the credibility of Scottish cricket, the rain continued and at about 1.30 p.m. a car load of embarrassed and angry Arbroath men arrived to swell their team to seven. By the time that the rest of the team reached Grange Loan, the rain had intensified, the game had officially been called off, and the "freak show" cricket did not happen.

Sometimes scoring can be a little unusual. In a Small Clubs Cup game between Kinloch and Renfrew, a Kinloch batsman scored a 7. He skied one to the outfield, but hit the ball so high that the batsman had crossed for their third run by the time the ball came down to the waiting fieldsman. The hapless fielder dropped the ball, and was so disgusted with himself that he tried to kick the ball back. Sadly all he could do was lob it over the boundary line, and the net result was that the batsman who should have been caught earned 7 runs.

At a game between Stonehaven Thistle and Laurencekirk in the 1930s, a batsman was given out l.b.w. when the ball hit his chest. A strange decision, it would seem, but the Umpire was dead right, for his chest was on the ground at the time! The Stonehaven batsman had obviously had a wild night the night before and had taken more than a few hairs of the dog which bit him to cure the hangover. He had a terrible job getting his pads on, staggered out to the wicket, had to be pointed in the right direction and, as the ball was bowled, he lost his balance. His chest was right in front as the ball hit him. The Umpire duly raised his finger, and the batsman was carried off, "out" in several senses of the word.

A bizarre dismissal occurred one day when Almond Valley were on tour in Campbeltown. Mick Niven of Almond Valley played exclusively on the off side and could hit a ball mightily. Campbeltown's captain posted a fielder (unprotected) at silly mid off. Mr. Niven's brother, who happened to be Umpiring at the time, suggested tactfully that this was not a wise field position for this batsmen. The advice was ignored. The first ball was a wideish long hop outside off stump. Mick smote mightily, the fielder was hit on the head and the ball looped gently to the gully fielder. The fielder recovered and Mick trudged off, the victim of a brilliant piece of team fielding. At least, it would have been brilliant if it had been intended. It recalls the times when Brian Close of Yorkshire and Somerset who was at one point manager of Scotland, used to field at silly mid on, his bald pate glistening in the sun. Not only did Close disdain all helmets, he actually said to his slip fielders "Be ready for the rebounds!"

BLACKBURN, Hector – one of the great characters of Scottish cricket, Hector was a much loved and respected Umpire who died in 1995. His last big game was the Scotland v. West Indies game of that year.

He was a kind man, but stories of his inability to suffer fools gladly went the rounds. In one game when a fielder appealed for an l.b.w from cover point, Hector walked slowly across to the man, put his arm round him, looked at the wicket and said "Aye, right enough, from here, it looks as if he might have been out".

BLAIN, J.A.R.

On another occasion in a game between two English public schools at the Loretto Festival in Musselburgh, Hector was faced by a flamboyant appealer who shouted loudly with arms flaying. The gentleman tried Hector four times in the one Over. The first was answered with "Not Out", the second with a little stronger "Not Out", the third one a little stronger yet with irritation now apparent and the fourth with "Away and f—!"

BLAIN, J.A.R. (1979 –) John, who now plays for Northamptonshire, was the youngest ever player to be capped for Scotland for 106 years when he played his first International in 1996.

Steve Crawley of West Lothian and Grange bowls as umpire, the late Hector Blackburn, looks on.

He was brought up in Penicuik, but it was Heriot's F.P. with whom he was playing when he was given a two year contract with Northamptonshire. He turned his back on a promising football career to do so, as he was signed by Falkirk F.C. John has now earned 18 Scottish caps.

BODDAM – a small village just south of Peterhead which has had a cricket team called Boddam Victoria since 1878. They played in the Buchan League and the Peterhead and District Churches League before joining the Aberdeenshire Grades in 1936.

BONE, D. – author of "Fifty Years of Scottish Cricket" published in 1898, a highly entertaining if occasionally fanciful account of last century's cricket history. On 20th February 1895, for example, Glasgow Wanderers played Vale of Leven Wanderers on a frozen Loch Lomond. At another game in Kirkintilloch, the Umpire's concentration was disturbed by the presence of a few "village wenches". Well worth a read, but not to be taken too seriously!

BOROUGHMUIR – an East of Scotland League team, who have been around since 1921 when they were founded for former pupils of Boroughmuir School. Initially they played only friendly cricket, and the club folded temporarily in the mid 1960s, but resurrected itself in 1971. In 1983 they joined the East of Scotland League. Their golden spell was between 1993 and 1995 when, in successive seasons under the captaincy of the excellent Joe Telfer, they were promoted from Division 3 to Division 1.

Boroughmuir have struggled in recent years, not least because of the unhelpful attitude of Edinburgh Corporation. Their pitch at Meggetland in the Colinton district of Edinburgh, which has been their home since 1921, was widely regarded as unsatisfactory and dangerous, and after a game was abandoned in 1996 because the Umpire and both teams considered it unsafe, the team moved temporarily to Riccarton. They have now returned to Meggetland, but sadly there has been no great improvement in playing standards as they were relegated from Division One in 1998. Nor was the pitch always to everyone's satisfaction and several games towards the end of the season had to be relocated. It will be a good quiz question in years to come however "What have Sabina Park, Jamaica and Meggetland, Edinburgh got in common?" Answer – both places have had games abandoned because of an unsuitable pitch! It is to hoped however that a total redevelopment of facilities at Meggetland may be on the cards as we approach the millennium.

Spirits however remain high and Boroughmuir contain several weel kent faces on the Edinburgh scene, notably Robin Welsh, who has served the club for almost 25 years, and there are also Chris Sprott, Alex Lamb, George Thomson, Dave Templeton, Richard and Paul Pegg and Jimmy "the Hoover" Rutherford who have served the club well.

BON ACCORD – there is now an Aberdeen side called P.O. Bon Accord, which has no apparent connection with the one which had its floruit in the mid 1880s, round about the time of the founding of the Aberdeenshire Cricket Association.

It is possible that this team may have played a somewhat ignominious role in the early history of football as well. Football record books will tell that the record score in a football match was on 12th September 1885 when Arbroath beat Aberdeen Bon Accord 36-0 in the First Round of the Scottish Cup. Those who joke about this and say "it was a cricket score" may be closer to the mark than what they think. There is a certain amount of evidence to suggest that when Arbroath wrote to Bon Accord's secretary offering him a financial inducement if Bon Accord would waive home advantage, the letter was sent to the secretary of the cricket club, not the football club. The secretary thought that this was strange as no fixture had to his knowledge been arranged so late in the season, but accepted the suggestion. Bon Accord travelled down, and rather than go home again without any sport at all, agreed to play a game of football. In fairness, it must be pointed out that the real football team might not have done much better, for the development of football in Aberdeen trailed far behind that of cricket. On the same day Aberdeen Rovers lost 35-0 to the crack Dundee Harp.

BOORISHNESS – there can be little doubt that some cricketers experience a character metamorphosis as they step on the field of play. Conversation seems to come to a halt, and monosyllabic grunts are the order of the day. Bad words are sometimes spoken, however, and directed at no-one in particular. The jersey given to the Umpire is snatched back with a grunt rather than a "Thank You". When the captain suggests ever so gently that if he were to pitch the ball up a little more, he would be less likely to be hit for 4, the suggestion is apparently ignored, except for another grunt.

One is somewhat surprised to learn that the gentleman concerned may have a job off the field like a hotel manager, a public relations officer or even a speech therapist. For such people, cricket seems to be his Saturday revenge on the rest of the week.

BOREDOM – the charge most often laid at the head of cricket by those who no little about it. Sadly, it has to be admitted that the charge is not always without foundation, and the points structure of some Leagues does not do enough sometimes to encourage positive attacking play. There are times when the bowling is ordinary, the batting dull, the fielding pedestrian and the captaincy uninspiring. Even when the cricket is good, there are times when one side or other simply has to dig in for a spell. But the charm of the game is surely that it can change suddenly and irrationally.

BOUNCER – one of the few good aspects of Scotland's predominantly wet climate is that it makes the bowling of bouncers very difficult. Some people, notably the Kerry Packer Circus of the late 1970s in Australia, which did so much harm to the game, think that it is a great tourist attraction to see batsmen having to fend off short pitched bowling. This is arrant nonsense, for cricket is a game of skill and there really is no place for such brutality in the game. But because of Scotland's damp pitches, it is seldom an issue here.

There was one famous occasion in 1956 when Keith Miller tried to bounce Jimmy Aitchison, ironically enough on a damp pitch at Hamilton Crescent. It was the end of a long tour during which the Australians had lost the Ashes and they gave every sign of not taking the game seriously. Rain delayed play, but when it did start and Aitchison came in with Scotland at 30 for 1, Miller decided to bounce him. The bounce was so slow that Aitchison theatrically ducked and the ball sailed harmlessly past. "Nugget" (as Miller was nicknamed), tried again, Aitchison hooked him for 6, "Nugget" tried a third time and Aitchison belted him once more, the ball bouncing back off the spectators' seats. At the end of the over Miller, who was acting captain, took himself off, and Aitchison went on to score the first century for Scotland against the Australians since 1921.

BOWL-OUT – cricket's answer to football's penalty shoot out. Players from each side take it in turns to bowl at an unguarded set of stumps. This must be used to provide a winner when bad weather prevents the proper game. Of course it is unsatisfactory, but there are times when there is no alternative, given Scotland's weather. Grange, for example, were eliminated from the 1998 Abbot Ale Trophy by this method and Prestwick won the Scottish Counties Cup in similar fashion.

BOX – the necessary abdominal protector for batsmen, wicket keepers and close in fielders. Although often a source of much mirth when someone is hit by a cricket ball in the nether regions, those of us who have had such an experience will confirm that it is no joke. A box is therefore absolutely essential for any player.

Don Bradman leaves the field at Mannofield in September 1948, having scored 123 not out. This was his last innings in Britain.

BRADMAN, D.G. – (1908 –) very few people are aware that Sir Donald's last innings on British soil was at Mannofield, Aberdeen on September 17th and 18th 1948. Wisden tells us that "before a record crowd of 10,000 Bradman marked his last game in Britain with a brilliant innings which included seventeen 4's and two 6's." He was cheered to the echo as he reached 123 not out in 80 minutes. McCool also scored a century and the Australians won by an innings and 87 runs. Bradman himself always liked Scotland and was known to have a few days off in Scotland during one or other of his four tours to the British Isles. He also came to Scotland to recuperate from his life threatening illness and operation in the autumn of 1934.

BRECHIN – a very old club, founded in 1849, who have played in the Strathmore Union since its inception in 1929. In fact they won the Competition in the first five years of its existence, and again in 1937 (shared) and 1956. After a brief spell in the ascendancy in the mid 1970s, they have tended to drop away, but still play very competitively producing Scottish Internationalists like Kevin Thomson. Their ground is called Guthrie Park, the lease of which has caused them some problems

*Brechin C.C. 1884 – By the looks of things, cricket was a serious
business in Angus in these days! Macartney, (back row centre) is as
close a lookalike of W. G. Grace as you are likely to get!*

in the recent past. It is one of the best grounds in the country with a nice pavilion
and a scorebox built in the 1960s which was away ahead of its time.

There is an excellent book on the early days of Cricket in Brechin called
"The Annals of Brechin Cricket" by Alfred O'Neil which gives a detailed and
methodical account of the Brechin clubs (for there were others like the Volunteers,
East Mill, Lower Tenements, the Trades Union and Y.M.C.A) from the foundation
in 1849 until 1927. It appears Brechin were founded in 1849 as a direct result of
the popularity of a game at Montrose between Arbroath and Aberdeen, a fixture
well attended by Brechiners who enjoyed the novelty of travelling on the recently
arrived railway.

The first game was played at Kinnaird Castle on 8th June 1850 between
Kinnaird and Brechin C.C., and Brechin's first ground was Trinity Muir, a mile
out of town. Practice was at 6.30 a.m. and members would be fined for failing to
attend. Practice at such a time is not surprising in view of the fact that quite a lot
of "peep o'day" cricket seems to have been played in Angus in these days, the
idea being that the game would be over before workers went to their job. Yet this
practice, if true, would have done much to prevent jute factory workers from
playing the game, for the jute mills of Brechin (as evil as their Dundee counterparts
if less numerous) would have insisted on a 6.00 a.m. start, six days a week. Perhaps
in the 1850s and 1860s the jute industry would not yet have arrived in Brechin,
however.

There seems to have been a great deal of cricket played in Brechin in the Victorian era, but a perpetual problem in finding a permanent home. Bearshill, Viewbank and Cookston were all used for a while, until Nursery Park was acquired in 1892. At about this time, Brechin were considered to be one of the finest teams in Scotland, holding their own against Carlton, Grange, Perthshire and Aberdeenshire. They had many fine players including the Ferrier family, no fewer than 6 of whom played for the club, but the best ever was perhaps J.W. Sorrie who later moved to Carlton and was capped 12 times for Scotland between 1912 and 1924.

The First World War brought an end to Nursery Park, for the ground was required for the war effort and never regained. Alfred O'Neil talks poignantly of the last game played there on August 1st 1914 against Montrose where "there was something in the atmosphere which suggested that more weighty matters than cricket were in men's thoughts. As soon as the only decision possible had been come to (by the British Government) three days later, every club was affected, as one after another of the players responded to the military call. The remaining fixtures were cancelled."

Brechin, like many small towns, suffered grievously in the War and lack of manpower would have made it difficult to resume even if the ground had still been available. One or two sporadic fixtures were played in the early 1920s, but it was only when Guthrie Park was officially opened in 1924 that cricket really began again in the town. In 1926 Brechin and Y.M.C.A. amalgamated, and Brechin C.C. became once again one of the best in the country. With players like Bob Laing and Davie Chapman, it was no surprise that Brechin dominated the early years of the Strathmore Union, winning it in the first five years of its inception from 1929 to 1934.

Since the Second World War, the team have tended to do less well. They have had fine players, notably professional Geoff Wilkins and fast bowler Stuart Wilson, who was capped 20 times for Scotland between 1957 and 1964, but have never as a team emulated their excellence of the pre-War era. Apart from a brief spell in the mid 1970s, they have gradually lost the Angus battle to Arbroath and Strathmore. But cricket is well established in this small Angus town with a long history of the game. Considering the smallness of the town and the proximity of Scottish League teams like Aberdeenshire, Strathmore, Arbroath and Forfarshire, Brechin do very well "to keep the show on the road" as their excellent Secretary Gordon Morton (himself no mean player in the 1970s) says.

BRINKLEY, James – (Essex and Scotland) James is qualified to play for Scotland because he was born in Helensburgh, although he learned most of his cricket in Australia. He played 19 times for Scotland in season 1998. Before joining Essex, he was five seasons with Worcestershire.

BROWN, Douglas

BROWN, Douglas – one of Scotland's successful exports to England. Douglas learned his trade with Clackmannanshire, winning 5 caps for Scotland in the process, and now plays for Warwickshire, and has even played one day Internationals for England.

BROWN, James – (Perthshire and Scotland) – won 85 caps for Scotland (many of them as captain) between 1953 and 1973, and was responsible for 159 dismissals, including 7 in the one game against Ireland in 1957. He took 674 dismissals for Perthshire, and, under his guidance, Perthshire throughout the 1950s and 1960s were never far away from the County Championship.

BRUNSWICK – now defunct but founded in 1830, Brunswick were the oldest team in Edinburgh. They played on Bruntsfield Links and the Meadows as they never had a permanent home of their own. Their function in latter days seemed very much to be that of a "nursery" for young players, and they prided themselves from their earliest days of being "artisans". They provided a welcome opportunity for young men of a not particularly rich background to learn how to play cricket. As early as June 1831 they played a game against a Glasgow side for £25, an early example of the rich rewards of professionalism. They won the game and the large purse by scoring 106 "notches" for 2 wickets, as distinct from the Glasgow team's total of 104 "notches".

BUCKIE – play at Linzee Gordon Park. Their foundation is uncertain, but the earliest records are in 1882. Recent years have seen their best performances in their history in that they won the Small Clubs Cup in 1995 and 1997. They have also been consistent performers in the North of Scotland League, winning it in 1993 and 1994 and being runners up another five times in the 1990s, including 1998. Prior to this decade, they had been joint League Champions in 1973 and runners up in 1948. They are quite clearly a team with ambition, and much of what they have achieved is due to the efforts of Bill Flett, who excels with the bat, behind the stumps and with his administrative expertise as Secretary.

In their early years, Buckie played only friendly games but in 1910 played in the Banffshire Cricket League for a year before moving to the Morayshire Junior League. They still competed however in the Banffshire Cup, called the Herd Challenge Cup and indeed won it by defeating Fochabers in the Final at Keith.

After the First World War, they opened their present home in 1924, although it was known as the Cluny Public Park until 1935, when it was changed to the Linzee Gordon Park. In 1927 they joined the North of Scotland Cricket Association, and with the help of players like George Coutts and Alex Smith remained a respectable team, albeit with no great playing success, for over 50 years. They had, for example, the misfortune to lose in the Final of the Knock Out Tournament to Northern Counties on three separate occasions in 1949, 1950 and 1972.

Parallel to their League successes in the 1990s have been four successive Knock Out Cup triumphs from 1992 -1995 and a Cup Final defeat in 1997. Their greatest successes however have been the Small Clubs Cup triumphs of 1995 and 1997.

But they do not seem to wish to stay a small club. In 1998, they raised £75,000 to build a lovely new pavilion and they now are able to run a second XI. An ambitious team, well organized and structured, who deserve our plaudits for enhancing the game of cricket in this nice part of Scotland.

BURNTISLAND – a Fife team sadly now defunct. Their early days are wrapped in obscurity, but they played at Links Park until the mid 1950s, then moved to East Toll Park until the late 1960s when they could no longer carry on. They played in the Forth Valley League and the Fife League without having done particularly well in either. Notable achievements include the 10 wickets taken by George McGaughay against Kennoway and Windygates, another Fife team which is sadly no longer with us.

BUTE COUNTY – a team who deserve commendation for keeping the game alive on the island of Bute. They are possibly the only (or certainly one of the very few) island teams in Scotland. They are based at a ground called The Meadows in Rothesay and play in the Strathclyde Cricket League, using a fishing boat as a method of transport to fulfil some fixtures, a point highlighted by a full page in the "Sunday Times" on one occasion.

Bute County were formed in 1898 by naval personnel and local gentry. There are still scorebooks with many games played against visiting naval ships, including for example H.M.S. Britannia. The local Academy was the epicentre of the club sustaining cricket in this unlikely part of the world until 1963 when the club went defunct in spite of the efforts of people like R. MacIntyre, the current President of the club. Thanks to the efforts of MacIntyre and others and recruitment from the local pub teams, the club was re-launched in 1987, wearing the colours of Yorkshire C.C.

Indeed they are a cosmopolitan bunch who have been served by Pakistanis, Kenyans, New Zealanders, Australians (one of whom was a woman), Irishmen, Welshmen and Englishmen as well as the indigenous population. They have not featured prominently among the winners of the Strathclyde Cricket League, nor the Small Clubs Cup, but they deserve a great deal of credit for keeping the game alive in difficult geographical circumstances.

C

CAIRNDOW – possibly the youngest club in Scotland, in what seems to be a mini growth area of Argyll. They were founded in 1996, the original intention being to play one fixture to assist with fund raising activities for the refurbishment of Cairndow Village Hall, but a second fixture was played that summer against a team called St. Catherine's. In 1997 and 1998 they managed to play about six or eight fixtures per season against teams like Innellan, Carradale, and Mid-Argyll. They are now an integral part of Cairndow Village Hall and Recreation Club. They play enthusiastically and sociably, if occasionally lacking the finesse of more established clubs, and play their games at Clachan Farm, watched by a large crowd, sadly most of them sheep. Cairndow face problems of lack of members and of course the almost perpetual Argyll rain, but they are to be commended and encouraged, and some day we may see a team like this winning the Small Clubs Cup.

CALEDONIAN – there have been two Aberdeen teams of this name, but this one was founded in 1969 by ex-members of the YMCA club and the staff of the Rowett Research Institute.

CARLTON – founded in 1863, Carlton are one of the oldest clubs in the country, and certainly one of the best documented. Their foundation however was very much an after-thought. Four young men had been expelled from the Y.M.C.A for

Carlton CC 1st XI 1897

arranging a dramatic performance which did not please the establishment of the said organization. The four men then formed a Literary and Debating Society, which kept them occupied during the winter, and for the summer formed a cricket club as well, and according to Robert H. Christie's early history of the club "...the promoters, being very Tory, named it the Carlton Cricket Club, after the Carlton Club in London".

They play at a place called Grange Loan (not to be confused with Grange C.C.) on the south side of Edinburgh. Grange Loan has a distinctive slope, and is a lovely ground, surrounded by trees and desirable properties, although the pavilion does seem to be a little inadequate for modern needs. The ground has been described as *rus in urbe* – the countryside in the city. They have played there since May 17th 1905, their previous ground being called Old Grange Loan.

The club are well served by histories, the best being "Play" published in 1946 and written by Dr. N.L. Stevenson, a player and captain of the club, a man described by one club member as the Scottish equivalent of W.G. Grace (both in character and playing ability). Carlton had an undeserved reputation for exclusiveness, but tried hard, according to Dr. Stevenson, to lose this tag, including, for example, the provision of free teas for all spectators in the early 1920s in what Dr. Stevenson describes as the "Tea Offensive". They also worked hard to bring cricket to other parts of Scotland, both under the name of Crustaceans and sometimes under the name of Carlton itself, going on tour to places like Deeside, and all detailed for us in sundry books written by the prolific Doctor.

One of the best and most poignant cricket books is written about Carlton under the name of *Carlton Redivivus*, redivivus meaning "restored to life" and much used by early Christians about Jesus and indeed Nero who was meant to be Satan redivivus. This small and delightful book tells us about Carlton's first few games after the First World War.

Great players in the past have included Scottish Internationalists like G.W. Jupp and J.W. Sorrie. Their best season in recent years was 1988 when they won both the East of Scotland League and the Masterton Trophy, a trophy which they have lifted on three occasions in the 1990s. Currently they have an outstanding Scottish Internationalist opening bat in Bryn Lockie and play in the First Division of the 1999 Scottish National Cricket League.

Their motto is *"Tu ne cede malis"*, meaning "Do not give in to evil", a fitting motto for such a long-standing and resilient club.

CARRUTHERS, Chris – a formidable figure who has done a great deal for Scottish cricket for many years. He is a teacher of Classics at Fettes College, and is a respected Umpire. He has been Chairman of the S.C.U. and was a Selector in the early 1990's. He has also been manager of the Under 19's Scotland team, which has included taking the youngsters abroad. He has played a crucial role in the development of Scottish cricket.

"Wha Daur Meddle Wi Me?"
The formidable Chris Carruthers

CASTINGS – a now defunct Falkirk team, founded in 1899 and originally confined to workers in the Falkirk Iron Company. Their early years saw them have a somewhat nomadic existence but, in 1922 they moved to a place called Thornbank.

CENTURY – what every batsman aspires to making. The difference between 99 and 100 is a vast one in cricketing terms, although in truth, most club batsman never make 99 more than once in their careers! 78 Centuries have been scored for Scotland and, in an average season, about 160 batsmen can expect to have a place in next year's Scottish Cricket Guide for reaching a ton. The record number of centuries is 56 scored by Rev. Jimmy Aitchison in his lengthy career for Carlton, Grange and Kilmarnock.

CHEATING – it would be a brave man who would say that cheating does not occur in Scottish cricket, but it would perhaps be sensationalist to claim that it is widespread. Allegations of cheating in, for example, tampering with the ball are often made but seldom substantiated and it is difficult to see how any organized cheating can actually take place on the field of play. Occasionally, a fielder will claim a catch when he knows that the ball touched the ground, and might fool the Umpire, but he also knows that the opposition will retaliate when it comes to their turn.

Perhaps there is more cheating off the field in the playing of illegal players or the employment of some "amateurs" who are not what they claim to be. Pitches may be doctored to suit one particular bowler but then again that plan would have to depend on the captain winning the toss.

It is so often a grey area to define what cheating is. The batsman who does not "walk" when he knows he is out and is supported by "his" Umpire (i.e. a member of his own side) is a despicable creature but, if the Laws of the game are strictly applied, he is in fact doing nothing wrong.

Very often, one finds that some professionals will actually draw the line at cheating, however hard they play the game. One recalls a game in which the Australian professional shouted at the Umpire, was warned for dissent, sledged the batsman, argued with his own captain, mouthed obscenities at his fielders who dropped catches and generally lived down to the Australian stereotype. At a crucial stage of the game, the ball came to him in the gully at or about ground level. His fielders appealed, the Umpire hesitated, the batsman began to walk when suddenly the Aussie threw the ball on the ground and said "Didn't carry!" When looked at quizzically by his team mates he said "Foul tempered Ozzie bastard I may be, cheat I am not". To say that everyone suddenly warmed to him would perhaps be an exaggeration, but he did earn their respect.

CHISHOLM, R.H.E. – (1927 –) an opening batsman whose career lasted an extraordinary length at the highest level in Scotland. His Scotland career comprised 80 caps, the first in 1948 and the last in 1971 (including captaining Scotland v.

M.C.C. at Lord's in 1960), scoring 3175 runs (including a century), second only to the Rev. J. Aitchison. His best batting performances were in 1953 when he scored 55 not out, 43 and 41 against the Australians captained by Lindsay Hassett.

He was also a more than useful leg break and googly bowler, capturing 44 International wickets, and over 1,000 wickets for the various elevens he played for during his career, including the East of Scotland XI in representative matches against the other geographical districts. His best bowling performances were 5 for 57 for Scotland v. M.C.C. at Lord's and 4 for 21 against Warwickshire, both in the 1960s. At club level his bowling, alliteratively described by Douglas Barr as "f— ing, flighted filth" was responsible for the downfall of many batsman who simply could not read him, notably in 1960 when he captured 4 Grange wickets in 4 balls in an East League game when playing for Melville College F.P.

In his lengthy playing career which went on into the 1990s, Ron played for Gordonians, Aberdeenshire, Melville College, Stewart's F.P., then the merged Stewart-Melville, scoring a grand total of 15,870 runs. He was always a fine ambassador for the game and encourager of younger players, especially those who passed through his hands at Daniel Stewart's and Melville College.

CLACKMANNAN – founded in 1868 and traditionally known as the "Wee County" when they played in the Scottish County Championship which they won in 1924 and 1960. They play at a delightful ground called "The Arns" just to the west of Alloa, where they have been based since 1890, although they played in Alloa itself before then, firstly near the recently refurbished Alloa Tower which was used as a pavilion, and then between 1887 and 1890 at Bellevue. The move to the Arns was thanks to the courtesy of Lord Mar & Kellie.

The first recorded match was against Stirling County in 1868, but we know that an Alloa Cricket Club played and beat a team called the Oriental Club of Stirling in June 1863. They joined the Scottish County Championship in 1905 and, like many other clubs, suffered terribly in the Great War during which 29 members of Clackmannan County Cricket Club paid the supreme sacrifice. Their names are inscribed on a simple plaque in the clubhouse with the inscription, "They Played the Game".

Happier times came in 1924 when the Wee County won the Championship, thanks to the impressive bowling of N.M. Halley, who took 43 wickets during the season at a cost of 8.39 each (including 6 for 7 against Fifeshire) and A. West, who took 63 but slightly more expensively at 11.27. The 1924 season was remarkable for good weather and large crowds and a most unusual tie in the game against Perthshire. Perthshire were chasing 117 to win and reached 116 for 7 to level the scores and then lost their last three wickets without further score. In addition to the success in 1924, Clackmannan also won the title in 1960 and have come close on several other occasions, notably the years immediately after their triumph in 1960.

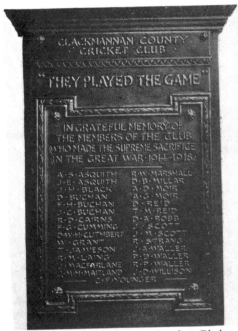

*Clackmannan County Cricket Club
War Memorial*

In recent years they have found life difficult. In 1993 they were once dismissed for 12 all out by Strathmore (not a record, for Linlithgow dismissed them for 9 in 1890!) and in 1997 they were relegated from the Scottish League in spite of the valiant efforts of professional Haravinder Sodhi. They now play in the East of Scotland League, from which they were unable to escape in 1998. A visit to "The Arns" however is one of Scottish cricket's more pleasant experiences, for the scenery is outstanding and the teas exceptional. Their scorer is Len Bell, a knowledgeable and informative character, who is now approaching his 80th birthday and one of the grand old men of Scottish cricket. He has the distinction of having played for the club in 5 decades (one more than the legendary Freddie Titmus of Middlesex) in that he started playing for them in 1947, and as late as 1995 played in a friendly match, batting low down the order.

Famous players over the years have included Harry Bolton, the professional from 1894 to 1897, an early example of a player taking all 10 wickets in an innings, against Heriot's F.P. in Edinburgh; T.A. Bowie was capped 6 times for Scotland and played between 1891 and 1934; the tragic C.F. Younger, who won one cap against South Africa in 1912 and perished in the First World War, and between the wars Mark Wilson and H.A. McLeish won Scottish caps. A.M. Dowell was three times capped for Scotland in the 1950s, and of course in recent years, there has been Dougie Brown, who was capped for Scotland in 1989 before his move to Warwickshire and England honours. Bryn Lockie of Carlton and Scotland started life with Clackmannan, and there has also been the Cousin family, notably father Alan who was of course a member of the Dundee F.C. team the only time they ever won the League in 1962.

They are a team with a noteworthy past and a tremendous sense of history, as was proved when in September 1985 they celebrated in period costume the bicentenary of the first ever recorded Scottish cricket game played at Schawpark, Alloa between the Earl Cathcart's XI and the Hon. Col. Talbot's XI. It is sad to see this grand club, traditionally known as "The Wee County", no longer in the top echelons, but it is hard to believe that glory days will not some day return to the Arns.

The Cathcart Family Group who played such an important role in the first recorded Scottish game on 3rd September 1785.

CLASS – a ticklish and sensitive issue, but one which must be addressed. Sadly it is the opinion of too many Scottish people (and occasionally some who are educated enough to know better) that cricket is the prerogative of the rich and the leisured. At its crudest this is seen when a bunch of not very bright young men happen to be passing Leith Links, for example, during the progress of a game and start to shout things like "Snobs" or "Poofs". They are usually careful to be well out of reach of the big Australian fast bowler when they shout such remarks, and one should always be careful not to get angry at ignorance, but such remarks are often sad and hurtful.

There are several reasons for this erroneous assumption. In the first place, it is certainly true that historically cricket owed a lot to the patronage of the aristocracy, who gave the cricket club a piece of land on their ground or their "policies". This did in fact necessitate more than a little "cap in hand" "forelock touching" behaviour from the lower orders. Another reason is the prevalence of fee paying schools and their former pupils teams who play the game in the big city areas, particularly Edinburgh, and the comparative dearth of local authority schools who do so. Yet another is the cost of the game. Equipment is grossly overpriced, as any spring catalogue will indicate, and subscriptions and match fees are none too cheap either, far too expensive for quite a lot of people, and crucially a lot more expensive than the cost for a young lad of playing football.

This disparity in wealth also happens at club, as well as individual level. A club to continue in existence must have funds. Funds are required to pay for groundsmen, professionals, rates, sightscreens, equipment and general upkeep. Some of this can come from a successful bar, but the rest needs to come from subscriptions, unless the club is lucky enough to have a few legacies or enjoy the benefits of aristocratic patronage.

There are sociological reasons as well for the apparent preponderance of the bourgeoisie. One is the media presentation of the game. Scottish cricket, more or less, does not exist on TV, and frankly is far too subtle and sophisticated a game to lend itself to the tabloids, unless of course there is some controversy involving violence or umpire-slagging which does not really help the game at all. Thus the high proportion of the Scottish public who read nothing other than the tabloid press, read virtually nothing positive about the game, being compelled even in the middle of June and July to read some inane drivel about the latest fictitious transfer gossip and the "I only ever wanted to play for Celtic/Rangers" sort of cant.

In this respect, it has to be said that Scottish society to a certain extent mirrors that of England. Simplistically (but remember it is the simplistic and superficial level that is presented to the public by the media) cricket is played by rich people around London, even richer people in places like Hampshire, Sussex and Somerset where there is sometimes a hint of aristocracy, and it is only in the tough, raw Northern counties of Yorkshire and Lancashire that the lower orders play the game. Now, as Yorkshire people tend superficially on television, to play up to their stereotype of being arrogant, selfish and boorish, the Scottish working people cannot relate to them any more than they could to the Peter May/ Mike Brearley upper class toff. Scotland thus lacks a positive role model in England.

This is of course a gross over-simplification, and those of us in the game can see that. But can the average Scottish person who has no previous pre-disposition towards the game see that?

And there is the schools factor. Since the tragic teacher dispute of the middle 1980s a whole generation of boys has turned into men with little or no practical experience of playing cricket. The dispute affected the local authority sector particularly badly, for in most cases schools cricket which was suspended during the dispute never started again.

CLYDESDALE

Yet to say that Scottish cricket is class-ridden is emphatically not true. In rural Scotland, class divisions are certainly not evident. Freuchie and Strathmore, to name but two, are excellent examples of that. Aberdeenshire and the Aberdeenshire Grades have seldom been accused of any sort of class bias and, even in the big cities, old school ties and the "Members Only" type of exclusiveness, although not entirely absent, are less pervasive than they once were. Very few "F.P." clubs are nowadays entirely restricted to those who once attended that school.

Public Parks cricket on a fine summer evening is a perfect social leveller. The Meadows in Edinburgh will often reveal men in ordinary trousers with perhaps a white·shirt and trainers coming out to bat. This is good, for the Meadows are on a bus route and people should have the opportunity to see that Scottish cricket is for everyone. Another excellent example of "working class cricket" (if I may use such a politically incorrect term) may be found in places like Fauldhouse in West Lothian. To describe Fauldhouse as "run-down" is perhaps to state the obvious, for in the 1980s it had to endure the worst of the Thatcher v. Scargill argument about mining in which there has been no winner and many losers. Yet the cricket club Fauldhouse Victoria survives. Not only does it survive in adverse circumstances; it has provided a rallying point for the community.

Something that certainly works in rural areas to break down barriers and to interest more people in cricket is the holding of six-a-side tournaments between local pub teams and even football teams. All this is a good laugh, and the takings at the bar certainly rise on that particular Sunday. It would help if more of the well-established city teams would be prepared to do that sort of thing. It might bring enormous benefits.

Another idea that certainly worked with Carlton in the 1920s was the "Tea Offensive" as Dr. N.L. Stevenson put it whereby all spectators were given their tea. It would have been interesting to see it tried out in the 1930s in an area of high unemployment, but perhaps the class barriers would have been too high.

CLYDESDALE – a famous Glasgow team, formed in 1848 and based at Titwood in Pollokshields, Glasgow since 1876, having played previously at Kinning Park. In 1904, their ground was extended and a new pavilion opened. It is a fine pavilion as well, and the ground is a genuinely a nice urban ground, even though the building of tennis courts and other sports facilities recently have perhaps detracted from its appearances and endangered its International status. Space has had to be taken from the cricket area, but it remains a fine venue. The clubhouse has also been recently redeveloped.

They were founded by Archie Campbell of Hawick as an amalgamation of the Thistle and Wallacegrove clubs. (Thistle had been in action since 1832 and probably earlier – one of their games in 1832 having descended to a riot) Their first recorded game was against "a Greenock XI" (in which they wore green and yellow ribbons on their bowler hats) and on September 16th 1998 they marked their sesquicentenary (150 years) with a game against Greenock, played in Victorian costume.

In 1851 at Kinning Park, they attracted 8,000 to see an International between 22 men of Scotland and 11 of England. The Scotsmen with numerical superiority won, but an interesting statistic was the 20 wickets taken by one John Wisden, who 12 years later would produce the first of his Wisden Cricketers Alamanacks. Wisden was referred to as "the little wonder" in 1851, and seems to have been a fine bowler.

Clydesdale's most notable contribution to Scottish sport, other than cricket, is the football team called Clydesdale who played in the first ever Scottish Cup Final of 1874. Sadly they lost to Queen's Park. They have also played rugby and hockey. In 1875, when they moved from Kinning Park, the Kinning Park ground was taken over by a football team called Rangers.

In 1893 Clydesdale introduced a junior section at the price of 5 shillings (25p), and this junior section has enjoyed continuous existence ever since, producing many fine players for both club and country. 27 Clydesdale players have played for Scotland, the most famous being Terry Racionzer, who played 65 times between 1965 and 1984, and current Internationalists are Greig Williamson, Ian Stanger and Bruce Patterson, although Patterson of course now plays for Ayr. Titwood has played host to countless Scottish Internationals over the years, although recently it has tended to lose out to other venues, notably Grange in Edinburgh, and recent ground changes have made it less likely to be used in the future.

Clydesdale's playing record is second to none. They have been winners of the Scottish Cup on six occasions, and counting shared championships they have been fourteen times champions of the Western Union, doing particularly well in the 1920s, and the 1970s. (1893, the first year of the competition, is still in doubt – Clydesdale claim it was shared with Greenock, whereas Greenock claim to have been the sole winners). Terry Racionzer, writing in the Match Programme for the 150th Anniversary week (sadly ruined by rain) sums up Clydesdale's consistent success during his time by saying, "if you did not come to training, you did not play in the team".

Sadly for Clydesdale, they did not quite make it into Division One of the Scottish National Cricket League for 1999, but they will be an asset to Division 2, and it is hard to imagine them not being in the First Division for long.

COACHING – a successful team will often be so because they have spent long hours in the nets coaching and encouraging youngsters. If they are lucky enough to have a rich crop of talented boys developing simultaneously, they will reap the benefit.

Yet it is sometimes an eye opener to see just how many clubs apparently neglect this side of the game. It should, for example, be a part of the professional's contract that he coaches, say, four hours a week – two with the under 12s one night and another two with the teenagers another night. So many professionals get their money too easily, and show little interest in coaching. An example of how successful coaching can be would be seen in the late 1950's, 1960s and early

COMMONWEALTH GAMES

1970s at Strathmore, Forfar, where Nigel Hazel produced a seemingly never ending stream of talent for the team.

Coaching can be done along the orthodox lines of the MCC Coaching Manual by anyone who knows a little about the game. The coach need not be a great player himself. What certainly matters however is his willingness to spend time and to show an interest in the youngsters. There must be in every club someone who is called the coach. Boys must never be given a bat and ball and told to play themselves. That way the bullies take over, and the younger boys soon become discouraged.

A coach should be encouraging, but not effusive. He must be tactful, yet firm. Above all he must have patience, and he must do it because he enjoys doing it. Unhappy people seldom do their job well, and kids can spot a reluctant coach with the same degree of accuracy that they can a useless teacher at school.

COMMONWEALTH GAMES – Scotland entered the 1998 Commonwealth Games; the first year that cricket had been offered. England didn't, mainly because their season was still in full swing.

The Games took place in Kuala Lumpur. Scotland's first game was a draw against Pakistan on September 9th. Pakistan batted first and scored 201 for 5 from 50 Overs. Scotland were 31 for 3 when the rain came down. Sunday September 12th however saw a huge and disastrous defeat at the hands of New Zealand, a team which Scotland might just have defeated. New Zealand, after losing a few early wickets, reached 278 for 6, and Scotland collapsed to 101 all out. Then two days later, Scotland lost again, this time to Kenya. Scotland reached 156-7, an undemanding total which Kenya reached with the loss of only 5 wickets to bring an end to an ignominious campaign for Scotland, from whom more had been expected.

COMRIE – a team who play at The Laggan, Comrie, a picturesque ground which lies to the east of the village. They were founded in 1906 from a temperance society. In 1998, depopulation compelled Comrie to amalgamate with Crieff for the purpose of entering a team in the Perthshire League, but Comrie still retains its separate identity.

COPLEY, S.H. – (1906 –) professional of Cupar from 1932 – 1938. He took over in mid season following a tragic accident to the previous professional Clowes who was hit in the head by a ball in the nets. Copley was the groundstaff boy who took a famous catch at Trent Bridge in 1930 to dismiss Stan McCabe off the bowling of Maurice Tate.

CORSTORPHINE – a comparatively recently founded team (1957) who play in the Scottish National Cricket League. They play at Union Park in Corstorphine on the west side of Edinburgh. They have not been without their troubles in recent

Pakistan international Shadid Saeed of Corstorphine in action

years. Like some other clubs in Edinburgh, they have suffered because they play on a Corporation pitch which sometimes isn't maintained as well as it ought to be. Vandalism and yobbery have been a problem as well, even on occasion attempts to disrupt a game. They have also had an unhappy knack of attracting controversy and the wrong kind of headlines, notably in their alleged playing of illegal players which prevented their admission to the inaugural Scottish League in 1996, (a charge still hotly disputed by the club) and in 1988 an indiscretion within the club led to the suspension of their professional. They are a pleasant and hospitable club nevertheless.

They were founded in 1957 as Elldee Cricket Club and were the social club of the engineering firm Laidlaw Drew (the same Laidlaw who was Whittle's partner in the development of the jet engine). They joined the East of Scotland League and the now defunct Scottish Midland League, playing their fixtures at Sighthill.

COWAN, David

In the early 1970s when the then Corstorphine team folded, Elldee moved to Union Park and changed their name when they amalgamated with the Corstorphine Rugby Club. In 1997 they did join the Scottish National Cricket League, and will be in Division 3 in 1999, following a none too successful season in 1998's Conference.

Alan Spiers has captained Scotland at Under 16 level, and notable players have included Mike Yellowlees, who is a GB Hockey internationalist, Hearts footballers Norrie Davidson and Henry Smith, and Sky TV presenter Robert McCaffrey. Professionals have included Pakistani Internationalists Shahid Saeed, Akram Raza, Basit Ali and Indian Surender Khanna. In scorer Geoff Allen they possess one of the nicest men in Scottish cricket.

COWAN, David – (1964 –) Freuchie and Scotland. A fine fast bowler and aggressive left handed batsman who has performed particularly well for Freuchie in the Village Trophy. He is a talented football player as well and was once on the books of Raith Rovers. He made his debut for Scotland in 1989 and his best performance was 5 for 45 against the MCC in 1994. He has won 25 Scottish caps, but has been struggling with injuries recently.

CRAMOND – A very new team on the Edinburgh scene. They were formed in autumn 1996, and in their first season played in the East League Division 3 and won promotion to Division 2. Clearly a team to watch for the future.

CRATHIE – an Aberdeenshire Grades team who play their fixtures within the grounds of Balmoral Castle. Their Patron is the Duke of Edinburgh and they were founded in 1948. They also participate in the Village Cup.

CRAWLEY, Steve (Grange and Scotland) – played for Scotland four times in 1995 and again another 11 times in 1998. Steve is an aggressive opening bat and a good slip fielder. He has also played for West Lothian. He was on the Lancashire staff between 1982 and 1984 but never made a great impact.

CRESCENT – the oldest of the city of Aberdeen clubs who still play in the Aberdeenshire Grades. They were founded in 1880, and have the distinction of being the first owners of Pittodrie Park where Aberdeen F.C. now play. When Aberdeen were formed in 1903, part of the deal of buying Pittodrie was that Crescent would still play their games there in the summer months. Sadly, the pitch deteriorated under the constant pounding of footballers and Crescent had to move back to the public parks.

CRIEFF – a fine old club, who play at George V Park, Braidhaugh, Crieff. They were founded in 1853, but sadly very little is now known about their early years because their early records were donated to the authorities as waste paper to be recycled for the war effort in 1939! In the early years friendlies were played against other Perthshire teams, as most villages did have a cricket team, sadly many of them no longer with us. Crieff hit a low point in the early 1930s because of the prevailing economic conditions of the time, something which hit the rural communities of Scotland as hard as it hit the urban ones, and it seems that little cricket was actually played in the 1930s.

But with the end of the war, there came a huge increase in interest in the game. The club was re-activated in 1947 and games took place at Simpson's Field which was part of Duchlage Farm. At that time interest was sufficient to allow the fielding of two elevens. In 1949 they moved to their present home and in 1978 joined forces with the local rugby club in order to construct proper pavilion premises.

In the 1960s, with the arrival of the Perthshire League and the re-emergence of the Perthshire Cup, cricket became more competitive. Crieff won the League on five occasions and shared it once, winning it three years out of four in the early 1990s. They have also done well in the Perthshire Cup, and have on two occasions been the unlucky finalists in the Small Clubs Cup, a competition that they have entered since its inception. On one occasion the great de Silva, when playing for a Sri Lankan under 19 team, was dismissed for a duck by Crieff. Great players of the past have included D.N. Watters (14,337 runs and 912 dismissals behind the stumps), A.W. Sinclair (1210 wickets) and A.T.S. Forster (13,349 runs).

Sadly, Crieff have come upon difficult times of late. A paucity of players resulted in the club having to withdraw from the Perthshire League in 1997, but bravely they have kept going, still playing Sunday cricket. In 1998 they decided to amalgamate with neighbours and rivals Comrie for the purpose of entering the Perthshire League, although both clubs still retain their separate identity. Like many teams from smaller areas of population, Crieff are perhaps going through a phase where the players are simply not there and it is becoming difficult to attract youngsters from local schools such as Morrison's Academy and Crieff High School. Hopefully, it will only be a temporary phase.

CRUSTACEANS – this word in English means animals like crabs which hang around sea shores, but in a cricket context it refers to a team formed in 1933 by Dr. N.L. Stevenson. It was based at Carlton, but included players from other teams and they played what Stevenson benignly but patronisingly calls "missionary" matches, going to mining areas perhaps with no great tradition of cricket and spreading the gospel of the game there.

CULTS – Cults have been around since 1893 and are one of the many strong teams in Aberdeenshire. They play at Allan Park in Cults, where they have been since 1900. Cults can justifiably claim to be the strongest team in the

*Cults Cricket Club 1948 (First and Second Elevens with
Founder Members). Note the unconventional dress of some
players, including the polo neck "goalkeeper" jerseys.*

Aberdeenshire Grades at the moment, for they have won Grade "A" 12 times
out of the last 13 (losing out only to Dyce in 1989), as well as a host of other
local trophies, such as the Aberdeenshire Cup. The question has been asked
if they dominate the Grades as much as all that, why don't they do as Inverurie
and Stoneywood-Dyce have done, and apply for the Strathmore Union?
Apparently, the idea has been floated within the club, but the feeling is that
they might struggle in such exalted company.

At a national level they have won the Small Clubs Cup in 1989,1993 and
1998, becoming the first team to win it three times when they beat Queen's Park at
Forfar on August 9th 1998 by dismissing their opponents for 110, even though
they were four bowlers short. They have frequently been indebted over the years
to Harry Milne for fine performances with both bat and ball and a feature of the
team is that they are a family team with 3 Gillanders, 2 Alexanders, 2 MacDougalls
and 2 Milnes all actively involved. Jerry Gomez, who played for the West Indies
in the 1950s and the 1960s, had two sons Greg and Steve who both played for the
club, Greg in particular being a brilliant batsman who once scored 99 not out at
Ellon in the pouring rain.

CUPAR – formed in 1884, Cupar play at Duffus Park, a pleasant ground in the
west of Cupar. They have been there since their official formation in 1884-5 but
before 1910, Duffus Park was known as Bonvil Park.

1884 could be best described as their re-constitution. Cricket was probably
introduced by English soldiers guarding French prisoners in the town during the
Napoleonic Wars. A cricket club is mentioned in the Fife Herald as being formed
in 1836, and they played at Cart Haugh, a space next to the River Eden to the east

David Bell, captain of Cupar

of the town centre. The club had a somewhat piecemeal existence and were banned from time to time from playing on the Cart Haugh, presumably because of disorderly behaviour. Bonvil Park however was discovered in 1884 and officially opened on 16th May 1885 with a game against Forfarshire.

Great players in the past have included W.G. Innes, D.S. Cooper (who in 1905 hit 207 against Forfarshire at Forthill which is still a club record) and H.L. Stewart. Hugh Stewart, an all-rounder, was capped for Scotland 4 times in the 1930s but was not the first Cupar man to do so as W. O'Brien Lindsay won one cap in 1929. In 1932 their professional Clowes met his death in one of cricket's rare accidents after being hit on the head with a ball at net practice. This tragic occurrence happened on 13th July 1932. He was hit on the back of the head as he bent down to pick up a ball, but apparently recovered and went home, a little shaky but with no other damage. He was found in his bed the next morning.

One of their great characters was wicket keeper/batsman Peter McLaren, who scored 19385 runs in his lengthy career with the club (sixth in the all-time run scoring records), and is currently an Umpire. Another famous Cupar character is "The Scribe", otherwise known as Dr. Allan Baxter, the scorer who will cheerfully confess to being a total pedant in the keeping of records.

Cupar joined the East of Scotland League in 1961, had a yo-yo existence between Division One and Two, and, in 1997, were disappointed not to reach the Scottish National Cricket League, losing to Stoneywood-Dyce in the Play-Off on a wet day at Forfar. At this point a meeting of their players opted to leave the East of Scotland League in favour of the Strathmore Union, where they felt that the standard of play and particularly of pitches is a lot better. In the Strathmore Union they underperformed in 1998 and expect to do better in 1999.

Cupar are a friendly club, playing at an attractive ground and with a good reputation for sportsmanship.

D

DALGETY BAY – formed in 1975. Dalgety Bay is a "new town" on the north shore of the Forth. Unlike other "new towns", it is exclusively residential housing and caters for Edinburgh commuters. The team plays in the East of Scotland League.

For less than half the length of its existence has the club actually played in Dalgety Bay. In their early years they played at Rosyth Public Park, but in 1978 moved to the grounds of Donibristle House, an almost idyllic setting for a game of cricket. At this point the club really took off in terms of interest and membership, but a severe body blow was dealt to the club when the use of the Donibristle ground was denied them. For a while they had to play on opponents' grounds but in 1986 they moved to Pitreavie in Dunfermline (alongside Dunfermline Carnegie) where they stayed until 1994.

In the 1980s on Sundays they played in the Forth Cricket Union, and in spite of their unsettled home life managed to win the League in 1989. This encouraged the team to apply for entry to the East of Scotland League. They were immediately successful in that they won the 4th Division in 1990 and managed to stay in Division 3 until 1993 before a return to Division 4.

The nomadic existence came to an end with the development of the Dalgety Bay Leisure Centre in 1995. Immediately there was a growth in membership and interest and the club's performances began to improve. In 1998 Dalgety Bay won the 3rd Division Title (the 3rd Division was the equivalent of the old 4th Division before the defection of the top teams to the Scottish National Cricket League) and will therefore in 1999 play in Division 2 of the East of Scotland League.

The club are indebted to some fine players who have given loyal service. John Meadley for example, a product of the youth development scheme in the 1980s, has now topped 7,000 runs for the club and Keith Pearson has bagged 500 wickets with his seam bowling. They have also been fortunate in having good captains like Hector Smith, Stuart Gibson, Rod Burns, Alan Pearson and Murray Forbes as well as hard working Committee men like Ben Douglas and Peter Franklyn.

DAVIES, Alec – (West Lothian and Scotland) currently Scotland's wicketkeeper and a stylish batsman as well. Plays for West Lothian, but has also played for Grange. In 1998 he picked up the Famous Grouse award as Wicket Keeper of the Year, a thoroughly deserved accolade for this fine player. He has earned 59 caps for Scotland.

DENNESS, M.J. (1940 –) Mike Denness remains the only Scottish born player to have become captain of England. He was unfortunate in that his tenure of the England captaincy coincided with two not entirely unrelated events. One was the undeniable fact that 1974-5 Ashes series saw the Australian duo of Lillee and Thomson at their best, bowling fast, hostile, intimidatory stuff, and the other was that Denness's England team had to face them without their best batsman Geoff Boycott, who declared himself "unavailable" in the middle of the 1974 season for reasons that never convinced anyone, and which the cynics thought had a lot to do with not wishing to go down a "corridor of uncertainty" with Lillee and Thomson at the other end of it.

Mike Denness's house at Ayr

This must not however obscure the excellence of Denness's cricketing career. He was born in Bellshill, but it was at Cambusdoon, Ayr that he learned his trade as a cricketer, living in a house that was on the boundary. He played his first game for them as a schoolboy in 1954, and won the first of his 19 Scottish caps in 1959.

Largely through the good offices of E.W. Swanton, then cricket correspondent of the "Daily Telegraph" and a hugely influential figure, Denness joined Kent in 1962. By the late 1960's he was captaining the side when Colin Cowdrey was playing for England. He played a large part in Kent's winning of the County Championship in 1970, then became captain in 1972. He won the John Player League with them in 1972,1973 and 1976, the Benson and Hedges Cup in 1973 and 1976 and the Gillette Cup in 1967 and 1974. In Denness's time, Kent could well lay claim to being the "Kings of One Day Cricket" as the banners of their supporters claimed.

Following a dispute with Kent in 1976, Denness crossed the Thames to Essex, and there his success continued, being part of the Essex team which won their first ever honours – the Benson and Hedges Cup in 1979 and then the County Championship of the same year. There was of course another fine Scotsman in that team – Brian Hardie of Stenhousemuir. Denness finished playing for Essex in 1980. He had a variety of jobs after that in cricket, including in 1998 being the Chief Inspector of a Panel which deducted 25 points from Northants for having a pitch that was not suitable.

His test career is sadly associated in public memory with that dreadful Ashes Tour of 1974-75, but it should not be forgotten that in his captaincy England won a series against India and New Zealand, and drew with Pakistan and West Indies, the latter opponents in the Caribbean! His 28 Test Matches included 4 Centuries. In fact, one of his centuries was on that fateful 1974-75 tour of Australia. Granted it came in the last Test at Melbourne with the series lost and with Thomson out of the side and Lillee injured during it, but still, not many English batsmen can claim to have scored 188 against Australia.

He can possibly claim to be the Scotsman who has done the most for English cricket on the playing field.

DENNIS, W.H. – (1923-1991) – a famous player and coach. He played for many teams, notably Kirkcaldy and Stirling County, but his main contribution was at Glenalmond School where he coached youngsters.

DOUNE – a Perthshire village team, founded in 1886 who play at a place called Moray Park. They compete in the Small Clubs Cup and the Village Trophy, but with as yet no great success.

DRAMATICS – Umpires often feel that some cricketers fill in their winter evenings by performing in the local amateur dramatic society. This is excellent training for cricket, for one can then with conviction hold up and examine the bat to persuade the Umpire that the ball hit the bat before it hit the pad, or do a brilliant "double take" in feigned astonishment at being given out, or if the wicket-keeper and the slips all take part in the chorus of an opera, they will be able to rise up together with a brilliantly orchestrated and synchronised "How's That?". Other tricks can include the look of feigning concern for an injured batsman, contrition after the bowling of a bouncer, and hurt, moral rectitude, righteous indignation and injured innocence when the cruel Umpire turns down an l.b.w. appeal.

The problem is that several of the Umpires have themselves dramatic experience, and at least one of them is a well known Producer of plays. They are therefore able to weed out the ham actors without any great difficulty.

DRAW – It is often confusing to a non-cricketing person that if side A scores 230 for 3 declared and side B only scores 89 for 9 (i.e. is not All Out), the result is a draw. I recall talking to a Chilean friend of mine about cricket. He said "You put on TV in the morning and there is cricket. You put on TV in the afternoon and there is still cricket. You put on TV in the evening, and there is still bloody cricket! You watch it for five days, and then nobody wins! It is a draw!"

In Scotland, it is even more confusing. In a Cup game (normally played on a Sunday) there must be a winner, which means in the above mentioned scenario of side A 230-3 and side B 89-9, side A would indeed win, both teams having batted for 50 Overs. Many people feel that this should happen in League games as well, but as it is, a draw can normally be achieved by preserving wickets intact. Then comes into play a somewhat complicated system of awarding bonus points.

DRINKS – a necessary interruption to play on a hot day. The players and Umpires can be out in the heat for up to three hours at a time (a lot longer incidentally than what would normally be expected in a First Class game in England) and it is usually agreed that drinks will be taken after 25 Overs. The time for drinks is normally not counted in the time allowed for bowling. It is not unknown for one of the captains to object to drinks on the grounds that it breaks the momentum of concentration (Geoff Boycott would often blame the drinks interval for a lapse in concentration) but normally they are very welcome. They are normally of orange, lemon or lime juice, but if the bar has not yet opened or if the game is played on a public park, it can be just water! Contrary to all the jokes, there is very seldom any alcohol and certainly no arsenic.

There are of course the other kind of drinks, namely the ones consumed in the bar after the game. It is difficult for a teetotaller to enjoy totally the social life of a team, for so much happens around the subject of the consumption of alcohol after the game. According to some accounts, "going on tour" to the Borders, the Highlands or the north of England is little more than a glorified orgy of drunkenness.

One must however beware of automatically accepting as true the stories that one hears. Some people, notably insecure young men, are prone to assume that their drunken exploits are so spectacular that it is worth adding an extra wee bit here and there!

DRUMMOND – an East of Scotland League team, normally to be found in the lower reaches thereof. They play at Inverleith Park, Edinburgh.

DRUMPELLIER – one of the most famous clubs of the west of Scotland. They have played at Langloan (at one point called Drumpellier Policies) in Coatbridge since 1880 although they were formed in 1850. Langloan has played host to some representative games, notably Scotland v. India in 1974. It is odd to record of a club which now plays in one of the grimmest parts of industrial Scotland that they were founded by the aristocracy, but this is exactly what happened. Some local

Drumpellier team 1992

enthusiasts approached Sir David Carrick Buchanan for the use of a field on his estate. This was granted and money was given to level the pitch and engage a professional on condition that the club was called Drumpellier. Not only that, but the benign Laird provided his butler, gamekeeper and coachman as players for the club, granting them time off to do so.

"Drumps" have produced many players for Scotland over the years, won the Western Union on many occasions and lifted the Scottish Cup in 1979, 1981, 1982 and 1995, the last occasion seeing a rare phenomenon in Scottish cricket, namely crowd disturbances in the Final against West of Scotland at Hamilton Crescent. In the Western Union, Drumpellier shared the title in 1896, and won it on another nine occasions. Famous players of bygone days have included Alex Watson, who was born at Coatsbridge (sic, according to Wisden 1921) in 1844 and played for Lancashire for over twenty years from 1871 to 1893. He might have earned an England cap but for a doubtful bowling action. In the 1970s and 1980s they were much indebted to Sandy Brown, who played 48 times for Scotland and who played for Drumpellier all his career apart from a four year spell as professional with Uddingston. Sandy's best International score was 104 not out against Warwickshire. In more recent times Alan Stevenson, who earned 14 Scottish caps, has been a fine competitor for "Drumps".

In 1999, they play in the Second Division of the Scottish National Cricket League.

DUMFRIES

DUMFRIES – one of the outposts of Scottish cricket, but also one of the oldest clubs, being formed in 1853, although they enjoyed a precarious existence in their early years owing to the lack of suitable opposition and the difficulties of transport. Some sources date their foundation from 1885. Their original colours were maroon and blue, which are still in use to this day.

Dumfries play at a lovely ground called Nunholm, where they have been for well over a hundred years. Nunholm boasts facilities which are on a par with anything in Scotland and which contain, as well as a good cricket wicket, all-weather tennis courts with floodlights, 4 squash courts and a fitness suite. Important games which have been played there include two one-day Internationals between Scotland and India in 1987, the 100th game between Scotland and Ireland, and several Scotland "B" games against the likes of Durham University and the Central Lancashire League.

They have been members of the Western Union since 1996, having left the Border League the previous year. They had joined the Border League some time after the First World War and won this competition in 1938 and 1993. They joke that the first success precipitated a war, but the second was more important in that it put an end to Kelso's nine in a row run of successes.

Since their move to the Western Union, they have enjoyed some success. They won the Scottish section of the Abbot Ale Trophy in 1997, (although their proficiency at bowl-outs and coin-tossing stood them in good stead as well as their cricketing ability, it must be conceded) but have as yet to make it to the Scottish National Cricket League, and indeed enraged some other teams in Scotland by their failure to fulfil a fixture in the 1998 Scottish Cup. Clearly, their remoteness does cause them problems.

They cannot boast any Internationalists, but in 1981 were able to provide as S.C.U. Chairman the late Tom Farries. Alex Ritchie, the present General Manager of the S.C.U., is a former player of Dumfries.

DUNDEE HIGH SCHOOL FORMER PUPILS

DUNDEE HIGH SCHOOL FORMER PUPILS – An ambitious club who play in the Strathmore Union and have ill concealed desires to join the Scottish National Cricket League. Well coached by Lindsay Ancell, the club is no longer strictly for men who are former pupils of Dundee High School and they have done well in recent seasons, winning the Strathmore Union in 1978, 1989, 1993 and 1995 and being second on a number of other occasions. That they are a little short of the top grade was proved however in their Scottish Cup campaign in 1998. Chasing a huge Heriot's total at Goldenacre, they slumped to 10 all out!

A character associated with them for many years is Graham "Spider" McLaren, an after dinner speaker of some note and also a seller of cricket equipment. His advertisement shows him talking to Mark Waugh, but then adds that he also supplies Rossie Priory Second XI ! He is no mean player himself, although now in the veteran stage. He recalls with amusement an occasion at Kirriemuir when DHSFP had restricted the home team to a paltry 30 all out.

Victory was assured but the Dundee men managed to snatch defeat from the jaws of victory by reaching 29 all out!

Efforts are being made to find out when exactly they were formed so that they can organize a Centenary Tour to Sydney! It seems that 1901 is the year, but there is a certain amount of doubt. They have always played at Dalnacraig and for the first half of their existence they were a "closed" club with membership confined to former pupils of the school. In 1951 however they joined the Strathmore Union, which compelled a relaxation of this policy. In their early years in the Strathmore Union they were much indebted to Jack Stark, the School's Janitor/Cricket Coach, who took 74 wickets in the club's inaugural Strathmore Union season. Dundee High School F.P. have now played in the Strathmore Union for almost fifty years, and they have had a Second XI in the Second Division for most of that time as well.

The club have done well in the midweek knock-out competitions. They have won the Three Counties Cup on 6 occasions, the most recent being 1997 and the Second XI have had 3 successes in the Two Counties Cup. In 1987, the club appointed their first professional Jayantilal Kenia from Bombay, who scored 1,119 runs in his first League season. He played for another 3 seasons, and since then the post of professional has been filled by a succession of young cricketers from Sydney clubs, notably St. George C.C. for whom Don Bradman once played.

No player has ever earned a full cap for Scotland while still at the club, but Adam Heather, Kevin Ancell and Daniel Bunce have all done so at youth level. Sadly, there is a tendency for talented DHSFP players to move on to Forfarshire. A case in point is the late Earl Reoch who had played at Dalnacraig, but by the time that he earned his three Scottish caps in 1973 was already a Forfarshire player.

DUNECHT – an Aberdeenshire Grades team who play in the picturesque grounds of Dunecht Castle. They were founded in 1932.

DUNFERMLINE – sometimes called Fifeshire, and not to be confused with Dunfermline Carnegie. They were formed in 1862, but that was more of a re-formation for there had been a team called Fifeshire previously. Some sources date their foundation from 1857 when they played a game in Kirkcaldy against Dunnikier on August 20th of that year. They play at McKane Park in the south west of Dunfermline, and in 1992 opened a nice new pavilion.

For the first years of their existence, they played at a ground near the Lower Station, in the east end of the town not too far away from where East End Park of Dunfermline Athletic Football Club now is. In 1879 they moved to Ladysmill Park, opening their new ground with a game against Grange on June 7th of that year. For a spell, Dunfermline hit a severe trade recession, and many Dunfermline people followed the example of Andrew Carnegie and tried their fortune in the U.S.A. This clearly denuded the club of some players, but there was

Dunfermline/Fifeshire 1939. Note the dog under the left hand seat. Note also the grim faces – as this must have been taken towards the end of the season, were they thinking about Hitler and Poland rather than cricket?

a good side effect when in 1906 one of the emigrants, one John McKane then living in Nevada, returned with his wealth and bought the ground on which they were playing and promptly gave it to the club. This is why it is now known as McKane Park.

Up to the First World War they had no great success, although men like P.E. Morfree and J. Paton earned Scottish caps. They joined the Scottish Counties Championship in 1906. As Fifeshire they won the Scottish County Championship twice in the 1920s, but their heyday was quite clearly in the 1930s when they won the Scottish County Championship six times out of seven in the years leading up to the Second World War. They had great players like Tommy Spowart, the legendary Classics teacher at the local High School who was five times capped for Scotland, and the mighty Willie Anderson, who captained Fifeshire during its glory years and was capped for Scotland 25 times. In four seasons 1923, 1927, 1931 and 1934 Willie took more than 100 wickets. The very use of the name Fifeshire tended to cause a little resentment in Kirkcaldy and Cupar, but the sustained success of the 1930s tended to take the edge off their arguments.

Since the Second World War, any success has been short lived, although there have been some fine players, none more so than the ill fated Murray Peden, who played for the club from the mid 1960s until 1972 before moving on to Stenhousemuir. Murray scored 1032 runs in season 1972, but it was when he was with Stenhousemuir that he caught the eye of the Scottish selectors. He died in

Dunfermline Abbey (Robert the Bruce and all) looks down in admiration as Mike Yellowlees off drives Andy Bee in the Corstophine v Stoneywood Dyce play-off at McKane Park, Dunfermline in 1996.

1978, and Dunfermline and Stenhousemuir have an annual fixture in his memory.

In the 1990s, in spite of fine players like Ross Mitchinson and professional Mansoor Elahi, they have struggled a little in the Scottish National Cricket League, and are currently in the Third Division after a shocking season in 1998. With new professional Shahid Aslam, who formerly played for Heriot's, Dunfermline are hopeful of doing well in 1999.

Their ground at McKane Park in the south-west of Dunfermline is a fine one with its nice new pavilion, but their wicket always looks bare. It usually plays better than it looks however.

DUNFERMLINE CARNEGIE – founded in 1909 and played their first games on the site of Queen Anne High School in the north of the town. They owe their name, like so many institutions in Dunfermline, to capitalist and philanthropist Andrew Carnegie. Since the 1950s they have been playing at Pitreavie to the south of the town on a pitch that is generally regarded to be one of the better ones in the East of Scotland League. Carnegie have struggled in recent times and are currently in Division 3.

Famous players include Jim Govan, who went on to play for Scotland, having begun his career with Carnegie, but one man alone stands out above all others in the last 40 years of Dunfermline Carnegie. He is D.W.D. Bain, who played over 900 games for the club, and on one famous occasion against Burntisland in 1964 managed to take all 10 wickets.

DUNLOP – a village team in Ayrshire who play in the Strathclyde League, the Village Cup and the Small Clubs Cup but as yet with no great success. Their ground is called Netherhouses, and they were formed in 1930, although there had been a previous team of that name from 1906 – 1910.

The team was formed in 1930 by two brothers David and John Carruthers and thanks to their sterling work, the club was soon well established. John Carruthers in particular has played a great role over many years in keeping Dunlop Cricket Club not only alive but active and healthy. The ground at Netherhouses was given to them by the late Andrew Howie, who also a couple of years later built a pavilion. The first game was actually played in 1931, but the foundation is correctly dated to September 1930, because that was when the decision to from a club was taken.

They played in the Kilmarnock and District League (which became known as the Ayrshire League) and the Dick Trophy, but it was not until 1958 that they

The famous Carruthers of Dunlop – John, David and James

first tasted success, winning both trophies and then the Dick Trophy again in 1959. In 1966 they joined the Glasgow and District League Division 4 and made steady progress up the Leagues until promotion to Division 1 in 1977.

In the 1980s however, Dunlop suffered more than most from lack of youngsters because of the teachers' dispute. The dearth of youngsters compelled them to withdraw from the Glasgow and District League in the late 1980s, but they later joined the Strathclyde League. Even in the years in which they didn't play League cricket, they still continued playing friendlies and competed in the Small Clubs Cup and the Village Trophy. They achieved no great success, but that does not seem to bother them, for they play their cricket for enjoyment rather than the win at all costs mentality which is sadly so prevalent elsewhere in Scottish cricket.

One of their more unusual claims to fame is that they had a wicket keeper who once stumped the great John (Jack) Berry Hobbs of Surrey and England. Billy McDowall was captain of the Glasgow Schools in 1930 in their game against Harry Rowan's touring XI. "The Master" had scored a century, then grew careless, or perhaps wanted to give a youngster his moment of glory, and was stumped. This happened at a ground called Golfhill which is now closed thanks to the actions of vandals. Billy McDowall then joined Dunlop and was a great servant to them both as a wicket-keeper and batsman until the Second World War.

DUNNIKIER – a fine old team from Kirkcaldy, and now Kirkcaldy's only surviving team following the demise of Kirkcaldy C.C. in 1998. They were formed in 1856, and at their Centenary Dinner in 1956, they were addressed by no less a person that Douglas Jardine of "Bodyline" fame. Their origins are interesting. The building that is now the Dunnikier Hotel was known as Oswald House, and the staff of that aristocratic mansion played their cricket there on a Saturday with tea provided by the Master. They continue to play on the same ground.

In recent years they have been enthusiastically led by the Cutter family – Alan the father and wicket-keeper batsman, Lil the mother, secretary and tea lady and two sons Brian and David. Currently in the Second Division of the East of Scotland League, they have done well in recent years in the Forth Union, a tournament competed for on Sundays. Dunnikier won this tournament in 1995 in addition to three times in the 1980's. They are an enthusiastic, friendly team with much expected in future years of the promising Alan Budd.

DYER, Nick – (Edinburgh Accies, Chichester and Scotland) a spinner who has now played 16 times for Scotland.

E

EAST OF SCOTLAND CRICKET ASSOCIATION – this organization does a great deal to keep cricket alive in the Edinburgh district. With the arrival of the Scottish dimension and national Leagues, the East of Scotland League has lost a great deal of its prestige, but from the 1970s until the early 1990s it was correctly regarded as the most difficult League to win, gradually overtaking the Scottish County Championship in prestige. It was inaugurated in its present form in 1953, although there seems to have been a similar competition at the end of last century which Carlton claim to have won in 1897 and 1898. In 1953 the first winners were Grange.

As from the year 2000 there will be an amalgamation of the East of Scotland League with its associated Grade Leagues (i.e. the Leagues in which 2nd XI teams normally play). Such a move has been on the cards since the creation of the Scottish National Cricket League, and the advantage will be that it will give more opportunity for East of Scotland teams to play on good wickets like Goldenacre, Myreside etc. The exact formation of East Leagues in 2000 will depend on achievements in 1999, but it is envisaged that there will be nine Divisions in total. The top team in Division 1 will then go into the play off set-up for promotion to the Scottish National Cricket League, provided that the top team is not a 2nd XI team. In that case, the play-off opportunity will go to the highest placed 1st XI team.

The administrators of the East of Scotland League deserve great credit for what they do in keeping the game alive for, thanks to their efforts, well over 1,000 people are involved in cricket in the Edinburgh District every Saturday. The change to be brought about in 2000 is imaginative and deserves success.

EAST KILBRIDE – founded in 1962, this team deserve credit for keeping cricket alive in the sometimes none too sympathetic atmosphere of a "new town". They play at Calderglen Country Park in the grounds of Torrance House and in 1998 won the Western Union. Their other honours include the winning of the Glasgow and District League in 1990 and 1991. Their best known player is Asif Mujtaba, Pakistan International and vice-captain at one point.

The early years of the club were precarious ones, but there was a determination to keep going. The first games all had to be played away from home, but gradually hard work gave them a home of their own. In 1965 a site agent's hut was purchased which gave them some primitive accommodation, although water for the tea urn had to be taken from a standpipe on the opposite side of the ground. Also in 1965, the team decided to enter the 4th Division of the Glasgow and District League, finishing second in their first year of entry.

In 1968 the Sports Club was opened and the club has never looked back. Also in 1968, East Kilbride played a friendly match against the Lisbon Lions of Glasgow Celtic, a fixture which attracted a large crowd. East Kilbride have continued the honourable tradition of playing friendly games against, for example, psychiatric hospitals as well as the serious side of playing League cricket.

It is not too fanciful to imagine this enthusiastic bunch of cricketers playing some day in the Scottish National Cricket League.

EDINBURGH ACADEMICALS – a long established Edinburgh club who were founded in 1854, although some people think that they did not play in their present form until 1884. They were originally exclusively for former pupils of Edinburgh Academy, although that restriction has now been relaxed. They play at Raeburn Place (across the road from Grange), a ground that they share with their Rugby club. Their ground is famous in that it was the venue of the first ever rugby International between Scotland and England in 1871 and the home of Scottish rugby for some years after that.

Edinburgh Accies 1935

For a spell, Accies found it difficult to assert their identity from the Grange, and this became a particular problem when the Grange became their next door neighbours in 1872. Players like Balfour-Melville played for both teams, often in the same season. Now there is no such problem, and the teams continue their friendly rivalry.

*David Loudon of Edinburgh Accies, commonly known as
"Large" for obvious reasons.*

Success has eluded the Accies in recent years, but they did win the Scottish Cup in 1974 and the Masterton Trophy in 1970 and 1977. Tragedy struck the club in 1995 when, in a game against Carlton, their long standing player Ian Moffat collapsed and died on the field. The club has always had a certain reputation for quirkiness, and earned a certain amount of national ridicule when their first game of the season in 1998 had to be cancelled because a floodlight pylon (used by the rugby club) was on their pitch, only some 15 yards from the wicket. It was one of the more unusual examples of light stopping play! It did however highlight (if one pardons the expression) the undeniable fact that cricket tends to be the poor relation of rugby at Edinburgh Accies.

Accies play in Division 3 of the Scottish National Cricket League. In spite of their comparatively poor recent form, they remain a strong team and enjoy a reputation among Umpires of accepting decisions without question. A stalwart of Accies over the past 20 years has been Dave Loudon, commonly known as "Large" for obvious reasons. He is a much loved figure on the Scottish scene and bereft of the snobbery of which Accies are sometimes unfairly accused.

EDINBURGH INSTITUTION – one of the forerunners of Royal High Stewart's Melville. They were formed in 1872 and in 1937 changed their name to Melville College. They then amalgamated with Daniel Stewart's to become Stewart's-Melville, and a further amalgamation with Royal High followed in 1997.

EDINBURGH PUBLIC PARKS ASSOCIATION – under the enthusiastic guidance of Secretary Norman Berger, this Association does a great deal to keep cricket going in the Capital. Currently there are 24 member teams rejoicing in such unlikely names as C.L.O.G (Coopers and Lybrand, Oil and Gas), Cockburn Lords, Edinburgh Beige, Botanics and Maccabi.

The Public Parks Trophy has been played for since 1891, the latest winners being Standard Life. In recent years, the Final has been played at Carlton's Grange Loan, which has helped to give players the feel of a "real" cricket ground, even though it detracts somewhat from the purity of parks cricket, as an inverted snob might say. There is also the Brunswick Trophy, a six-a-side tournament normally played at the Meadows over two nights, a trophy which the Biblical sounding Maccabi won in 1998. In addition to this there is a Midweek League, and this organization deserves credit for encouraging people from a broader social base to play the game, as cricket, especially in Edinburgh, sometimes has the undeserved reputation of being exclusive and snobby.

EDINBURGH UNIVERSITY – play at Peffermill on the south side of Edinburgh. They were founded in 1877, although sporadic cricket had been played before then by the students, and for a long time played at Craiglockhart before the University purchased Peffermill.

EDINBURGH UNIVERSITY STAFF

EDINBURGH UNIVERSITY STAFF – like their student counterparts, this team plays at Peffermill, and are currently in Division 2 of the East of Scotland League.

ELGIN – a strong team in the North of Scotland. They were founded in 1853 and played originally on the Links at Stotfield. Since 1902 they have played in the Cooper Park. At one point in their early days they advertised for more members and made the statement that *"Cricket braces the nerves, hardens and deepens the muscles and gives tone and vigour to the whole man. It is a rational amusement without which men become peevish and morose as Monks in a Cloister."*
Clearly young men of Elgin did not relish the prospect of the monastic life, and the club became a strong and healthy one. There were at one point several cricket clubs in Elgin, but by 1892 they had all merged as one. In 1893 they joined the North of Scotland Cricket Association and, along with Forres St. Lawrence, have the distinction of unbroken membership since its inception. They were the first winners of the North of Scotland League in 1896 and have won the competition on 13 occasions, their best years clearly being the era before and after the First World War. Their last success was 1991. Recent years have seen the club as respectable rather than brilliant.

ELIE – founded in 1989, Elie play in the Small Clubs Cup. They are based at the Ship Inn, whose "mine host" Richard Philip is the driving force behind them. The difference is that Elie play on the beach! They had played a few games at

Cricket on Elie Beach

neighbouring Largo and St. Andrews before having their first beach game in 1991 against Edinburgh Accies whose professional Nehemiah Perry, being a Jamaican, must have felt at home.

Before play begins, the pitch has to be raked before it is rolled. "Windballs" are the best form of ball to use on this surface, and the fixture list is dictated by the tides. In 1998, for example, only seven home games could be arranged on Sunday afternoons, but some other games were played away from home. Sadly the rules of the Small Clubs Cup prevent any home games being played on Elie beach, but it is nice to see cricket being played in such an unconventional way and also to see tourists gathering to watch such an occasion. Teams played against range from the august Grange to the Fat Beardies, who must be exactly what they say they are!

ELLON GORDON – founded in 1862, Ellon Gordon play in the Aberdeenshire Grades. Their home is at Gordon Park in Ellon, Gordon being the name given to the area round about the Aberdeenshire town, and indeed the name of the family who gifted Gordon Park to the town in 1907. The team's early years are not well recorded, and the only reason for giving 1862 as their foundation is that they held a 50 year celebration in 1912.

They have done reasonably well in the local competitions in the 1970s and 1980s, and they have two successes in national tournaments. One was in 1973 when they won the Scottish section of the Village Trophy by beating Kintore, Crathie, Freuchie (before their stranglehold of this tournament) and Rossie Priory. Sadly they lost to Tudhoe of Durham whenever they crossed the English border. The other was in 1986 in the second year of the Small Clubs Cup when Ellon Gordon beat Marchmont of Edinburgh at Duffus Park, Cupar in the Final. It was a remarkable game for Ellon's 100 did not look all that great a total, but Marchmont with players like Malcolm McNulty and the Sardesai brothers collapsed to 15 all out! Colin Addison took 7 for 11 and Alan Middleton 3 for 3 in the most remarkable exhibition of bowling in the history of the club.

Captain David Buchan of Auchmacoy, who is their Honorary President and who played for them once or twice in the 1940s, is extremely well connected in the cricket world, for his godfather was none other than Douglas Jardine, the author and originator of the Bodyline form of attack on Australian batsmen in 1932-33!

ENGLAND – a ticklish one this for the fans of Scottish cricket! Do we support them in Test Matches or do we not? Opinion is very much divided on this one, and it is not easy to give a clear answer, unlike for example the England football team, whose misfortunes are greeted with undisguised glee, and whose triumphs (almost as seldom as those of the Scotland football team) are greeted with scorn and belittlement. Those of us old enough to remember 1966 will recall the cemetery silence that Kenneth Wolstenholme's "They think its all over – it is now!" produced in Scottish households. The funereal atmosphere continued for the next winter until the 3-2 at Wembley and the capture of the European Cup by Jock Stein's Celtic righted the balance somewhat.

But to return to cricket. The issues are less clear cut in this sport, given that Scotland cannot yet really be considered a rival to England or indeed any Test playing country, with the possible exception of New Zealand in a bad year. And it cannot be denied that England does provide the best possibility of a Scotsman playing Test Cricket. One thinks of Mike Denness who was actually captain of England, I.A.R. Peebles a great cricketing player, personality and journalist of the 1930's and one entertains hopes for Dougie Brown, Gavin Hamilton and others. Do we not have more in common with the Englishmen than with any other Test playing nation?

Well, yes and no. It must be stated that it is difficult for us to identify with the English cricketing establishment with all its aristocratic overtones of Lord McLaurin or indeed the Thatcherite entrepreneurs of recent years. Moreover, even further down the social scale, do we have much in common with the hard, brutal, blunt Yorkshire "Call a spade a spade" way of thinking? Or the "horny handed sons of rustic toil" of wherever they come from?

It does, I suppose, depend who they are playing against. Old Trafford in 1961 when Richie Benaud turned the Test Match, bowling Peter May (the personification of the English upper middle class) round his legs for a duck then persuading the demented Brian Close to hole out at deep Third Man would probably have won many Scotsmen over to Australia. Indeed Bobby Simpson, who seemed to dive for the slip catches before the batsman played his stroke, is of undeniably Scottish descent.

Yet half a generation later in the mid 1970s, when the "ugly" Australians were in Britain before they sold out to Kerry Packer and his money, might have been a different matter. Similarly the West Indians of 1980 and 1984, who bored everyone rigid by their slow over-rate and besides outclassed England and everyone else into the bargain, were also difficult to identify with. What of the Pakistanis of the early 1990's and the ball tampering allegations?

It is an open question this one, whether Scottish people can bring themselves to support England. It would however be resolved if only Scotland had a good Test Cricket team of their own. That however is still hard to imagine, although the welcoming of teams like Zimbabwe into the Test playing fold does lower ever so slightly the threshold of improbability.

EQUIPMENT – some of it outrageously expensive these days, but it is very important to have the gear that suits you. Youngsters often find it difficult to learn how to run with pads and box on, and there is always the thrill of excitement as they put on their pads – a job that is so much easier now with the velcro rather than the buckles of yesteryear.

Helping a youngster on with pads can remind one of the Iliad of Homer. Achilles (as Geoff Boycott would do in later years) was "sulking in his tent" and would not fight for the Greeks. Eventually under pressure, he allowed his friend Patroclus to wear his armour in the fight – something that it is less easy to envisage the mighty Yorkshireman doing. Achilles however counsels Patroclus not to go up to the walls of Troy, but to stay by the Greek ships. Patroclus however is so excited about putting on the armour that he does not heed the advice. He does go up to the walls of Troy and meets his death at the hands of Hector.

In similar vein many a coach or teacher has told his charge, whose trembling hands are donning the equipment, "Watch for the spinner from the far end" or "Play straight for the first Over" or "No risky singles to that red-headed chap with the good arm". The youngster will nod impatiently, savouring the moment of walking out to bat. Then disaster occurs... All part of the rich tapestry of cricketing life!

EVENING GAMES – in most parts of the country, there is a midweek knock out tournament, and in Glasgow an Evening Cricket League. In Edinburgh and District there is the Masterton Trophy, in Strathclyde the Rowan Cup, and Angus, Perthshire and Aberdeenshire combine to compete in the Three Counties Cup. These games are played over 25 Overs, usually, and often produce great excitement in the gloom of a 9.30 p.m. finish. Because of the need to have a winner, Umpires are usually more lenient towards ground and light conditions than they might otherwise be. This type of cricket is not for the purist, it must be admitted, but is thoroughly enjoyed none the less.

F

FALKLAND – Scroggie Park is one of the most beautiful grounds in Scotland, dominated as it is by East Lomond Hill. The ground is owned by Ninian Crichton-Stuart, who is the hereditary keeper of Falkland Palace where died in 1542 James V a few days after the birth of his daughter who became Mary Queen of Scots. The ailing James, wounded at the Battle of Solway Moss uttering the immortal phrase "It cam wi a lass and it will gang wi a lass". It is also said that the chamberlains and butlers of the palace would dismiss beggars with the phrase "awa tae Freuchie", which was a considerable drop down the social scale in medieval Scotland. Nowadays however Falkland and Freuchie enjoy a keen but friendly rivalry on the cricket field without any great feelings of social inferiority or superiority.

Falkland C.C. was founded in 1860, but it is only in recent years that they have taken part in national competitions. Under the benign Presidency of Bob Nellies, the club had a deserved reputation for hospitality, as well as an excellent youth development structure. They are very much a family club, with loads of people called Watson, notably captain Brian Watson whose fine batting has perhaps deserved more national recognition and whose two sons now both show a great deal of promise.

Today with their very impressive youth structure Falkland remain very enthusiastic about their cricket. Their clubhouse, which was opened in 1957, has been extended in 1968, 1981 and 1992, so that it now has a restricted licence. Until 1979, the club played mainly friendly cricket, but joined the East of Scotland League in that year and in 1994 reached the First Division. They were thus in at the start of the Scottish League when the East amalgamated with the Scottish Counties.

In Cup competitions, Falkland have done well in the Fife Cup with a certain amount of success and on three occasions reached the Scottish Final of the Village Trophy without sadly emulating the sustained success of their near neighbours Freuchie. Falkland were disappointed by their own performances in 1998 and as a result play in Division 3 of the Scottish National Cricket League in 1999. This may be no bad thing, however, for it will give them a chance to develop more of their young talent. .

For a casual visitor to Fife, there exists no finer sight than the view from the top of East Lomond (Falkland Hill) on a fine summer's day, and the sight of tiny white figures running about the field. It is obvious when a wicket falls, for you can see the long trudge back to the pavilion for the disconsolate batsman and, if you look closely (with binoculars) you can tell the end of the over as the Umpire strides purposefully to or from square leg. For these and many other reasons, quite a lot of people are happy enough to admit that Falkland is one of their favourite teams.

FAULDHOUSE VICTORIA – a team with an interesting pedigree who have performed miracles in keeping cricket alive and thriving in a town which has long since lost its source of income. Fauldhouse is in West Lothian, and are the furthest West team to play in the East of Scotland League. Their foundation is given as 1855, although there is a certain amount of evidence that cricket may well have been played in the area before that. The suggestion given by their own history book (Fauldhouse Victoria Cricket Club by Lee and McKenzie) is that the inhabitants were introduced to the game by some Yorkshire miners who came up to help sink a shaft at the Victoria Pit. From there the game spread to other West Lothian villages and cricket was a thriving concern in the Victorian era. Their current Eastfield ground was opened in 1902.

They have played in the Glasgow and District League, the East of Scotland League and many other minor leagues and are one of the few clubs in Scotland of whom it can be said that they have an entirely working class base. They have been indebted to three generations of the Cruickshanks family and have had fine players like Grant Johnston (who played 28 times for Scotland), Peter Reid and the Allan brothers. In 1985-86 they were involved in a *cause celebre* when they were expelled from the East League, (but subsequently re-instated) for allegedly playing an illegal player.

A very interesting club with deep roots in the Scottish game and an excellent counterblast to those who accuse cricket of being a game which thrives on social snobbery. The history book mentioned above is a fascinating read, because it contains everything one would wish to know about Fauldhouse Victoria C.C. and so much more beside, particularly the fortunes of their football team but also a fascinating account of the development of this West Lothian village

FERGUSLIE – founded in 1887, and play at Meikleriggs in Paisley. They first won the Western Union Championship in 1905 and now are members of the 1st Division of the Scottish National Cricket League in 1999. They are well organized by the brothers Ian and Stuart Kennedy and in recent years they have had fine professionals like Dawnley Joseph of the Windward Islands and Mike Hussey of Australia.

Their first game was on May 19th 1887 against the already established Kelburne, who allowed them to field 17 men. Paisley seems then to have been a hotbed of cricket, for there was also a team going by the name of St. Mirren. Ferguslie, who enjoyed the patronage of the Coats family, also in their early days organized a fixture against the Barlinnie Prison Officers and other interesting teams. It was the Coats family who in 1889 provided them with their splendid ground at Meikleriggs. The turn of the century saw that tremendous sporting character James Welford join their ranks. James played right back for Celtic and, until recently, was the only Englishman to have won both a Scottish and an F.A.

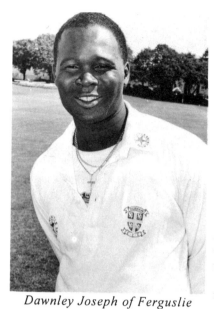

Dawnley Joseph of Ferguslie

Cup medal. He had also played first class cricket for Warwickshire.

They entered the Western Union in 1903. In 1905, quite clearly their *annus mirabilis,* Ferguslie won the Championship and remained undefeated. They won the Championship on another seven occasions, and have always been considered one of the stronger sides in the West. Great players in the past include Scottish caps like Sam Thomson and Fred Colledge of the era immediately following the Second World War. But their greatest successes came in 1969 and 1983 when they won the Scottish Cup. In 1969 they beat Strathmore in the Final at Hamilton Crescent and in 1983 Watsonians were the defeated finalists.

One of their best ever players, Peter Reid, wrote a good history of the club in their Centenary year.

FLOODLIGHT CRICKET – one of the disadvantages of Scotland's climate is that whenever it gets dark, it usually gets cold as well. This has meant that no-one has ever tried to introduce floodlight cricket matches in Scotland in any serious way, although there was once a friendly played for charities at Stark's Park, Kirkcaldy.

It is probably a blessing for traditionalists that no entrepreneur has ever tried this one, for it would probably involve coloured clothing, a white ball and black sightscreens.

> *And oh may Heaven our simple lives prevent*
> *From luxury's contagion, weak and vile!*

FOCHABERS – founded in their present form in 1947, Fochabers have one of the most attractive grounds in Scotland and compete in the North of Scotland League. The area has a long tradition of playing cricket for in the 1850s the Duke of Richmond did a great deal to foster cricket in Gordon Castle. It says a great deal for the enthusiasm of this club that they have kept the game alive in such a sparsely populated area.

Widely recognised as playing on one of the most picturesque of grounds (and there are many which could fit that bill) in Scotland, they are situated on the banks of the River Spey and opposite the gates to Gordon Castle. They were probably first founded as Fochabers Cricket Club in the 1880's, and originally their pitch was within the grounds of Gordon Castle. Their players tended to be members of the Duke of Gordon's family and staff but they were supplemented by the pupils from Milne's Institution (then a lantern of learning in the North) whose schoolmasters were very enthusiastically pro-cricket.

The present ground, originally a cattle grazing area, was first used for cricket in 1937. The club went into abeyance during the Second World War, but started again under its current constitution in 1947, one of its founder members being Ivor McIvor who has been with the club ever since and merited a mention in Wisden 1995. Gordon Baxter OBE has also had a long association with the club.

On at least two occasions the club has hosted cricketing personalities. In 1976, to celebrate the bi-centenary of the village, Mike Denness (whose grandmother came from Fochabers) brought a team of Kent cricketers to play a game against Scotland and, in 1997, Mike Atherton took time off the pressures of captaining England to coach Fochabers youngsters and relax with some salmon fishing.

The club plays in the North of Scotland League, but has no great record of success other than in the 1960s when they won the Reserve League and Cup on several occasions. But there are grounds for optimism in the performance of the youngsters, especially the Under 12's who have done very well under the inspired coaching of John Cockbain.

FOG – although not the most prevalent cricket hazard, fog can occasionally be enough to knock out a game. It depends however on the teams concerned. There is a well documented account of a game in 1965 between East Kilbride and Fauldhouse when the ground was enveloped in a pea-souper "like the monster in the old Quatermass films of the 50s" as East Kilbride's historian puts it. But both teams wanted to continue, even though both scorers couldn't see what was going on and had to come out onto the field, books in hand, to stand at short square leg in order to see the game!

FOOTBALL – Nobody can ever deny that in Scotland cricket plays a very poor second to football, although in view of recent International and European performances by Scottish teams (and by multi-nationals whose only claim to Scottishness is that they are based in Glasgow and play under the name of what used to be a Scottish team)! It is hard to see why this is the case.

But a Scotsman is obsessed by football. This was not always necessarily to the detriment of Scottish cricket, however, for the seasons used to be complementary. The football season used to finish at the end of April and resume in the middle of August, and the cricket season could live with that. Indeed many players played both games, sometimes at a very high level. One thinks of Scot Symon, Donald Ford, James Welford and many others. Moreover, the football teams themselves would play cricket on a fun basis. Celtic, a year after their greatest hour in 1967, played a cricket game at East Kilbride, Hearts have played at Carlton

FORFAR

and Hibs used to be regular visitors to Leith Links. This was beneficial to both sports.

The problem now is that football has suffered its "Invasion of the Body Snatchers" by media moguls and entrepreneurs who care little about the welfare of any sport (least of all football itself) and are interested in little other than the fast buck. They have the power and the will to make sure that football is played in the summer. If that happens, cricket will inevitably suffer, unless of course there is a backlash against this excessive, saturation coverage of football. Yet, there is surely room in Scotland for sports like cricket, and indeed many others.

FORFAR – town in Angus, home of Strathmore County, not to be confused with Forfarshire. The small market town however is one of the centres of Scottish cricket with a lovely ground on which have been played Internationals and a fine team called Strathmore (q.v.)

FORFARSHIRE – team who play in Broughty Ferry, Dundee at a ground called Forthill. They owe their name of Forfarshire to the fact that the county of Angus was so called until 1931, and that good players from towns like Forfar and Brechin would tend to gravitate towards the "Shire" team, which was based in the town with the largest population (i.e. Dundee), not the County town, which was Forfar. They were founded in 1880 and they were the first winners of the Scottish County Championship in 1902. They won that Title 15 times in all, the most recent being in 1992.

Famous professionals that they have had over the years include Peter Higgins, Frank Smailes, Alf Pope and Clairmonte Depeiza, but Depeiza caused a lot of ill feeling by his habit of running out the non striking batsman as he ran up to bowl if the batsman was out of his crease. This is technically legal, but is "not done" without a warning in polite circles and one particular incident against West Lothian in 1957 caused distress.

Great amateurs that have played for the Broughty Ferry team include G.K. Chalmers, a fine wicket-keeper in the early days, R.G. Tait, who joined the club from Aberdeenshire, as well as locals from Angus, namely M.R. Dickson and R.W. Sievwright from Arbroath and various members of the Ferrier family from Brechin. Special mention must also be made of Drummond Robertson, the highest ever accumulator of runs in Scottish cricket with 29,748, most of them (but not all) scored for Forfarshire. The club also produced in the 1970s Scotland stars like wicket-keeper Alex Steele and the hard hitting Peter Rhind.

Their ground, Forthill, has staged many Scottish Internationals over the years, including the famous game against Worcestershire when Hugo Yarnold, (see separate entry) Worcestershire's wicket keeper and later a distinguished Umpire, claimed 7 victims in Scotland's second innings on July 2nd 1951. Six of the victims were stumpings, four of them from Roly Jenkins, and the six stumpings in an innings remains a world record.

68

The well dressed Edwardian cricketer – W.R. Sharp, Forfarshire

FORRES ST. LAWRENCE

Throughout the years, Forthill has had a good reputation as a fine batting strip, and certainly facts would tend to support this claim. In 1926 for example, in a County Match against Clackmannan, Forfarshire scored 366 for 4 in 2 and a half hours with three batsmen Young, Ferrier and Russell all reaching centuries. In more recent times two Antipodean batsmen have reached a double century – Watsonians' Kim Hughes in 1976 and Forfarshire's New Zealander Jon Philips in 1996 in a SCU Cup game against Livingston in 1996. Under groundsman Douglas Walker, who won the Groundsman of the Year award in 1998, this reputation has been enhanced.

In recent years, Forfarshire's one great success has been the winning of the Scottish Cup in 1994. They had won the County Championship in 1992 but since 1968 the Scottish Cup had eluded them. They won the trophy at Hamilton Crescent in a game against Poloc in which their total of 225 for 8 owed a great deal to a half century by New Zealand professional Jon Philips and a late assault by Angus Hay. When Poloc batted, they were going well until David Johnston removed the two threats of Sajid Ali and Keith Sheridan.

Forthill has a fine, extensive modern pavilion, opened in 1972 and hanselled with a game against the Lord's Taverners who included Trevor Bailey. It remains one of the great grounds of Scottish cricket with an impressive gateway in memory of W.R. Sharp, who was captain of the club for an astonishing 40 years from 1885 to 1925. Yet there is about the place now a residual sadness, a yearning almost for the great days of the late 1940's and before the Second World War when crowds used to throng to see games against Aberdeenshire and Perthshire.

To counteract this dangerous wallowing in nostalgia, the club have tried hard to involve youngsters under coach Alistair Murray and more recently Peter Drinnen, who has been described as a "Development Officer" although he is the professional as well – and a good one.

FORRES ST. LAWRENCE – founded in 1861 to join at least two other clubs in the Forres area. They played on various grounds in their early days, but by the time that they joined the North of Scotland Cricket Association in 1893 they had found a fairly permanent home at Roysvale Park. In 1903, and again in 1905, they won the North of Scotland Championship under the captaincy of Alex Grant (in 1903) and Grant Peterkin (in 1905).

It was the same Alex Grant who donated Grant Park to them in the 1930s, a ground that was officially opened when the Australians played the North of Scotland Select on September 15th 1934. There is a certain amount of evidence to suggest that the Australians did not take this fixture too seriously, but it did give the people of Forres the chance to see the likes of Bradman and McCabe. Playing for the North of Scotland was I.A.R. Peebles of Middlesex, the famous son of a Forres stalwart, the Rev. G.S. Peebles.

The game is significant as far as Don Bradman is concerned for several reasons. One is that Forres is the most northerly ground in the world on which he played cricket. Another is that it was the only time he ever bowled on the 1934 tour. As it was a non-First Class match, it is not mentioned in Wisden but he did bowl 3.5 Overs and took 1 wicket for 20, the unfortunate batsman being J.I. Kemp. But it was immediately after this game that Bradman, who had been struggling with health problems for some time, suddenly was taken very seriously ill with an unusual and life-threatening form of appendicitis, which prevented his return home to Australia. The Don happily recovered after an operation but not without rumours spreading through both England and Australia on several occasions of his death.

Forres St. Lawrence won the League three times after the Second World War, but have not won it since 1953. They are a strong club nevertheless with a great tradition.

FRASERBURGH – founded in 1862, the "Broch" joined the Aberdeenshire Grades in 1891. They won the Aberdeenshire Cup in 1973.

FREUCHIE – famous village team in Fife. Founded in 1908, it is said, by an enthusiastic local dominie to prevent good players going to nearby Falkland with whom there has existed a long standing but friendly rivalry. For most of their life they played mainly friendlies, but the club were surprised fairly recently to discover a trophy calling itself the Fife League with Freuchie's being the last name on it in 1939. Certainly from the Second World War until 1980, they played friendlies although they did from time to time attempt to join the Strathmore Union and the

Three generations of Christies in Freuchie: Brian, David and Graeme.

FRIENDLIES

Perthshire League. But in 1980 they made the historic decision to join the East of Scotland League. After working their way up through the Second Division, they won the First Division in 1989, admittedly with more than a little help from opponents having points deducted and rain on the last Saturday, but it was a great achievement.

Their greatest moment, however, came in 1985 when they won the Village Trophy at Lord's, the first and to date only Scottish team to do so. Their captain that day, Davie Christie, has the honour of having a street (The Christiegait) named after him in Freuchie. They have done consistently well in the National Village Trophy since 1985, only on two occasions failing to win the Scottish section. The problem has come in not being able to progress further.

Their devotion to the Village Trophy has certainly earned the club national recognition, and indeed a great deal of revenue. The atmosphere in the village on Cup day is something that is hard to parallel in Scottish cricket, but there is a problem in that to take part in the Village Trophy, Freuchie are not allowed to engage the services of a professional, even for games other than the Village Trophy! This draconian prohibition clearly has implications for their ambitions in the Scottish National Cricket League, and it may be that a professional will have to be engaged, even though it means an end to the Village Trophy forays.

In recent years, Freuchie has provided Scottish Internationalists like Dave Cowan and Scott Gourlay. In 1998, they came very close to gaining a place in Division One of the Scottish National Cricket League, but Division Two will be their lot in 1999.

FRIENDLIES – a sad side-effect of the increase in competitive cricket, particularly on a Sunday, in recent years has been the decline of the "friendly" fixture in which the cricket should theoretically be a little more adventurous, less cut-throat and indeed more "friendly". Mind you, there have been "friendlies" which have been anything but friendly and in any case, it is surely a sad comment on human nature if competitive cricket cannot be played in a "friendly" spirit, or at least if relationships in the bar afterwards cannot be cordial.

Sadly, however, friendlies tend to be played half-heartedly with weakened teams, and often a player is unwilling to risk the wrath of his wife and subsequent withdrawal of favours by playing in the League on Saturday and then a friendly on Sunday.

FUTURE –

But och I backward cast my e'e
On prospects drear,
An' forrit, tho' I canna' see,
I guess an' fear!

The future of Scottish cricket is difficult to predict. Certainly, in terms of popularity, there can be little doubt that the game took a dip in the 1960s and 1970s. The teacher's strike and its aftermath in the mid 1980s also had its effect on the playing of the game in local authority schools.

Yet the game has remained strong in private schools, in local villages, in traditional areas like Aberdeenshire and, very noticeably in recent years, in the ethnic communities of the west of Scotland and in Edinburgh. Much will depend on how the Scottish International team do in the various competitions in which they take part. There can be little doubt that the game received a tremendous shot in the arm on June 24th 1998 (the day after the football team lost to Morocco in the World Cup) when Scotland recorded their first ever victory over a county side in the Nat West Trophy beating Worcestershire at Grange.

Politics may now play a part as well. It is clear that Scotland will become less dependent on England in the near future with the imminence of the Scottish Parliament, even if full independence is not achieved. What effect this will have on Scottish cultural and sporting life is not easy to imagine, and cricket, so often wrongly and hurtfully perceived as an "English" game, may well suffer further in the eyes and minds of the Scottish public.

Much clearly depends on how resilient the clubs prove to be in the face of the new attractions of the early 21st century. The quality of "stick-at-it-ness" will be much needed, and what would really help would be a few spectacular Scottish successes on the cricket field, along the lines of the high-profile win over Worcestershire in the Nat West Trophy of 1998.

G

GALASHIELS – a good Border League club who play at Meigle Park (formerly Mossilee) in Gala, a ground with an "antique" clubhouse which has been extended and refurbished over the years. In 1996 they regained the Border League which they had not won since 1975. Their history in that competition is nothing short of phenomenal, the 1996 success being their 30th. They won the competition as far back as 1896 (the second year of its existence) and won it every year from 1950 to 1962 with the exception of 1959 when Hawick broke the sequence. Such success led to three brothers called Nichol being capped for Scotland – W. Nichol 40 times (although his career was mainly with Kelburne), R.J. Nichol 9 times and D. Nichol once. There was also a Sandy Nichol who played representative cricket but did not quite manage to attain a full Scottish cap. This is a astonishing rate of success for one family.

The early years of Gala are well documented in a booklet written by R.A. Anderson which chronicles the development of the club from 1853 until the outbreak of the Second World War. The tweed industry in Galashiels saw the influx of many unemployed weavers, particularly from Yorkshire, and they played a large part in the establishment of cricket in the town. Their first game was played at Selkirk on August 20th 1853, and it would be fair to say that Gala's development was a slow one. There is a record of one game against Selkirk in 1863 being abandoned following a dispute over a catch. The odd thing here was that, although there were two club Umpires, it was the Gala Umpire who said "not out" against a Selkirk batsman, and the Selkirk Umpire who reversed the decision!

In 1882, Gala opened their new ground at Mossilee, having had to leave their original Abbotsford Road ground because of its unsatisfactory condition, with a game against Grange. The new ground seems to have given a tremendous impetus to the team and indeed the rest of the area, for in 1895 the Borders Cricket League was formed.

Gala would win the League in 1896, the second season of its existence, and part of the reason would be the excellence of their professional, a young Yorkshire all-rounder by the name of Wilfred Rhodes, whose slow left arm round the wicket bowling was particularly impressive, as was his distinctive habit of bowling with his cap on. He took 169 wickets in his two seasons at an average of about 7 runs. At the end of 1897, however, Rhodes returned to Yorkshire and by 1899 had won the first of his 58 Test Caps in his lengthy career.

The years leading up to the First World War were vintage ones for Gala, although success in the Borders League was hard to come by. Gala had a fine all-rounder in the Rev. F.H. Hoggarth and in 1911 the club was paid two great compliments when Gala man A.M. Grieve was made President of the Scottish Cricket Union, and Mossilee was chosen as the venue for the (sadly rain-ruined)

International game Scotland v. All India. Not only that, but wicket-keeper J.R. McDougall was chosen to play for Scotland in 1912 against Ireland.

In 1921 another Gala wicket-keeper, A.M. Aikman, was chosen to play for Scotland against Ireland, as Borders cricket continued to flourish after the resumption. Another representative game was awarded to Mossilee in 1927 when the New Zealanders comprehensively outplayed the South of Scotland. In 1930, Gala finished second to Carlisle in the Borders League, although according to their own calculation they had won. The official reckoning was done through percentages and Gala objected to the Secretary's arithmetic, but were over-ruled. By 1934 Willie Nichol, now with Kelburne, had won the first of his 40 caps for Scotland, a tradition that would be followed by two other members of the Nichol clan in the 1950's.

The 1950s and early 60s were a time of phenomenal success for the club, with the team winning the League regularly on an almost annual basis and doing consistently well in the Border Knock Out Cup. Since then things have not been quite so good, although there was a brief bright spell in the 1970s. As professional in recent years they have had Australian Jason Arnberger, who has also played for a few other Scottish clubs, and in 1998 they employed the talented young New Zealander Kane Rowson, who is reputed to be on the fringes of International recognition. They still remain however a strong and vibrant team in the Borders League.

GARGUNNOCK VILLAGE – an unpretentious village team who were formed in 1983 (although it was not until 1984 that they played their first game) and as yet have had no great national success. Gargunnock is near Stirling and their ground is called Meiklewood. For their first seven years they had no home and either played away or borrowed a ground, usually Williamfield, the home of Stirling County, but in 1990 they opened their splendid new ground which has fine facilities and a splendid view of a lovely part of Scotland. For a spell between 1988 and 1993 they had playing for them the great Irvin Iffla, the veteran West Indian who had contributed so much to Scottish cricket, notably Stirling County in the 1950's and 1960's. Iffla in fact had a tournament named after him, a winter tournament played on astroturf under the floodlights of Stirling Albion's Annfield Stadium, and Gargunnock were the hosts of this.

Gargunnock played in the Perthshire League between 1991 and 1995. They then joined the Strathclyde Sunday League, and won Division 5 of that tournament in 1998. They reached the Quarter Final of the Small Clubs Cup in 1996.

Gargunnock are a fine club who play their cricket with enthusiasm, but the problem is one of ageing membership, as the average age is well over 40 with one or two over 60. Veteran David Anderson, quondam of Stirling County, has topped the batting averages for the past two years.

Gargunnock 1998. Clearly an enthusiastic team of all ages! The dog bears the illustrious cricketing name of Hobbs.

GARROWHILL – one of the saddest stories of Glasgow cricket in the 1990's has been the decline and fall of Garrowhill, sadly unable to play in 1998 and now defunct.

The club was formed in 1951, playing for a year on a far from level football pitch at Barrachnie before the adjacent ground, shared with Shettleston Harriers, became available. Early records have largely been lost but an early stalwart was Jim Salmond, a leading fast bowler in the Coatbridge area before the war, who took wickets for Garrowhill well into the 1960s.

Admitted to the Glasgow League in 1964, the club played in Division 3 for a few years, but were relegated and spent over a decade in Division 4 until the reconstruction of the late 1980's took them into Division 3 and ultimately Division 2. The club was successful in evening knock-out competitions, winning the Glasgow Public Parks Cup on six occasions, including a particularly successful spell of four wins between 1972 and 1977.

The leading batsmen were Don Bell, who scored for the club the first 6,000 runs of his career aggregate of 15,400, and Phil Fitzpatrick, who scored over 1,000 runs in 1975. Two bowlers have taken 10 wickets in an innings, Roy Layton in 1967 and George McArthur a remarkable 10 for 5 against Jerviswood in 1972. Sandy Robertson, Secretary of the club for 25 years and Secretary of The Cricket Society of Scotland for even longer, took over 900 wickets. Another administrator from Garrowhill is John McGregor, who has been Secretary/Treasurer of the West of Scotland Association of Cricket Umpires and Scorers since 1991 and of the Western District Cricket Union since 1995.

The club moved from Barrachnie, initially to Mount Vernon, then to Huntershill at Bishopbriggs, then to the Old Aloysians' Ground at Millerston. Circumstances compelled a merger with Strathclyde in 1996, but this was not a success and the club is sadly no longer with us. A great deal of credit however is due to the club for keeping cricket going in a none too friendly environment and the hope is expressed by quite a few people in Glasgow that Garrowhill will one day rise again.

GIFFNOCK NORTH – formerly called Thornliebank, they folded in 1993 after over 60 years existence.

GLASGOW ACADEMICALS – play at New Anniesland and compete in the Western Union, in which they came second to East Kilbride in 1998. They were founded in 1866 and played their first games at Burnbank before settling at New Anniesland in 1919. Their most famous player is Douglas Lockhart who has been captained over 20 times for Scotland. Other great players of an earlier vintage are A.D. Innes, G.G. Crerar and A.R. Forrester.

GLASGOW HIGH KELVINSIDE – play at Old Anniesland, and compete in the Scottish National Cricket League. Glasgow High School Former Pupils were founded about 1870 but lacked a permanent base until after the First World War, when they moved to Old Anniesland. They had shared Titwood with Clydesdale for a spell.

Following their amalgamation with Kelvinside at the end of the 1980s, GHK joined the Western Union and from there onto the Scottish National Cricket League where they compete in Division 3 in 1999. Their long standing professional Zahid Ahmed continues to be a success with both bat and ball, and they have also had great service from Richard Young over the past few seasons since he joined them from Clydesdale. Both these men are left arm spinners and, when used in tandem, they can be quite effective.

In 1998, GHK attracted a certain amount of national notoriety when their captain ran on the field when his team were batting to complain about the bowling action of an opponent!

GLASGOW UNIVERSITY – have struggled to maintain a team under the constrictions of the University set-up but in 1998 they played in the British Premier League of Universities. The loss of the Garscadden ground in 1993 has meant that fixtures have had to be played away from home, but it is hoped to open a new ground at Garscube in 1999 with six well-laid grass pitches, something which should encourage the development of university cricket.

Cricket has been played at Glasgow University since the 1880s and there have been times when they have had a very strong team indeed but, as is the way with a transient student population, standards have fluctuated from year to year.

GLASGOW UNIVERSITY STAFF

Notable players include Colin Mair who captained the University side in the 1970s and was for many years afterwards a stalwart with West of Scotland C.C.

GLASGOW UNIVERSITY STAFF – a Strathclyde League team who should be selling "The Big Issue", for they have been homeless for a year or two, but there is now the possibility that they will be moving to a new ground at Garscube in 1999. Prior to 1993, they played at Garscadden but for Sabbatarian reasons, it was always closed on a Sunday by order of the University Divinity Department! Eventually they had to give up this ground when the Garscadden facility was closed down

They were founded in 1946 or shortly afterwards, playing a regular programme of friendly matches on Saturdays and midweek against local clubs and the Staff teams of other Scottish Universities. One of their leading lights in those days was Ogilvy MacKenna, the University Librarian who had played 8 times for Scotland when with Kelburne before the Second World War. In the early 1970s the club extended its commitment to beyond the end of the University term and they also entered the Strathclyde League.

A feature of the team (not surprisingly perhaps given the preponderance of older men) has been the strength of its spin bowling with David Evans, George Abbott, Stephen Phillips, Roger Downie, Gordon Curry, Richard Cogdell and Neil Rollings all doing well in this department. The club has never won an honour in the Strathclyde League but has had two close things – second in 1993 and the defeated finalists of the Cup in 1982.

It is to be hoped that this team, like their student equivalents, will be given a new lease of life when their new ground opens.

GLENDELVINE – a team who play at a beautiful ground in the Perthshire League, a competition which they have won on three occasions in 1974, 1983 and 1995.

GLENROTHES – a fine Fife team who have kept the flag flying for over 40 years since 1957. They play on the Town Park and have survived many problems of vandalism and so on. They play in the East of Scotland Division 1 and currently have some fine local players like Geoff Sampson, Robert Hutchison, Darren Bremner and Michael Donaldson, all products of the local High School. They also have a father and son combination in Keith and Steve Rowley and a good bowler in Mike Page, like the Rowleys, ex-Kirkcaldy.

They have always been very good at developing youngsters, but have had several disappointments in their attempts to find themselves a new home. In 1998 they put the seal on 41 years of existence by winning the East of Scotland Division One. Sadly, this particular year, there was no automatic promotion to the Scottish National Cricket League, but it does give them a slot in the Scottish Cup.

Glenrothes Cricket Club Presentation to Mark Mitchley to commemorate Mark scoring 10 Hundreds for the club

Their first home games were played at John Dixon Memorial Park, Markinch, then they had a few seasons at Dovecot Park and Carleton Park in Glenrothes itself before in 1976 moving to the Town Park, or as it is sometimes grandiosely styled, Riverside Park. They joined the East of Scotland League Division 3 in 1978 and were promoted to Division 2 the following year. In the 1990s for a spell they had a professional called Mark Mitchley, son of the South African Test Umpire Cyril Mitchley.

There was a team last century called Rothes Cricket Club who were founded in Leslie 1855 by the Total Abstinence Society. This team was resurrected immediately after the Second World War and played on Leslie Commonty, but were absorbed into the new town team of Glenrothes.

GODDARD, George (1937 –) one of Scotland's greatest ever players and entirely worthy of the M.B.E. that he earned. He played 63 times for Scotland in full Internationals and 15 times in limited over competitions. He was a good batsman (over 1,000 runs at International level), but a greater contribution was made by his off spin with which he took almost 1,400 wickets in club cricket and 154 at International level. He retired at the end of the 1994 season in which he had played no small part in his side Heriot's winning of the East of Scotland League championship.

George Goddard, M.B.E. – ex-Heriots

GOLFHILL – a now defunct club from the East End of Glasgow. They were in existence from 1890 till 1967 and played at Meadowpark in Dennistoun, where Whitehill Secondary School now stands. Despite repeated attempts, they were never admitted in to the "closed shop" of the Western Union, even when their performances suggested that they could do well. This was particularly true in the mid 1930's when they had a fine professional called Horace Wass, who earned 8 Scottish caps. Horace also played football for Chesterfield and cricket for Derbyshire, as well as a spell with West of Scotland. Sadly, Horace is one of the few people who quite simply disappeared, as his death has never been recorded, and not even his family know what happened to him.

GORDONIANS – an Aberdeen team, originally former pupils of Robert Gordon's High School, who play at Countesswells since their move from Seafield. They play in the Strathmore Union which they won in 1994 (their only success). They are four times winners of the Three Counties Cup – 1939, 1949, 1950 and 1953 but have had no recent success. They also play Aberdeenshire Grades cricket. Their best ever player was R.H.E. Chisholm, who started his career with them before moving on to Aberdeenshire.

GOURLAY, Scott – (Freuchie and Scotland) an all rounder who has now played 19 times for Scotland. Scott was just a little on the young side for Freuchie's great day at Lord's in 1985 but he is one of Freuchie's fine young players that they have unearthed since that day.

GRACE, W.G. – the great Victorian doctor appeared several times in Scotland. He twice appeared at Raeburn Place, Edinburgh in 1890 and 1891, attracting a large crowd just to see him. These were not however his first appearances in Scotland. He also appeared in 1877 at Langloan in Coatbridge when a United South of England XI played 22 men from Drumpellier. He scored a first innings half century, but then was run out (or thrown out, as it was then recorded) for 0 in the second as the Englishmen collapsed to 39 all out!

GRAMMAR F.P'S – as they call themselves in the Aberdeenshire Grades, they are better known as Aberdeen Grammar School Former Pupils. They play at Rubislaw, and participate in the Strathmore Union, a title that they narrowly failed to win in 1998 when they went down to Cupar on the last day.

GRANGE – one of Scotland's most famous clubs since their foundation in 1832. They were formed (not unlike the circumstances of Carlton 31 years later) when some members of the Edinburgh Speculative Society tired of debating issues like the First Reform Act and the Abolition of Slavery and started a cricket club on a piece of ground given by Sir Thomas Dick Lauder on his Grange Estate, hence their name. In 1833 they were in action playing a Glasgow XI on Glasgow Green, a game which they lost although one of their players called Henley hit a 17 (there were no boundaries then). In the same year they made the decision to employ a professional, one John Sparks who had played for M.C.C. and All England.

Sparks was a great success throughout the 1830s and 1840s and their then ground at Grove Street became known as "Sparks' Ground". In the early 1860s they lost their ground because of the needs of urban developers, and were homeless for some time before they made the momentous move to Raeburn Place in 1872. Their impressive and distinctive pavilion was opened on 29th June 1893 by Lord Moncrieff.

Great events in their history include a score of 590 against a Newcastle XI in 1896, and a fine victory by an innings over the Gentlemen of the M.C.C. in 1901. Between the wars, they were much indebted to B.G.W. Atkinson for his fine batting, and in the immediate aftermath of the Second World War, G.L. Willatt scored five consecutive centuries in 1949, as well as many other fine achievements. They were the first winners of the East of Scotland League when it was formed in 1953, and won it 11 times in all, including 4 in a row from 1990 to 1993.

Raeburn Place has been the host to many Scotland games over the years and has seen almost all the great players in world cricket from W.G. Grace and Victor Trumper onwards. The Australians have played there on at least 15 occasions, the South Africans 5 times and the West Indies and the Pakistanis in recent years as well. Not only that, but Grange played host to Scotland's first ever win in the Nat West Trophy against Worcestershire in June 1998.

In recent years, Grange have been indebted to Ian Beven, a somewhat irascible Australian but a fine off spin bowler who has played as both professional and amateur. Other fine players include George Salmond, Roddy Smith, Steve Crawley and Peter Steindl and the sheer depth of talent has made it small wonder that they won a Scottish League and Scottish Cup double in 1997, and have won the Scottish Cup another four times in the early 1990s. The only fly in the ointment was 1992 when bad weather prevented the Final against Strathmore being played and the Cup had to be shared. In 1998 when there could not be a Scottish League Champion because of the Conference structure, Grange nevertheless by winning Conference "A" and also carrying off the Scottish Cup for the sixth time (equalling Clydesdale's record) earned themselves the title of "Team of the Year" at the Famous Grouse awards evening. A further source of pleasure for Grange was the nomination of left handed Roddy Smith as the "Batsman of the Year"

They are clearly a very rich club and the visitor is immediately impressed by the fact that their ground is very clearly a specifically cricket ground. Other sports like tennis and hockey do take place on their premises, but are clearly subsidiary to cricket. They have been called the M.C.C. of Scotland, and indeed before the formation in 1909 of the second Scottish Cricket Union, Grange's ground was the "de facto" headquarters of Scottish Cricket. Another similarity to Lord's is that Raeburn Place has a Pavilion End, and a Nursery End, for the Inverleith Nurseries lie adjacent to the ground.

GREAT DAYS – there have of course been many great games of cricket played every season, and hopefully there will continue to be. To qualify for a "Great Day", however, there needs to be something which compels the rest of the cricket world to sit up and take notice that Scottish Cricket exists. Victories over Ireland, for example, are hardly noteworthy, nor is the great moment of Victorian Edinburgh when the Gentlemen of Scotland beat the Australians at Raeburn Place in 1882. This was a one day game hastily arranged because Australia had already beaten Scotland in the first two days of the scheduled three days! I can at the moment list five truly great moments:

Sunday September 1st 1985 – Freuchie v. Rowledge in the Final of the National Village Championship at Lord's. Rowledge batted first in this 40 Over match and were restricted to 134 all out. This was due to fine bowling by Dave Cowan and Terry Trewartha in particular, and "tigerish Scottish fielding" as Wisden says which saw two Run Outs by Andy Crichton. But Freuchie's batting was none too impressive with 24 being the top score. At the end of the penultimate over Davie Christie was run out going for what would have been the winning run, leaving the score at 134 for 8 and his son Brian and George Crichton to see out the last over.

Ian Beven – Grange's Australian off spinner playing for Scotland

Freuchie knew that all they needed to do was to "door" the six balls to win on the fewer wickets conceded rule. Last man Niven McNaughton apparently might well have been "timed out" if he had had to go in, for they would "never have got him out of the toilet" as Davie Christie put it years later. Tension mounted as the over progressed, but then the Umpire miscounted and gave a seven ball over! Not that it mattered, for the game was won! It remains the only day in history in which Scottish flags and banners have been waved in triumph over the sacred turf of Lords'.

Rowledge

R.E.C. Simpson	c. A.N. Crichton	b. Cowan	6
A.P. Hook		b. McNaughton	28
N.S. Dunbar	run out		33
C. Yates		b. D.Y. F. Christie	10
P. Offord	run out		0
R.J. Dunbar	c Irvine	b. Trewartha	12
A.J. Prior		b. Trewartha	6
P.R. Cooper		b. Cowan	12
B.A. Silver	c. Wilkie	b. Trewartha	0
A.B. Field	not out		10
J. Reffold	lbw	b. Trewartha	0
		Extras (lb 9, w 7, nb 1)	17

Total 134 All Out (39.3 Overs)

Cowan	9	1	25	2
McNaughton	9	0	31	1
B. Christie	9	0	28	0
D. Christie	5	0	17	1
Trewartha	7.3	0	24	4

Freuchie

M. Wilkie		b. Field	10
A.S. Duncan	c. Yates	b. Silver	16
A.N. Crichton	lbw	b. Field	0
G. Wilson	c. Offord	b. Yates	14
D. Cowan		b. Silver	16
S. Irvine		c and b. Prior	24
G. Crichton	not out		24
T. Trewartha		b. Reffold	1
D.Y.F. Christie	run out		11
B. Christie	not out		0
N. McNaughton	did not bat	Extras (b 6, lb 8, w 2, nb2)	18

Total 134 for 8 (40 0vers)

Field	9	1	15	2
Reffold	6	1	25	1
Prior	9	0	31	1
Yates	9	0	31	1
Silver	7	0	18	2

Sunday May 11th 1986 – Scotland v. Lancashire at the North Inch, Perth in the Benson and Hedges Cup. It would have to be admitted that this was a particularly impoverished era of Lancashire history which bore little comparison to Red Rose sides of previous or subsequent years. Yet their side did contain many household names, and more than half of them participated in Test Match cricket at some point of their career. Full marks are due to Scotland for their bowling and fielding in this game. They had come within a whisker of beating Worcestershire the previous week.

The game started on the Saturday, but bad weather compelled the game to be held over to the Sunday. Scotland's total of 156 for 9, in which captain Richard Swan's 31 was top score, did not look enough. Lancashire got off to a reasonable start, but tight Scottish bowling, particularly by Peter Duthie, restricted them, then wickets began to fall. Jack Simmons looked as if he could win it for Lancashire, but was manoeuvred off the strike at crucial points and Lancashire finished three runs short before a small and incredulous home crowd. Lancashire actually reached the Final of the NatWest Trophy that year, but there can be little doubt that the defeat by Scotland played a large part in the dismissal of the management team of Jack Bond and Peter Lever.

Scotland

I.L.Philip	c. Fairbrother	b. Hughes	**28**
W.A.Donald		c and b. Patterson	**4**
R.G. Swan		b. Abrahams	**31**
O.Henry	c.Hughes	b. Watkinson	**9**
N.W. Burnett	lbw	b. Patterson	**27**
A.B.Russell		b. Allott	**8**
D.L. Snodgrass	c. Fairbrother	b. Patterson	**0**
D.G. Moir		b. Allott	**21**
P.G. Duthie		b. Allott	**8**
J.D. Knight	not out		**1**
A.W.J. Stevenson	did not bat	Extras (b8, lb7, w2, nb2)	**19**
		Total 156 for 9 (55 Overs)	

Allott	10	2	24	3
Patterson	9	2	31	3
Watkinson	11	3	25	1
Simmons	7	2	17	0

GREAT DAYS

Hughes	11	1	24	1
O'Shaughnessy	2	0	9	0
Abrahams	5	0	11	1

Lancashire

G.D. Mendis		b. Stevenson	30
G.Fowler	lbw	b. Duthie	1
J.Abrahams		b. Henry	31
S.J. O'Shaughnessy		b. Duthie	9
M.Watkinson	c. Moir	b. Henry	16
N.H. Fairbrother		b. Duthie	12
D.P. Hughes	c. Knight	b. Burnett	4
C.Maynard	st. Knight	b. Donald	7
J.Simmons	not out		16
P.J.W. Allott		b. Moir	13
B.P. Patterson	not out		3
		Extras (b3, lb3, w5)	11
		Total 153 for 9 (55 Overs)	

Duthie	11	4	31	3
Donald	10	0	40	1
Moir	11	0	36	1
Stevenson	11	3	20	1
Henry	11	4	19	2
Burnett	1	0	1	1

Thursday 10th May 1990 – Northamptonshire v. Scotland at Northampton in the Benson and Hedges Cup. A fine triumph for Scotland considering that the Northants team contained five Test players. Scotland did not seem to have the best of preparations for this game considering that their previous game against Notts did not finish in Glasgow until 7.30 p.m. the previous night and it was early in the morning before they checked into their hotel! But Scotland batted first and fine contributions by Gordon Greenidge (then playing for Greenock), Richard Swan and particularly Ian Philip gave Scotland their highest ever total in a Benson and Hedges Cup match – a very respectable 231 for 8. When Northants batted, Wayne Larkins scored 111 but the Aberdeenshire connection of Andy Bee and Dallas Moir disposed of him, and the rest of the Northants team under-performed in the face of fine Scottish bowling and fielding. There was one broken-hearted Scotsman, however. Jim Govan of Dunfermline who also played for Carlton had turned professional with Northants for a brief and unsuccessful time. He was playing for them that day and by scoring 30 looked as if he could win it for them, but, sadly for Jim, he was run out and Scotland won the day by 2 runs, Curtley Ambrose being unable to find the boundary off the last ball. Ian Philip won the Gold Award.

Scotland

I.L Philip	lbw	b. Ambrose	**95**
C.G. Greenidge	lbw	b. Capel	**32**
B.M.W. Patterson		b. Govan	**8**
R.G. Swan	c. Ripley	b. Ambrose	**44**
A.C. Storie	c. Larkins	b. Ambrose	**8**
A.B. Russell		b. Robinson	**0**
D.R. Brown		b. Capel	**16**
A.Bee		b. Ambrose	**0**
D.Cowan	not out		**4**
J.D.Moir	not out		**3**
C.L. Parfitt	did not bat	Extras (b2, lb7, w12)	**21**

Total 231 for 8 (55 Overs)

Ambrose	11	3	26	3
Thomas	9	0	52	0
Robinson	10	0	47	2
Capel	11	0	29	2
Govan	11	2	55	1
Wild	3	0	13	0

Northants

W.Larkins	c. Bee	b. Moir	**111**
A.Fordham	lbw	b. Moir	**0**
G.Cook	lbw	b. Cowan	**6**
R.J. Bailey		b. Cowan	**1**
D.J. Capel		b. Brown	**0**
D.J. Wild	c. Parfitt	b. Brown	**15**
D. Ripley		b. Brown	**9**
J.G. Thomas	c. Patterson	b. Cowan	**32**
J.W. Govan	run out		**30**
C.E.L. Ambrose	not out		**11**
M.A. Robinson	not out		**0**
		Extras (b1, lb7,w4, nb2)	**14**

Total 229 for 9 (55 Overs)

Moir	11	0	51	2
Bee	11	1	58	0
Parfitt	11	1	26	0
Cowan	11	1	36	3
Brown	11	2	50	3

A view of Ian Philip of Stenhousemuir and Scotland which is not instantly recognisable. The batsman is Rob Bailey of Northants.

Friday 11th April 1997 – Scotland v. Ireland at Kuala Lumpur in the Play-Off for third place in the I.C.C. Trophy. Scotland won this game to qualify for the 1999 World Cup to be played in the British Isles. The game began on the Thursday, but torrential rain compelled it to be continued on the Friday. Scotland batted first and reached 187 for 8 with Mike Smith being particularly unlucky not to reach his half century. Ireland's reply was a good bit short and Scotland owed their success to some fine catching in the outfield as Ireland's batting became increasingly irresponsible and desperate. Keith Sheridan's four wickets were particularly commendable. A feature of the game was the inordinate amount of Wides conceded in both innings.

Scotland

I.L.Philip	c. Doak	b. McCrum	11
D.R.Lockhart	c. Benson	b. Doak	21
M.J. Smith	run out		49
G.Salmond	c. A.Patterson	b. Curry	7
J.G.Williamson		c. and b. M.Patterson	27
M.J.deG.Allingham	run out		22
A.G.Davies		b. Heasley	17
I.R.Beven	c. A.Patterson	b. M.Patterson	3
S.R.Kennedy	not out		4
K.Thomson	did not bat		
K.L.P. Sheridan	did not bat	Extras (lb4 w22)	26
		Total 187 for 8 in 45 Overs	

Gillespie	5	1	10	0
McCrum	7	1	14	1
Heasley	8	0	44	1
M.Patterson	8	0	42	2
Harrison	8	0	34	0
Doak	6	0	28	1
Curry	3	0	11	1

Ireland

J.D.Curry	c.Salmond	b. Thomson	7
A.D.Patterson	c. Davies	b. Thomson	6
D.A. Lewis	c. Thomson	b. Allingham	11
J.D.R.Benson	c. Smith	b. Sheridan	26
N.G.Doak	c. Thomson	b. Sheridan	7
A.R.Dunlop	c. Salmond	b. Sheridan	10
D.Heasley	c. Lockhart	b. Sheridan	18
P.G.Gillespie	st. Davies	b. Beven	9

G.D.Harrison	c. Lockhart	b. Williamson	16
M.W.Patterson	c. Kennedy	b. Williamson	6
P.McCrum	not out		2
	Extras (b1, lb1, nb6, w15)		23
	Total 141 all out in 39 Overs		

Beven	9	0	35	1
Thomson	6	1	27	2
Kennedy	9	3	14	0
Allingham	3	0	13	1
Sheridan	9	1	34	4
Williamson	3	0	16	2

Wednesday 24th June 1998 – Scotland v. Worcestershire at Grange in the 1st Round of the Nat West Trophy. This was Scotland's first ever win over an English County in the Nat West 60 Over trophy and a gripping game of cricket it was! Worcestershire needed nine off Greig Williamson's last over, and with tension mounting, fell four runs short, Lampitt being bowled off the last ball. A seventh wicket stand of 131 between Lampitt and Haynes had made it look as if Worcestershire would pull the game out of the fire, but Scotland bowled steadily and fielded competently, with Alec Davies taking four catches to Craig Wright, notably the prize ones of Hick and Moody. Earlier Scotland had posted an excellent total of 244 which owed much to Patterson and Allingham with acceleration coming exactly when it was required. It was a victory made all the sweeter by the fact that Scotland's football team had been knocked out of the World Cup by Morocco the night before.

Scotland

B.M.W. Patterson		b. Lampitt	71
B.G. Lockie	c. Rhodes	b. Newport	10
M.J. deG. Allingham		b. Lampitt	54
G. Salmond	run out		27
R.A. Parsons	c. Leatherdale	b. Moody	30
J.G.Williamson	c. Leatherdale	b. Moody	4
I.M.Stanger	not out		23
C.M.Wright	not out		5
P.D. Steindl	did not bat		
A.G. Davies	did not bat		
Asim Butt	did not bat	Extras (lb12, w2, nb6)	20
		Total 244 for 6 (60 Overs)	

Newport	11	1	46	1
Haynes	8	2	10	0
Lampitt	12	1	44	2

Moody	12	3	55	2
Illingworth	12	0	48	0
Leatherdale	5	0	29	0

Worcestershire

W.P.C. Weston	c. Parsons	b. Steindl	6
A. Hafeez	c. Stanger	b. Wright	33
G.A. Hick	c. Davies	b. Wright	29
T.M. Moody	c. Davies	b. Wright	4
D.A. Leatherdale	c. Davies	b. Wright	3
V.S. Solanki	c. Davies	b. Wright	1
G.R. Haynes		b. Allingham	74
S.R. Lampitt		b. Williamson	54
S.J. Rhodes	c. Asim Butt	b. Williamson	6
R.K. Illingworth	not out		0
P.J. Newport	did not bat	Extras (b5, lb7, w8, nb 10)	30
		Total 240 for 9 (60 Overs)	

Asim Butt	12	9	43	0
Steindl	9	2	36	1
Wright	12	5	23	5
Stanger	7	0	36	0
Allingham	11	0	43	1
Williamson	9	0	47	2

GREENOCK – founded in 1862 and play at Glenpark in the reputedly rainy land of Greenock. There is evidence, albeit flimsy, of cricket having been played in Greenock as early as 1819, and certainly Clydesdale in their inaugural season of 1848 played twice in the town of Greenock. But Greenock C.C. were founded in 1862 and until 1864 they played at Wellington Park, but were given Glenpark in 1864 by Sir Michael Shaw-Stewart Bart. It was opened on May 7th 1864, and Greenock have played there ever since.

Glenpark is a small compact ground that has become renowned throughout Scotland as one of the finest places to play cricket. A walled ground, surrounded by houses on all sides, it is capable of creating a great atmosphere in which to play the game. It is also unique in that a six is only granted if the ball is hit out of the ground without touching any building or tree within the boundary walls. On a summer's day, with the sun shining off the immaculately whitewashed walls, there is simply no better place to play and watch cricket in Scotland. This ground has hosted Scotland v. Ireland games and other representative fixtures, including a game against the Australian Imperial Forces in 1919 which featured Herbie Collins, and a visit from Jack Hobbs, admittedly past his prime in 1935 when he scored 62 for H.B. Rowan's XI.

GREENOCK

In their early years Greenock struggled (twice for example they were dismissed for 9) but the perseverance of their founding fathers proved worthwhile. One of them was Dan Kerr, father of the famous John Kerr, and a feature of the club throughout the years has been their family dynasties – the Kerrs, the Adams, the Ballantines, the Walkers and others. Another feature of their social life has been their frequent tours to Ireland.

They were the first winners of the Western Union in 1893, and won it again in its Centenary Year of 1993, making it 16 times in all, as well as having considerable success in the two midweek Cups – the Rowan Cup and the West League Cup. 1984 was anything but the horrors that Orwell predicted for, in that year, Greenock won every trophy that they entered bar one. The exception was the Scottish Cup which they lost to Poloc in a closely contested Cup Final. What made 1984 even more remarkable was the fact that the team were at that point all amateur. They were captained by Peter MacKerracher and had in their ranks three particularly fine players in all rounders Tom Black and Peter Duthie and fast bowler Jack Clark, all of whom played for Scotland.

They are now members of the First Division of the Scottish National Cricket League, and in 1998 won the S.C.U. Cup, defeating Watsonians in the Final. Their famous players of the past include professionals Jarvis, Jenner, Hollingdale, Tobin, Mayne, Laughlin, Scarff and Clifford and of course in the early 1990's the great West Indian Gordon Greenidge, whose benefit match in 1990 gave the Greenock spectators an early glimpse of what they could expect from Brian Lara.

Their greatest ever player was John Kerr (q.v.). Greenock history is well served by a couple of excellent books called "Greenock Cricket Club Records

Greenock in 1894. The grim looking man second from left in the front row is Dan Kerr, father of the famous John Kerr.

1887 – 1937" by J.C. Riddell, and "Greenock Cricket Club – One Hundred Years 1862 – 1962" by the same author, both of which give a vivid insight into what is one of the truly great clubs of Scottish cricket.

GREIG, A.W. – (1946 –) Tony Greig (captain of England from 1975-1977) although born in South Africa is of Scottish parentage, his father coming from Edinburgh and his grandfather having owned shops in Falkirk and Bathgate.

Greig played for Sussex and came into the England team in the early 1970's as an aggressive batsman and versatile bowler. He was made captain following the demise of Mike Denness in 1975. Tony was a fine player but had the tendency to say a few silly things like his intention in 1976 to make the West Indians grovel. Unless you have players to back that up, there is a tendency for such words to be rammed down your throat. Viv Richards, Andy Roberts and a few others proceeded to do just that, as England went down to a 0-3 thrashing.

Showing considerable strength of character however Tony fought back from this, leading a very successful tour of India in 1976-77, during the course of which, incidentally, he and John Lever were wrongly accused of ball tampering. Sadly, however, he has gone down in cricketing history as the great Judas who was the front man of the Packer Revolution. His sins in this respect included attempting to persuade English players to defect from established cricket and join the Packer circus. Nothing wrong with that, one might say, except for the fact that he was captain of England at the time! He was rightly sacked for this in early 1977, and perhaps Tony's Scottish connections should be minimised!

Since his cricketing career finished, Tony has worked as a TV commentator in Australia.

GROUNDSMAN – a good groundsman is worth his weight in gold. Cricket, more than most other sports, does need a good surface on which to play. The outfield can be a little rough on occasion, thanks to the playing of football, rugby or hockey over the winter, but the wicket itself, for reasons of safety, must be perfect.

A good groundsman will look upon his 22 yards like a mother looks after her baby. It will need to be nurtured, fed and watered and will need to look good. Some grounds of course have a reputation for high scores, others are more likely to "keep low", which means that wickets are more likely to fall. A pitch with loads of green on it tends to help the bowlers, but the determining factor is, as always, the character of the people who play on it.

A groundsman will want batsmen, even visiting ones, to score on his track. That is what people term a "good" track. He must work hard, especially in the early months of the season, although it must be acknowledged that groundsmanship is not an exact science and much depends on the weather and indeed the pre-existing position of the ground, whether or not the club are rich enough to own covers and the quality of the tools at his disposal, particularly the roller.

The "Masters" of Scottish and English Cricket – John Kerr of Greenock and Scotland with Jack Hobbs of Surrey and England, taken together at Glenpark, Greenock on 25th June 1935.

H

HADDINGTON – founded in 1877, they play at Neilson Park, a public park in the south of Haddington. Recently there has been a welcome return to form resulting in promotion in 1997 to Division 1 of the East of Scotland League after a prolonged absence. They are still in that League in 1999. John Hiley has recently excelled for Haddington with bat and ball.

Their first game was played on 27th July 1877 when Haddington Working Men's Club played Scotia of Edinburgh at a ground called Clerkington Acredales. In 1882 they moved to Brewery Park, behind where the County Buildings now are, where they stayed until the First World War. Cricket seems to have been a popular and colourful occasion in the late 19th century in Haddington with bands playing and ladies admitted free, even though men had to pay 3d. Sometimes stumps had to be drawn early because of "railway exigencies", meaning that the opposition had to catch their train to Edinburgh. On one occasion Haddington played against the exotically named "Tropic XI", a team of Edinburgh University students from the West Indies and West Africa.

Brewery Park was requisitioned for the First World War and, immediately after the Armistice, the club was offered Neilson Park. It was during the inter-War years that Sandy Cruickshank began to make his mark as an excellent batsman and bowler. In the same way as Brewery Park was lost in the First World War, so too was Neilson Park, ploughed up for crop planting, and the Club moved to Knox Academy playing fields, where for a spell they played quite a few games against the various RAF bases in the area.

The war over, Haddington continued at Knox playing fields and Cruickshank continued his marathon career which would last until the late 1960s, only a few years before his death at the age of 74. By 1962, Sunday games were sanctioned at the Knox playing fields, although the Education Committee took a little convincing, and in 1969 Haddington joined the East of Scotland League, winning Grade "A" under the captaincy of John Bonnington in their first year. From then on, they have been members of the League, and in 1975 they returned to Neilson Park. They had a lean spell during the 1980s and early 1990s, but now that they are back in Division 1, they are optimistic about the future.

HAMILTON, Gavin (1975 –) – a young man of the same name of one of Robert Burns' friends
> *"Lord, mind Gavin Hamilton's deserts,*
> *He drinks and swears and play at cartes"*

says Holy Willie, but this Gavin Hamilton deserves nothing other than our praise and whole-hearted admiration. From West Lothian, Gavin attracted the interest of Yorkshire from a young age and has now spent several seasons down at Headingley. 1997 was a disappointment, but 1998, particularly the latter half of it, saw the rare sight of hard-bitten Yorkshiremen singing the praises of this young Scotsman. 10 wickets and 149 runs in a match against Glamorgan was the best all-round performance in a single game by a Yorkshireman since George Hirst in 1906, then came 6 for 50 against Essex, and even that was bettered by 7 for 50 against Surrey in a game which played a vital part in handing the initiative in the County Championship to Leicestershire and away from Surrey.

This is clearly International form, but here comes the rub. For whom is Gavin to play? Some say that by playing for Scotland (for whom he has played 11 times in all) in an International against Bangladesh in the 1998 season he burned his boats for playing for England. This does have a certain logic to it, but it is a grey area, and it seems hard that this youngster should be denied the chance of playing Test Cricket. One could point to the likes of Mike Denness, who played for both Scotland and England, but these were other times, other days when the regulations were different. It would of course be all different if Scotland had Test status! As it is, he is playing for us in the World Cup!

HAMMERINGS – Any history of Scottish cricket will be rich in hammerings, especially when Scotland take on any good professional side. It would be heartless and indeed exhausting to list them all, but there is at least one that is a collector's item. This was the game at Shawholm in 1919 when the Western District of Scotland took on the Australian Imperial Forces. In two days the Australians put on 733 for 6, then dismissed the Western District for 85 and 88, thus winning by an Innings and 560 runs. Adding insult to injury, Wisden tells us that the Aussies reached 638 at the end of the first day then adds, "they scored at a terrific pace on the first afternoon, it being nearly two o'clock before the game began".

HARDIE, B.R. – (1950 –) one of Scotland's most successful players who won 14 Caps for Scotland between 1970 and 1974 as a right handed batsman. He played for Stenhousemuir, and then went to Essex for whom he performed well on many occasions, helping them to their first ever County Championship in 1979. He made 1,000 runs in a season on eight occasions, and in 1975 topped the 1,500 mark. He was looked upon as a consistent performer, and considered unlucky not to have achieved a Test cap.

HAWICK AND WILTON – deep in Rugby territory, Hawick have done well to keep cricket going at Buccleuch Park since their foundation in 1849. They are members of the Borders League, but the most recent of their four successes is 1964, although they did win the Border K.O. Cup in 1985.

The earliest indication of cricket in Hawick comes in 1844 when hosiery manufacturers from Yorkshire played at Brewery Haugh, but the first real match came in 1849 when a Hawick team played Sir Frederick Millbank's XI at Borthwickbrae, and then in a return match at Upper Common Haugh.

From a plethora of local teams, Hawick merged with Wilton and they have been known as Hawick and Wilton ever since. They opened their ground at Buccleuch Park on September 22nd 1860 in a game against Langholm. They have had no great record of consistent success in the Border League, having won it on only four occasions, their purple patch being in 1910 and 1911 when they won the League two years in a row and when brothers Walter and James Storrie were capped for Scotland. Arguably Hawick's greatest ever achievement came in 1928 when Hawick and Wilton beat Kent on tour, bowling them all out for 74. One suspects, however, that it was not the County team at its full strength or its full commitment, and certainly Frank Woolley, now in the twilight of his career, had left the night before to play for "The Rest" against the County Champions.

It was the same year of 1928 when, the Centenary Review notes sadly, "the petrol driven motor mower displaced the old type machine pulled by the horse. Work horses were becoming increasingly scarce". It then develops the point about the particular problem in applying poultices to any sore that the beast might develop.

During the two Wars, because of the amount of military personnel in the district, cricket actually flourished, and Buccleuch Park has seen a great deal of cricket. Sadly, however, cricket in Hawick has lagged behind other Border towns of similar size, and will continue to be a very poor second to all-conquering rugby. But they would have been particularly proud of their team in 1959. They won the Borders League in that year. Had they not done so, arch-rivals Gala would have won the League every year from 1949 to 1962. As it was, Gala's domination was hard for a Teri to swallow, and black humour abounded about the famous statue in the centre of the town of the man coming back from Flodden Field in 1513. That was not what it was at all. It was merely a Hawick cricketer on his return from another visit to Mossilee in Gala.

HAZEL N.L. (1921 – 1996) – one of the greatest batsmen of the post-War cricket scene. Nigel was born in Bermuda and came to Aberdeenshire in 1947 as professional on the recommendation of his predecessor Alma Hunt. Nigel established himself as a fine attacking batsman and, when he moved to Strathmore in 1954, quickly became a local hero, winning over those who thought "cricket was boring" by his fine attacking batting and disarming racist bigots by his charm and dignity. For Strathmore, he amassed 19,430 runs, including 2 double centuries and 28 centuries.

As great a contribution as his batting was his willingness to coach boys, something that had a profound long term effect on this club culminating in the victory in the 1971 Scottish Cup with a team of men who were all born in Forfar, apart from himself now aged 50. In later years, he worked as barman and steward for the club that he loved, and the Scottish cricket world mourned his passing in March 1996. His son, also called Nigel, plays for the club.

HELENSBURGH – were formed in 1879, and play at Ardencaple. They now play in Division One of the Western Union, having previously played in the Glasgow and District League. Arguably their best ever season was 1994 in which they narrowly lost the Small Clubs Cup Final to neighbours Vale of Leven, but managed to win the Second Division of the Glasgow and District League.

HELMET – more or less a universal sight on Scottish grounds these days. Whilst one cannot really criticize someone for taking steps to protect their own health and safety, one really has to question whether they are strictly necessary in Scottish conditions. With Scotland's heavy rainfall, pitches are damper and tend to lack bounce, the "beamer" or waist high fast full toss is specifically outlawed by the Laws of Cricket and in a laudable attempt to prevent the "bouncer" the Scottish National Cricket League compels an Umpire to call "No Ball" if the ball passes above shoulder height of the striker standing upright at his crease. In these circumstances, one feels that a batsman could dispense with a helmet.

Often a fielder at Silly Point or Silly Mid Off/On or Short Square Leg will wear a helmet. When not in use, the helmet should be removed from the field, otherwise a helmet left on the ground (behind the wicket keeper usually) might lose the fielding side 5 runs if the ball hits it.

HERIOT'S F.P. – a famous and consistently strong Edinburgh team, founded in 1889 to play their first season in 1890. They were originally exclusively for former pupils of George Heriot's High School, but since 1974 have no longer restricted themselves to alumni.

Their first ground was at Logie Green near Powderhall, a ground that no longer exists but seems also to have staged the Hearts v. Hibs Scottish Cup Final of 1896, the only occasion when a Final has not been played in Glasgow. They now play at Goldenacre, a fine ground in Ferry Road with a pavilion whose balcony gives a tremendous view of Edinburgh. This ground had its first cricket match on May 3rd 1902, and legend has it that a Heriot's bowler, the luckless William White, dropped an easy caught and bowled chance to the Clackmannan professional J.D. Hirst off the very first ball.

Since then Heriot's have always been a competent side and have unearthed quite a few good players. Arthur Creber, for example, a Welshman who was three times capped for Scotland was a fine bowler on either side of the Second World War.

Since the Second World War, with the arrival of more competitive cricket (Heriot's were founder members of the East League in 1953), success has been frequent, particularly in the 1970s and 1980s when they won the East of Scotland

League seven years in a row from 1977 to 1983. They won the Scottish Cup in 1978 and the Masterton Trophy five times, the latest being 1997.

Arguably their most famous ever player is H.K. More, who played 45 times for Scotland between 1966 and 1980, and scored 15,397 runs for Heriot's. He was a fine wicket-keeper as well, although their games even at the height of their "7 in a row" spell were often marked by bickering and temperamental problems. Hamish's brother George, famous in the legal profession, also played at about that time and on one occasion in 1972 against Selkirk the brothers put on stand of 220 for the first wicket. (The Selkirk fielders were heard, in their agonies, to shout "No More!"). A slightly older contemporary of Hamish was George Goddard who won 63 full caps for Scotland. Other players of that era included Peter Rhind, Ken Scotland (better known as a Rugby Internationalist), Eric Thomson and J.E. Ker.

Euan McIntyre, their current captain, has played for them for a long time, and their professional up until 1998, Shahid Aslam, has a ferocious pace, something a little surprising in a man of slender build. Jim Love, Scotland's coach, plays for Heriot's and current Scottish Internationalists are Mike Allingham and Asim Butt. It is also interesting to observe that at least one More and at least one Goddard are beginning to emerge to continue the family tradition.

They have a reputation of being a friendly club and they deserve this reputation. Their teas are excellent, and with a callous and welcome disregard for healthy eating, Heriot's give pies with tomato sauce. Their centenary brochure of 1989 is a very comprehensive account of the history of the club.

HIGHLAND – a team who play at Fraser Park, Inverness. They struggle a little because of lack of local competition in the immediate area, but they compete in the North of Scotland League and the Small Clubs Cup, without however having had any great success in either.

HILLEND – a team who play in the Glasgow and District League.

HILLHEAD HIGH SCHOOL FORMER PUPILS – Under professional Grant Parmenter, this team have come on leaps and bounds in recent years, and are now members of the Scottish National Cricket League. They were, according to one account, founded in the somewhat surprising year of 1918, although there is a certain amount of evidence that there was a Hillhead Cricket club before then, and even a Ladies cricket club of that name. The idea of a cricket club before the First World War for the daughters of gentlefolk in genteel Glasgow is perhaps surprising, but then again it might perhaps keep them away from the riffraff and keep their minds off more pernicious things like men. Their ground is Hughenden (more famous in rugby circles) in Glasgow.

HOLY CROSS

Until recently they have had a none too distinguished history of performances in the Glasgow and District League but recent years have shown an upturn in their performances. They earned their place in the Scottish National Cricket League in 1998 by winning the Second Division of the Western Union in 1997, and then earned the further piece of good fortune that Kilmarnock did not wish to enter the Scottish League meantime, leaving a space for them. In 1999 Hillhead play in Division 2, having had a tolerably good season in 1998.

As yet no member of this club has been capped for Scotland, but they did produce for the SCU one President in Dr. J.C. Davidson who held office in 1976. They are also proud of the fact that they organize the oldest-established cricket tour in Scotland, their men having ransacked the Borders every peace time year since 1929.

HOLY CROSS – An enthusiastic team who play at Arboretum Road, off the Ferry Road in Edinburgh, not far from other teams like Royal High Stewart Melville and Heriot's. Arboretum Road has a reputation of being a good batsman's wicket since the days of groundsman Eddie Watson in the 1970's. Holy Cross were founded in 1950 by Jim Black, a teacher of English at Holy Cross Academy. The first game was on 27th May 1950 against a team called Colinton Mains Association at Oxgangs. The club was designed mainly for former pupils of Holy Cross Academy, but the club was never exclusive. Indeed the school itself disappeared in the welter of educational re-organization when the comprehensive system was introduced in the late 1960s.

In their early years, in spite of being repeatedly rejected by the "closed shop" of the East of Scotland League's top division, they played in friendlies and in 1962 won a now long gone competition called the Scottish Midland League. They had fine bowlers like John Toal, Roddy Regan and Stan Arthur and an excellent wicket-keeper called Alan Reid. In 1976, with the East of Scotland Leagues now open, they won the Third Division, then the Second Division in 1979 and 1984. They were never strong enough to survive in the old First Division, possibly because they have never employed a professional.

They still play in the East of Scotland League, usually not far from the top of Division 1, and with the ambition that they show, the day will surely not be too far off when they join the Scottish National Cricket League. In 1998 they finished third in the East of Scotland League, beating winners Glenrothes on the last day. Their Secretary is James Bradley, a man with a wide knowledge of the game, and the team enjoy a deserved reputation of being willing to play cricket in conditions which the more fastidious would spurn.

HUMOUR – an ingredient sometimes sadly lacking on the cricket fields of Scotland, where competitiveness seems to bring with it a dismal earnestness which tends to make people forget that cricket is a game to be enjoyed.

It is probably true to say that lower down the Leagues, light-heartedness is more in evidence than in the grim battlefields of the upper regions where Cups, Leagues, bonus points and potential Scottish caps all conspire to make the game a serious and dire affair. Yet there are occasionally exceptions. In the 1996 Scottish Cricket Union Cup Final between Stoneywood-Dyce and Ayr, there was a deliberate false start. Umpire Joe Breslin, a much loved and respected figure, has a distinctive way of signalling "Dead Ball" which players enjoy watching. By agreement between the two sides, Andy Bee, while running in to bowl the first ball of the Ayr innings dropped the ball and delivered a convincing monosyllabic, Anglo-Saxon grunt to convince Joe that it was an accident. Joe then delivered his party piece to the Scorers, and the cheers of the players. The game then resumed in its deadly earnestness.

In 1982, at Battery Park, Greenock, two young ladies were making their way to a nearby funfair by walking over the cricket field. They were wearing stiletto heels, and although the sight was by no means unattractive to the lecherous fielders, polite requests were made to the damsels to remove their posteriors from the field, in view of the damage that their stiletto heels could do. They ignored the requests, and observing the captain of the visiting side crouching at first slip in an intense and apparently uncomfortable pose, shouted "Hey, mister, are you trying to do a jobby?"

Scotland were playing at Old Trafford, Lancashire in the 1950s. They were doing none too well at 65 for 5 when captain Hunter Cosh walked out to face a fine left-arm spinner called Malcolm Hilton. Cosh edged his first ball to first slip who dropped it. The same thing happened second ball except this time the slip caught it. Cosh returned crestfallen to the pavilion. The atmosphere was tense and dispirited until Willie Nichol of Kelburne said, "Well, Hunter, you couldn't even call that a chanceless duck." Cosh took it in good spirit but quite a few captains wouldn't have. Imagine saying that in these circumstances to the likes of Ian Chappell or Graham Gooch!

On another occasion at the same ground, Ralph Laing was hit in an extremely tender spot by Colin Croft the West Indian fast bowler. Anyone who has ever played cricket will know all about this, and how it is no joke whatsoever. Ralph however smiled at the sympathetic fieldsmen and said, "And to think that the last thing my wife said to me before I left home yesterday was 'I suppose you're away yet again to enjoy yourself for another three days' ".

Jim Wylie was an outstanding attacking batsman who enjoyed a lengthy career with St. Michael's of Dumfries in spite of having lost a large chunk of his leg in a sawmill accident. This handicap did not bother him all that much for he had the services of a wooden prosthetic to make up for the bit that the saw had removed. It was not all that obvious although Jim did have a slight limp. Some opponents were not aware of Jim's handicap and were occasionally taken aback when he would suddenly limp off from the crease saying, "I've broken my leg. I'll be back in a minute". Jim presumably kept a substitute leg for such emergencies

Joe Breslin – umpire

and no doubt had to thole remarks about the Umpire giving him his guard and saying "That's two legs" or people asking him if he wanted a short square leg etc.

Stirling County were fortunate to have the services of Terry Butcher, the famous footballer of Rangers and England, for a few games in the mid 1990s. After a few well publicised incidents at McDiarmid Park and Parkhead where Terry had been known to vent his frustrations on a dressing room door, Terry arrived for a game at Williamfield to find that the groundsman had not yet arrived and that the players were locked out of the pavilion. Terry, on the strength of his reputation, offered his services to find a way through the door, but fortunately a key arrived before this was necessary.

On another occasion, Terry was fielding at silly point for a bowler who had the Christian name of Tim. The bowler at the other end had the equally un-Rangers name of Kevin, but Terry joked about it saying that he never thought he would be on the same side as a Tim and so on. Ah well, they say that cricket broadens the mind!

Once Kirriemuir had a fast bowler who gave up the game. He still had his expensive cricket boots which he felt he could use at his work. So he painted them black. Next season he had second thoughts about retiring and came back. So he painted his boots white again. Nobody really noticed the difference until the rain came on. The players then saw chameleon type boots which in the course of an over changed colour from white to black, then eventually by the fifth ball back to white again.

HUNT, Alma (1910-1999) – Bermudan-born professional of Aberdeenshire from 1934 until 1947, famous among other things for a game against West Lothian in 1935. He took 7 for 11 as West Lothian were routed for 48, then opened the batting and scored the required 49 runs himself!

HUNTLY – play at Castle Park, Huntly. They were founded in 1854, when Strathbogie amalgamated with some other local teams. They were encouraged by the fifth Duke of Richmond, who in 1836 had inherited the Gordon estates and was a passionate follower of cricket. Their first game was in September 1854 at Aberchirder.

Their early years are well documented in a book by Patrick W. Scott. This book contains a wonderful description of the behaviour of the jubilant crowd when Huntly won the Aberdeenshire Cup for the second time in a row in 1907;

For a while handkerchiefs were conspicuous in the breeze while hands, umbrella and walking sticks were for the nonce somewhat out of their usual places.

Indeed the Edwardian era saw Huntly do very well in their various competitions in the Aberdeenshire Grades Association. Since joining the North of Scotland League, they have done well there also, notably their "7 in a row" in the mid 1960s. Huntly have won the Championship 3 times in the 1990s. They have competed in the Scottish Cup but with no great success. They also play in the Aberdeenshire Grades, and are extremely proud of the fact that Willie Donald, who played 57 times for Scotland when with Aberdeenshire and Epsom, hails originally from Huntly. For the 1999 season, Huntly have gained membership of the Strathmore Union, and it will be interesting to see how well they do there.

HYNDLAND – a Glasgow team founded in 1922 but now defunct, having merged with Allan Glen's and Bishopbriggs. As late as 1991 however they won the Glasgow Evening League KO Trophy.

I

IFFLA, Irvin – (1925 –) one of the great characters of Scottish cricket who still lives in his adopted Stirling. His lengthy career has lasted from the 1951 until 1993. He was a Jamaican who might have played for the West Indies if it hadn't been for the presence of Ramhadin and Valentine ("These two little friends of mine" as the 1950 calypso went) at the same time. He was the professional for Stirling County for nine years, but also played for Ayr, Stenhousemuir, St. Modan's and latterly Gargunnock Village, for whom he amassed 13,377 runs and took 1704 wickets. His bowling success was due to his nagging accuracy, and his sometimes uncanny knowledge of where the next catch was going to go.

INDOOR CRICKET – cricket does not really lend itself to being played indoors. For one thing it is difficult to find a Hall or Gymnasium big enough for a full game. The Scottish Cricket Union has now however found money from the National Lottery to build one in the grounds of Mary Erskine's School in Edinburgh, a decision which caused a certain amount of political controversy including the resignation of John Colquhoun from the Scottish Sports Council. John felt that this was a decision which favoured a fee-paying school, but as long as the facilities are available to everyone, there need not be a problem. There are occasionally six

Indoor U16 cricket 1994

a side tournaments played indoors in winter, one for example in Shetland. There is also the Cricket Media Super Eights played at the Hutcheson's Arena in Glasgow in early January and won in 1999 by Clydesdale. Games of Kwik Cricket for youngsters with a tennis ball can be played inside.

The Scottish winter is a long one. Foreign visitors to Scotland frequently comment that spring is slow to arrive and the weather does not always improve consistently in March and April. Any good side therefore will fix up Indoor Nets at a neighbouring Gymnasium or Sports Centre in the months of February or March. These conditions cannot, of course, replicate what will happen outdoors, but they do serve to help restore confidence and fitness. The "wicket" is usually a matting one with a fairly predictable bounce, and therein lies another reason why Indoor Cricket has not taken off in a big way – the game would almost certainly favour the batsman.

INJURIES – as always one of the dangers of any sport, but cricketing injuries are seldom life-threatening. Being hit on the head is always liable to be a serious business, but fortunately in Scotland, the pitches are normally so damp that the ball seldom rises to that height when you are batting. Nowadays Umpires are instructed to be very careful about sanctioning play in conditions that are potentially hazardous, particularly damp patches in the bowlers' run ups. In youth cricket, particularly at Under 13 level, there is a rule forbidding close fielding. All this follows the legal case in rugby where a referee was sued for incompetence when a player was paralysed following the collapse of a scrum which the referee, it was felt, should have done more to avoid.

One of the dangers of cricket for the older man is painful, although hardly life-threatening. Hamstrings are pulled very easily among the over-40s. Other injuries can be sustained in the early years of one's life, but have their effect later. Fast bowlers are of course prone to all sorts of muscle strains and stretches, and spinners too can find problems of slipped discs because of years of turning and twisting the body. Wicket keepers have problems with their knees because of the perpetual crouching.

Umpires often have a problem deciding about the fitness of conditions when it is one of these days, particularly in the early part of the season when everyone is keen, but the ground has not yet dried out sufficiently from last night's rain. Sawdust can help the problem, of course, but not every ground has a supply of that simple but effective remedy. All Umpires know that a wet patch on a bowler's run up can be very dangerous, and yet it is hard to be seen to delay or prevent play when football and rugby are going on quite happily on an adjoining pitch. This is a problem the world over, but particularly so in Scotland with the heavy rainfall and the late arrival of spring and summer, so that the pitches do not dry out as quickly as elsewhere.

INNELLAN – a recently formed club who play at Castle Toward in Argyllshire. Their fixture card claims that they were officially formed in 1993, although there are some indications of a cricket team around 1978 in a fund raising exercise for the Village Hall which was seeking to hold licensed dances.

Their fixture card also (most unusually) gives details of Western Ferries (Clyde) Limited's sailing times from Dunoon to Gourock, and tells us that they play teams like Mid Argyll, Cairndow and Knockdow. They compete in the Small Clubs Cup and various other local tournaments, but the main cornerstone of their existence is friendly cricket, a good tea and a few drunken escapades on tour in Yorkshire and elsewhere. Clearly, a friendly and happy club who do a great deal to keep the game going in one of the less accessible parts of the country.

INNINGS – by their very nature, most games in Scotland are of a single innings per side, and completed on the same day on which they started. The only two innings games are representative games played over two or three days. But it was not always so. Last century, when bowling was clearly better than batting, a two innings match was often completed on a day. The agreement usually was that if a two innings game could not be completed, the team which was ahead on the first innings would be the winners. This could have the effect of making the team who were behind on the First Innings throw the bat to collect quick runs, and then attempt to bowl out the opposition in the twilight.

INVERCLYDE – formed in 1957 as Scotts Cricket Club (named after Scotts Shipbuilding Company), they changed their name in 1986 to Inverclyde, because Scotts had been amalgamated into British Shipbuilders. They felt that the name Inverclyde might make it easier to attract sponsors.

Until 1998 they played at Battery Park, Greenock, but have now moved up the hill to Gourock Park which is an enclosed arena, although the playing surface is not as good as that of Battery Park. They joined the Glasgow and District League in 1977 and have played in all four Divisions. Their current President John Blair is one of the founder members of the club, and has worked hard on the Youth Coaching Initiative which is beginning to show results. In late 1998, the team completed their first "overseas" tour i.e. a weekend in Arran. With cricket about to be re-structured in the West, Inverclyde are confident of their future.

INVERGORDON – Invergordon have had an intermittent existence since 1949, but they have participated in the North of Scotland League.

INVERNESS – it would have to be admitted that the capital of the Highlands is a waste land as far as cricket is concerned. This is in stark contrast to Aberdeen where it thrives. Highland survive but Northern Counties are struggling, and teams like Inverness Citadel, Inverness College and Inverness St. Andrews have long since perished. Until season 1957, Inverness boasted a strong and active Welfare League, but this has gradually disappeared.

It is a sad fact that cricket has never made any significant inroads into the Gaelic speaking population of Inverness and areas to the west. Shinty is, of course, the game there, but, although one can hear Urdu and Punjabi spoken on the cricket fields of Scotland, one never hears Gaelic.

INVERURIE – one of the success stories of recent years, particularly since they joined the Strathmore Union in 1993. They were formed in 1931 and play at Kellands Park where they re-built their pavilion to coincide with their arrival in the Strathmore Union. They have participated in the Scottish Cup, albeit with no great success, but they won the Small Clubs Cup in 1992.

Although the present Inverurie team can only date their continuous existence back to 1931, the town of Inverurie has been a hot bed of cricket for much longer than that. There have been teams like Hawthorn, Inverurie Union, Inverurie Loco Works, Inverurie Paper Mills and Inverurie Butchers, and the first mention of an Inverurie side comes in 1887.

The club's first outing in the Aberdeenshire Cricket Association was less than auspicious as they were bowled out for 19, but they soon made their mark on the Aberdeenshire Cup by winning it in 1932, then again in 1936 and 1946. Almost half a century would pass before they won it again in 1992 in what was the last game played by the club as an Aberdeenshire Grades team before their entry into the Strathmore Union.

Inverurie's success in the early years was built around bowling all-rounder David Reis and the elegant batsman Eddie Prosser. The club's fortunes took a dip in the 1950's and 1960's, but under the guidance of the enthusiastic Norman Brownlee, the trend was reversed in the 1970's. By the 1980's the club was back at the top of the Aberdeenshire Grades, winning it in 1981 and remaining continuously in contention with Cults for supremacy.

The winning of the Small Clubs Cup in 1992 and the entry into the Strathmore Union brought a new lease of life to the club. 1994 was a significant year for the club in that they toured Barbados for the first time, and then won the Three Counties Cup, beating Brechin in the Final.

Inverurie are a team who deserve success, coming as they do from a small town and having to contend with so many other attractions. They have retained since 1931 a very high local profile, and hope to respond to the new millennium by promoting notions of cricket as a game of fun and sportsmanship.

IRVINE – based at Marress Sports Ground, Irvine now play in the First Division of the Western Union.

J

JARDINE, D.R. – (1900-1958) the man who masterminded the Bodyline tour of 1932-33 and remains the most hated Englishman of all time in Australia, has connections with Scotland that are by no means tenuous. He was born in Bombay, but of Scottish parents and spent many of his early summer holidays in Scotland. In his later years he was quite happy to acknowledge his Scottish connections, doing things like speaking at the Centenary Dinner of Dunnikier Cricket Club in Kirkcaldy in 1956 and charming everyone by his sincerity.

It was often said that much of his dour, unapproachable character was inherited from his Presbyterian forebears, and particularly his father M.R. Jardine who played for the Fettesians. There is a record of the said M.R. Jardine scoring 217 for the Fettesian-Lorretonians against Liverpool in 1893.

JARGON – one of the things that definitely discourages someone with a casual interest in cricket is the sheer amount of jargon and cricketing technicalities. So much of it is inherited from the English public school tradition, which one has read as a boy in the adventures of Billy Bunter and others. One shudders when one hears that someone is having a "knock at the nets" instead of a practice and just occasionally a fine drive is referred to as "a spiffing good shot" when someone called "Roge" or "Symon" is batting.

Ladies who are introduced to the game by eager boyfriends will always find it difficult to comprehend why a bowler needs a "deep fine leg" when he already has a "short square" one. Foreign visitors too will very soon find themselves lost in the mire of cricketing speak. One German student attempted to write a Ph.D. on the subject, and it would be interesting to know what the examiners at Heidelburg University made of it.

There is the word "duck". Some of the infantile Australian Television companies have shown the motif of a duck walking off in tears when a batsman has "failed to trouble the scorers" as it is more euphemistically put and I suppose that perhaps helps some of the younger fans to understand. But there was one occasion at a well known Scottish ground when the three year old son of a player who had been dismissed without troubling the scorers greeted his mother who had arrived to make the teas with the news that "Daddy's had a duck". Unfortunately, the youngster had a speech impediment and the good lady's instant reaction of mortification and jealousy (I wonder which bitch it was this time?) was a sight to behold, before she corrected her son and told him to say the somewhat ambiguous "Daddy didn't score today". Both parts of the ambiguity, she claimed and hoped, were true.

But there are words and phrases which frankly do not make sense, even to someone who has mastered the difference between leg and off, and silly and fine. A youngster for example might be told to stand on the "45 and catching" or "saving one". A batsman who completes one run will tell his companion that he is "looking" or "if you like". An Umpire might say "left arm round going through – two coming" as a new batsman appears after the same batsman has asked for "two legs" or perhaps just "two".

All this is difficult for the simple souls who wish their cricket simple and it is refreshing when one hears the captain of an Aberdeenshire side who places his field with the simple instructions of "ower there, Erchie" and "up a wee bittie, Geordie", or the captain of the Fife schoolboy side who, realising that the big hitter was on strike, told all his men to get back to the "boondaries". And there is the true story of a Scotsman who was doing his bit for the less fortunate and reading aloud a cricket book which he was recording on a cassette to be sent to a blind man in Sussex. The earnest young Scotsman was making every effort to minimise his Scottish accent. Everything went fine until he played back his recording and heard himself say "...shortly before lunch Tony Greig threw the ball to Underwood and invited him to 'bool' from the pavilion end".

One of the great joys of listening to a real expert on cricket like Richie Benaud on TV is that he has the ability to explain things without excessive resort to jargon, or if he does, can use it in such a way that a layman can understand.

JERVISWOOD – a Paisley team, founded in 1949, who play at Allanton Playing Fields, Ralston, Paisley. Previously they played at a ground called Seedhill.

JOCK'S LODGE – erstwhile ground of Royal High School F.P., situated not far from Meadowbank Stadium in Edinburgh. When the property developers won the argument in the late 1980s, Royal High F.P. were compelled to move to Barnton, to the playing fields of Royal High School. This move was not a great success, for the wicket was not always what it could have been, and eventually in 1996-97, Royal High F.P. merged with Stewart's Melville F.P. and were called in 1998 Royal High Stewart Melville, and in 1999 Stewart Melville Royal High!

The loss of Jock's Lodge was much to be deplored, for there was a fine old pavilion there. Frequently, jokes were made about the masonic implications of the word "lodge", but when Royal High engaged a large number of Pakistani players, it was said that it would be an idea if the ground were now to be called not Jock's Lodge but Jock's Mosque.

JUNIOR CRICKET – in recent years there has been much development of junior cricket, and the Scottish Cricket Union has done much to counteract the collapse of cricket at school level in the public sector. There are District Competitions, often held on a residential basis at some place like Fettes or Merchiston Castle during the school holidays at Under 13 and Under 15 Level. From these competitions a Scotland squad is chosen to play at a Festival against teams like Ireland, Cumbria or Durham. In addition there are District Championships at Under 16 and Under 19 Level played throughout the summer, which give aspiring young talent the chance to attract the attention for selection for national teams.

At club level there are Knock Out Competitions at Under 13 and Under 15 level and Leagues for Under 15s and Under 17s. In 1998 the Cups were won by Clydesdale and Kelburne respectively, whereas the Leagues (which become Cups in the later stages) were won by a combined Edinburgh Accies/Grange team at Under 15 level and Arbroath at Under 17.

At International Level, Scotland have sides at Under 19, Under 16, Under 15 and Under 13 Levels who play against Ireland, Durham, Wales etc. at various festivals. At Under 19 Level, there is a World Cup in which Scotland competed in South Africa in 1998. The World Cup will be held every two years and in the year between, there will be a European Tournament. Scotland will host this tournament in 2001 and will compete in the 1999 tournament which will be held in Ireland.

It appears that European Tournaments will be the order of the day, for under the aegis of the European Cricket Council, European Youth Tournaments are being introduced annually at Under 15, Under 17 and bi-annually at Under 19 Level. The Under 15 Tournament in 1999 will be held in Scotland and will involve Scotland, Ireland, Denmark and Holland. The Under 17 one will feature the same opposition but will be played in Holland.

Scotland stars of the future?

G W Jupp

JUPP G.W. (1873-1945) – famous batsman for Carlton who also played for Scotland and Somerset. He was a prodigious hitter of the ball and scored many centuries for Carlton. On one occasion at Raeburn Place he actually hit a ball into someone's house through an open window on the other side of the road. Sadly, his *floruit* was in the Edwardian era and coincided with the time when the Scottish Cricket Union was in abeyance, so he was capped for Scotland only twice in 1909 (after its re-formation) and 1912. Being a native of Somerset, he was occasionally given a game for them, but he was never a regular.

111

K

KEITH – Keith are said to have been founded in 1862, through an amalgamation of Keith and Keith Mechanics. A couple of years later there is a record of a game against Huntly, which led to serious crowd unrest following some dispute about under-arm or over-arm bowling. They now play at Fife Park and the years since the Second World War have seen steady progress culminating in the victory in the North of Scotland Senior Knock Out Cup in 1990 and the North of Scotland League itself for the first and only time in 1996

KELBURNE – founded in 1860, Kelburne play at The Oval, Whitehaugh in Paisley. They have been there since 1899, having played at Blackhall before then. They are now members of the Scottish National Cricket League and play in Division 3 in 1999. They played in the Western Union, but were never considered to be one of the better teams and won the League on only three occasions, 1924, 1947 and 1951.

1947 also saw the first International at Whitehaugh when the South Africans drew with Scotland, the occasion being marked by Jimmy Aitchison's 106 not out. Kelburne themselves have produced a few Scottish Internationalists, notably Willie Nichol, who also played for Gala, but was so identified with the Paisley men that he became known as "Willie Kelburne"

Kelburne were the first winners of the Scottish Cup in 1966, but have had no great success in that competition or any other since that date. In 1995 they had as professional the South African with the lovely name of Roger Telemachus, a name which Classical students will immediately identify as the son of Odysseus.

KELSO – play at Shedden Park, Kelso and for many years were the kingpins of Borders Cricket. Like Gala, they have performed a "nine in a row" of League titles, in Kelso's case from 1984 to 1992, and won again in 1994. More recent success however has been confined to the Borders Cup, which they have won a total of 20 times. Their most famous player is J.E. Ker, who played 57 times for Scotland between 1977 and 1988 and another Internationalist is Andy Goram, who played 5 times for Scotland at cricket and many more times at football.

Kelso are apparently (given the lack of any information to the contrary) the oldest club in Scotland. The Minutes book of 1821 to 1830 is in the Scottish Borders Archive and Local History Centre in St. Mary's, Selkirk. Earlier Minutes books are now lost, but as 1821 is described as the Second Session, it may be that the club was founded in 1820. We are told that the club was founded on 13th June but, annoyingly, we are not told what year. The earliest entry is for 4th September 1821, when the club met for the first time after the "Recefs" (sic) (Recess,

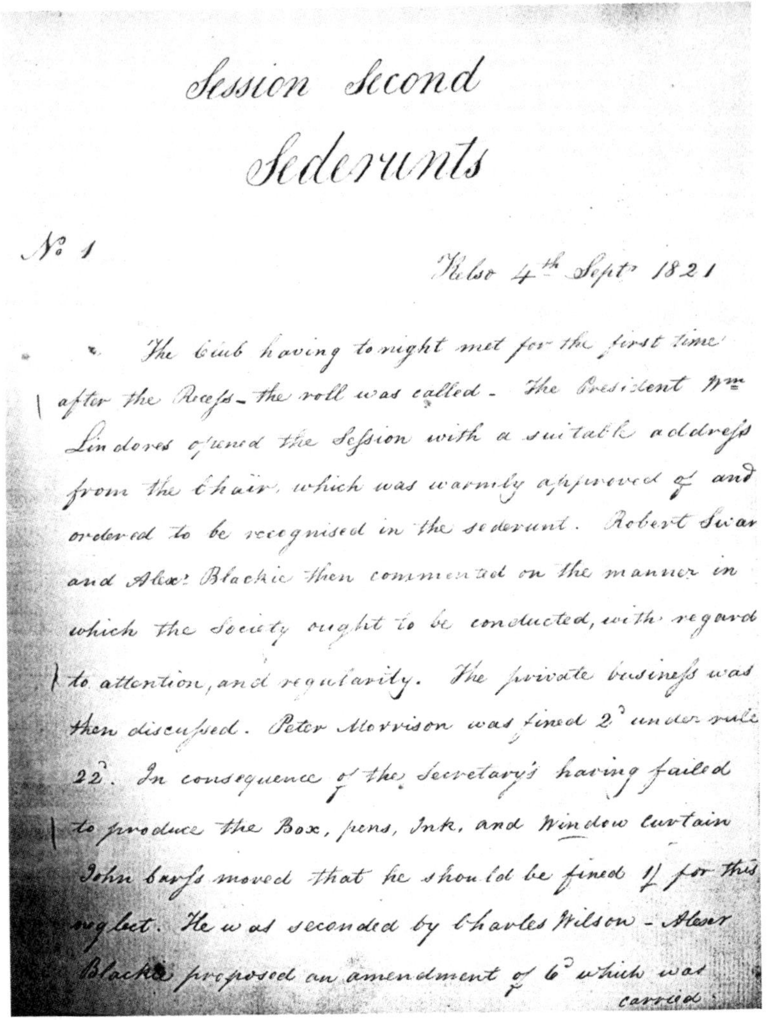

Session Second

Sederunts

Nº 1

Kelso 4ᵗʰ Septʳ 1821

The Club having to night met for the first time after the Recess - the roll was called - The President Wᵐ Lindores opened the Session with a suitable address from the Chair, which was warmly approved of and ordered to be recognised in the sederunt. Robert Swar and Alex: Blackie then commented on the manner in which the Society ought to be conducted, with regard to attention, and regularity. The private business was then discussed. Peter Morrison was fined 2ᵈ under rule 22ᵈ. In consequence of the Secretary's having failed to produce the Box, pens, Ink, and Window Curtain John Laws moved that he should be fined 1/ for this neglect. He was seconded by Charles Wilson - Alexʳ Blackie proposed an amendment of 6ᵈ which was carried.

The earliest documentary evidence of cricket in Scotland – the minutes book of Kelso for September 1821. Clearly the club had been in existence for some time before this. Note the spelling of the double s.

presumably) but the Minutes book tends to deal with internal club matters and does not tell us much about games played etc. It is however a wealth of interest. The Secretary, for instance, was to be fined 1 shilling, later reduced to 6 old pence, then 2 old pence for having failed to "produce the Box, pens, Ink and Window Curtain" for some unspecified occasion, but perhaps the said meeting on 4th September 1821.

There also seems to have been a great literary emphasis in these early days of Kelso Cricket Club – for example next meeting's discusfion (sic) was to be "Whether does Education or Climate tend more to form national character" and at the meeting on October 4th President Peter Morrison read Burns "Epistle to a Young Friend".

Ay free, aff han', your story tell
When wi a bosom crony;
But still keep something to yoursel
Ye scarcely tell to ony.

Debates took place on motions like "Was Brutus justified in killing Caesar" and (surprisingly considering that Waterloo was only a few years in the past) "Did the reign of Napoleon in France tend more to good or evil". It would be hard to find a hundred years later in the early 1920's anyone with anything good to say about the Kaiser! Indications however that the 1820's were far from peaceful times even in the idyllic Borders come on the 11th February 1823 when the club had to meet at a different venue "owing to the clubroom being commandeered into a guard room in the evening, for those on watch over the Church grounds".

Of more immediate and mundane concern to the club was the problem on November 27th 1821 for "the woman who formerly put on the fires now refused to do so" and someone else had to be found to do the needful. There is much evidence however of members "enjoying themselves over a tumbler of punch" and in 1824 it was resolved that at the marriage of any member "the club is to give him a dinner and half dozen (sic) of wine".

The emphasis on the literary side of things in Kelso need not surprise us too much when we bear in mind that many a cricket club in the 19th century, notably Carlton and Grange, owed their origin, at least in part, to debating and political clubs. Indeed, the first Wisden for 1864 gives us *inter alia* a list of canals, the Battles of the Wars of the Roses, the winners of the Derby and the rules for a bizarre and little known game called Knur and Spell! It appears that cricketers in the early days were seldom at a loss to find a way to wile away the long winter evenings.

There is mention however in the Kelso minute book of the Secretary "having presented a Board containing the rules of the game of cricket" and being thanked for it. Punishment was however also visited on miscreants like Charles Wilson who was fined an unspecified amount one week for non-attendance "no excuse being presented".

On the cricketing front, the club found a home under the unlikely name of Wooden Anna leased from a Mr. Macker, according to the minute of Hogmanay 1822. The same meeting also agreed to adopt a Tartan Uniform for the playing of the game. Fortunately or otherwise, the New Year brought a change of opinion and by January 7th 1823, the uniform was changed to Blue with a White necker and cuffs and mother of pearl buttons! The uniforms were ready for Saturday 29th March when *"the Jackets being completed, the Club with a number of Strangers adjourned to Wooden Anna the play ground where the game was played with great spirit for more than three hours."* They were less lucky three weeks later when *"falling of snow and general coarseness of the weather"* compelled a withdrawal to warmer places and, presumably, more bowls of punch.

What the Minute book does **not** indicate however is any indication of any game actually played against another club. It does seem that Kelso Cricket Club was a collection of gentlemen who met in the winter months for entertainment soirees, conviviality and punch and who played cricket among themselves when the weather permitted it in the summer months. They were rich enough to insist on the wearing of the cricketing uniform (6 pence fine for defaulters, according to the minute of 4th April 1824) and were blessed with a Minute secretary who was conscientious and wrote legibly.

Kelso's existence has been far from continuous, as far as documented records can prove, so any claim to be Scotland's oldest club must be somewhat tenuous, that honour being keenly contested by Perthshire. However that may be, Kelso have an outstanding chance of being the longest lasting cricket club, for their ground Shedden Park was gifted to the town by a resident who reputedly stated that he wanted cricket to be played there *in perpetuitatem.*

Seldom however in the lengthy history of Kelso C.C. can there have been a tenser finish to a season than in 1994 when with Kelso, Dumfries and Berwick all in the hunt for the Border League, Kelso had to beat Hawick on the last day. Professional Jason Arnberger, who had been so prolific early in the season, was already back in Australia, however, and Kelso struggled. Hawick required three from the last ball, couldn't quite get the ball away far enough, and were run out going for the second of the three required runs.

Other successes achieved by Kelso include the Under 15 Scottish Cup won in 1985 and the Scottish Indoor Sixes in 1986. They have produced two Presidents of the Scottish Cricket Union – D.J. Luke in 1965 and R.K. Maconochie in 1985.

KELVINSIDE ACADEMY – one of Scotland's strong cricketing schools, and they certainly feel that they should be for their Greek motto is Aien Aristeuein which means "always to be the best". In the 1980s they were coached by Omar Henry, and did the unusual thing of going on a tour of Barbados.

KEMNAY

KEMNAY – members of the Aberdeenshire Grades since 1887. They had their glory years immediately after the Second World War, winning Grade One in 1949, 1951 and 1952.

KERR, John – (1885 – 1972) (Greenock and Scotland) – arguably one of the greatest ever Scottish batsman. He is third in the list of all time great run scorers, amassing 21,558 runs, second only to Drummond Robertson of Forfarshire and Morrison Zuill of Stenhousemuir. His average is over 40. John was the son of a great Greenock player of the Victorian age called Dan Kerr and he made his debut for the club in 1900 while still at school. He also played a few games for Carlton but it was for Greenock that he made his name. Kerr scored 49 centuries in his lengthy career, including a century against every Western Union team. He won 33 full caps for Scotland (and a few other honours) in an International career which lasted from 1913 to 1933. His most famous Innings for Scotland was perhaps his 137 in 1928 at Raeburn Place against Ireland, during which time he passed his 1,000 runs in games against Ireland, but he should also be remembered for the 147 that he hit at Raeburn Place in 1921 against the all conquering Australians who included men like Warwick Armstrong and others who had recently wiped the floor with J.W.H.T. Douglas's England. Yet there were those who thought that his 40 not out on July 3rd 1919 against the Australian Imperial Forces on a crumbling wicket against the likes of Gregory and Collins was equally praiseworthy.

He bowled as well, but never reached the heights with the ball that he did with the bat. His captaincy was always astute and with Kerr in charge, Greenock were seldom far away from the top of the Western Union. He was a fine man, abstemious, good humoured and a worthy Elder in the Church of Scotland. He died on December 27th 1972 at the age of 87. His brother James Reid Kerr was also a fine player, but somewhat eclipsed by John. James nevertheless scored 9 centuries for Greenock and was once capped for Scotland.

KILMARNOCK – founded in 1852, when according to tradition, four gentlemen came together in a local inn for the purpose and it can claim with justification to be the oldest sporting club in the town.

Kilmarnock encountered severe ground difficulties in the mid 1990's. Kirkstyle, their home since 1904 (they had previously played at Holm Quarry), is no longer deemed suitable, having suffered the ravages of floods, fire and vandalism. Floods in particular have caused a problem, as the nearby river

No Play to-day! Kirkstyle, Kilmarnock, after the floods of August 1961.

overflows its banks with regularity, and in bad years like 1961, people reputedly have been seen on the Kirkstyle outfield in rafts, fishing! On other occasions, a sharp frost has made an ice rink out of their ground. All this has helped to explain the unpredictability of Kirkstyle's wicket! Their future home is uncertain, although they have now amalgamated with Kilmarnock Rugby Club. The prospect of having to play fixtures away from home was enough to deter them from attempting to join the Scottish National Cricket League in 1998, but they hope to have new facilities in place by the year 2000.

Their pedigree in the Western Union is a long and honourable one. They joined in 1907 and are still with the Western Union. They were the first winners after the resumption of cricket in 1946 and won it seven times in all (joint in 1949) with their best period being the 1950s and 1960s. They have won the Rowan Cup 10 times, and on four occasions have won a Cup called the McCulloch Cup. (This trophy was donated by the McCulloch family in memory of their son Stewart who was a Kilmarnock player.)

Their most famous player is the Rev.J. Aitchison, who played for them in the years from 1937 to 1967 and again in 1973 and scored for the club a total of 15,280 runs which included 33 centuries, 19 of which were in the Western Union – a record for this competition. Such was his affection for Kilmarnock that when he played for West of Scotland for one season at the end of his career, the good Rev. refused to play against Kilmarnock, opting instead to play for the Second XI that day!

Their best ever bowler was Jim Thomson, who was scandalously under-capped by Scotland (only 5 times) but who became in 1984 the first player to take 1,000 wickets in the Western Union. He took 2044 in all games for Kilmarnock. Other great players include R.G. Hill, T.N. Gallagher, M. Colquhoun of more recent vintage and W. Thomson, R. Hamilton, W. Douglas Sr., W. Smith and J. McCulloch of the Victorian era. There was also R. Ellis who won 20 Scottish caps between 1963 and 1974.

In 1971 they reached the Final of the Scottish Cup only to lose to Strathmore. Their professional then was Australian Bob Massie, who a year later would destroy England at Lord's by taking match figures of 16 for 137. This was little surprise to Kilmarnock supporters, for in his debut Union match in 1969, he took all ten Poloc wickets for 34. But their best professional all-rounder was Tony Riddington in the early 1950s who had played for Leicestershire. In 1937, the club almost landed the great S.F. Barnes as professional, but were dilatory in contacting him!

Kilmarnock are a great club, and all supporters of Scottish cricket will wish them well in their attempts to find a new home.

KINGSWAY – a Dundee team, founded in 1947, who play at the University Ground, after previously playing at Dawson Park. They play in the Perthshire Cricket League, and won it for the first time in 1997.

KINLOCH – the oldest surviving Dundee Public Parks side, although the accepted date of their formation in 1905 cannot be conformed with certainty. The side spent much of its formative years in the Lochee Park Cricket Association but were winners of the Dundee and District Cricket Trophy, a trophy which can still be seen in the Dundee museum.

The club continued to play mainly friendly cricket at weekends and in local parks Cup competitions until 1969 when they made a successful application to join the Strathmore Union. They made their debut in 1970 and in their first season were runners up in the Two Counties Cup, a trophy in which they have always done well.

The club's honours list however boasts three Strathmore Union Second Division League title wins in 1979, 1988 and 1995. They have competed in the Small Clubs Cup in every year since its inception and in 1992 they reached the Semi Final.

After years of playing at public parks like Lochee Park or University Grounds, Kinloch now intend to move to a new ground of their own in Elliot Road for the start of the 1999 season.

The club's most famous ex-player is current President Jack Hirst, who scored 12,259 runs and took 1570 wickets in his lengthy career with the club.

KINTORE – one of the more successful sides in the Aberdeenshire Grades, particularly in the early 1970s. They have also entered for the Village Trophy and enjoy a reputation of providing lavish teas.

KIRK BRAE – a small Edinburgh team who play at Double Hedges Road, Edinburgh. They are in the Third Division of the East of Scotland League, having finished 6th in 1998. They also have a Midweek XI. There is no great record of

The Hakka. Kirk Brae Cricket Club scaring the opposition on tour at Riverdale Hall.

outstanding performances other than the time they delivered a shock to Stewart's-Melville in the Masterton Trophy several years ago.

They were founded in 1980, and their emblem is a badger. The learned claim that this is because of their persistent presence around the Kirk Brae area of Edinburgh, but the more prosaic point out that a badger is on a label of a West Country beer bottle! They started off playing friendlies, but then graduated to the Grades of the East League, and from there to the League itself. In 1998, the first ever century in the club's history was scored by a man by the name of John Hobbs, who is not surprisingly nicknamed "Jack". It is to be hoped that he can continue to emulate "The Master".

In 1997 the club was unfortunate to lose John McDonald who died at the age of 46. John who was nicknamed "W.G." because of his beard, was a fine and

Ian Gavin – captain of Kirkcaldy in 1991, later to play for Freuchie and Scotland.

chivalrous man who "walked" if he nicked a ball, and was himself a scrupulously fair Umpire. He is much missed by the club.

Clearly a pleasant and cheerful club who enjoy the game, and who deserve the support of all who love cricket.

KIRKCALDY – one of Scottish cricket's saddest stories has been the demise of Kirkcaldy, who were unable to fulfil all their fixtures in 1997 and failed to appear at all in 1998.

Founded in 1867, although there is a certain amount of doubt about the exact date, Kirkcaldy first played at a ground called Newton Park in Nicol Street. They played at a ground called Robbie's Park in 1891 but Robbie's Park was engulfed by the Beveridge Park when it opened in 1892. Kirkcaldy played at Beveridge Park until moving to Bennochy in 1957.

Between the wars they had some fine players like Wattie Venters, who might have played for Scotland if he had had a more fashionable club, and professional Len Halstead. There are a few reports of large crowds flocking to see them and even a few unsavoury scenes when the crowd disapproved of a few decisions made by the Umpire who came with the opposition.

After the war Kirkcaldy continued to prosper with Bill Dennis as professional. In the 1960's they unearthed the talent of Alan Ormerod, an English-born lad whose formative years were at Bennochy before he moved on to a illustrious county career with Worcestershire and others. Kirkcaldy's great days, however, were in the mid 1980s when they won the East of Scotland League in 1984, the Masterton Trophy in 1985 and 1989 and were considered unlucky not to do better in the Scottish Cup. They were very fortunate in their professionals e.g. Ray Joseph, Bob Carter, Sundeep Patil, Gus Logie and had a fine bunch of youngsters as well.

But in the early 1990s their lease expired on the Bennochy ground and they had to return to the Beveridge Park, a blow from which they never really recovered. At the same time, several of their better players opted to go elsewhere e.g. Ian Gavin to Freuchie, Graeme Welsh to West Lothian and the slide began. Attempts on at least one occasion to amalgamate with Dunnikier came to naught and Kirkcaldy quietly disappeared, little more than a decade after being considered one of the best teams in Scotland.

KIRRIEMUIR – home of cricket fan J.M. Barrie, Kirriemuir, a team who have struggled in recent times, play at a lovely ground called The Hill to the north of the town. This ground commands a lovely view of the Grampian Mountains and the Sidlaw Hills and has a Camera Obscura on top of the pavilion so that one can see the bad weather coming. One can also turn the camera and get a wonderful TV type view of the game from behind the bowler's arm minus of course Richie Benaud and the action replay! It is also next to a cemetery and, in the days when funerals were held on a Saturday afternoon, tradition and decorum dictated that

"Mad Mike" – Kirkcaldy's eccentric wicketkeeper Mike McKenzie of the 1960's, 1970's and 1980's.

the cricket was not allowed to start until such time as the hearse entered the necropolis wherein lies Kirrie's greatest son J.M. Barrie.

Kirrie's origins go back to the middle of last century, for Barrie himself as a youngster was a scorer for them. They have a reputation for enjoying their cricket without perhaps the cutting edge that some other teams have. Their golden years were in the 1970s when they won the Second Division of the Strathmore Union on two occasions and the Two Counties Cup on three. In 1972 they won the Double. Since then their achievements have been less obvious, but they deserve a great deal of credit for keeping cricket going in this small and lovely Angus town and they have also produced the occasional noteworthy performance on the field, for example in 1976 at Dawson Park, Dundee against Telecoms when wicketkeeper Gordon Shepherd took seven catches in one innings.

Kirrie enjoy a keen but friendly rivalry with their Angus neighbours. There are at least two stories involving Brechin Second XI. One was when Kirriemuir at tea time had reached 140, and their captain Dave Torrie was approached by the shamefaced Brechin captain, "I'm very sorry, Dave, but we've been fielding with 12 men!" Brechin had listed 12 men for the game apparently just in case someone didn't turn up, as often happened. On this occasion, all 12 appeared, travelled to Kirrie and took the field. Nobody, neither Umpires, batsmen, nor fielders themselves, noticed! It was apparently a *bona fide* mistake, and accepted as such, but only eleven Brechin men batted!

Another occasion saw the Kirrie men in the field awaiting the Brechin batsmen to start the innings. No batsman appeared, and after a decent interval of time, a polite enquiry was made as to why. It transpired that one of the openers had locked himself in the toilet, the lock had jammed and the man could neither get out, nor could his mirthful colleagues open the door from the other side. Eventually, a few muscular fast bowlers were able to break open the door and play commenced.

Their ground has seen a great deal of unusual happenings. For example, a game once had to be abandoned because tinkers had lit a fire in the nearby quarry and billowing smoke made play impossible! On another occasion, a helicopter was spraying a potato field adjacent to their ground with fertilising chemicals and unfortunately for the cricketers, the wind just happened to be blowing from the wrong direction!

They had a fine wicketkeeper in the 1960s called Arthur McIntosh. Unfortunately, Arthur was also a member of the Kirriemuir Fire Brigade and when the siren went, Arthur had no option but to drop everything (ball, bat, whatever), remove his pads and other accoutrements and charge off the park to his bicycle, usually to the sort of cheer reserved for a hero going to save the day.

But it is the Pavilion at Kirriemuir that is the most remarkable thing. It was situated so far from any electric pylon that it was as late as 1995 that electricity was put in, some 65 years after its grand opening by the Dreamer of Thrums. But in the 1930s a pipe was laid from the pavilion to the edge of the wicket so that the

Young Kwik Cricketers in action.

square could be sprinkled. It was used until war came in 1939. In the 1950s everyone knew that there was such a pipe, but no-one knew exactly where, not even the amateur water diviners who tried in vain. Eventually in 1973 the Town Clerk arrived with a metal detector and found it! It was used for a couple of years, then local government was regionalised in 1975 and Tayside Regional Council, to satisfy the whims of pedantic bureaucrats, closed it down!

KWIK CRICKET – a game played with a soft ball for children, mainly of Primary School age. The idea is that children develop a feel for the game, and a certain amount of knowledge of the skills involved before graduating to the adult game with a hard ball. This game is particularly valuable in countries like Scotland where not every boy necessarily has a great background in the game.

In 1998 the Under 12 Kwik Cricket Coaching Scheme and Cup saw eight teams – Grange, West Lothian, Ferguslie, Clydesdale, Arbroath, Stirling, Kelso and Dumfries contesting the Finals at the North Inch in Perth in August. The competition was very keen and Grange turned out to be the winners. A similar tournament for Primary Schools at Softball Cricket had taken place earlier in the summer, also at the North Inch, and Timmergreens Primary of Arbroath emerged as victors.

L

LADS' CLUB – an Aberdeenshire Grades team. They first entered that competition in 1934.

LANG, Andrew (1844-1912) – Scottish literary figure, famous among other things for his History of Scotland and translations of Homer's Iliad and Odyssey. He was also a great lover of St. Andrews University, about whom he wrote a famous poem called "The College of the Scarlet Gown".

> *St. Andrews by the Northern Sea*
> *A haunted town it is to me*

His cricketing connections are less well known but he was born in Selkirk, and was related to the many Langs who played cricket for the "souters" in the 19th Century, and he recalls his cricketing youth in the simple verse:

> *Well, there's one word that moved me when a boy,*
> *That moves today:*
> *It's when the Umpire, to the general joy,*
> *Pronounces "Play"*

And in his work "Brahma" he uses cricketing imagery to prove his own omnipotence when he says

> *If the wild bowler thinks he bowls,*
> *Or if the batsman thinks he's bowled,*
> *They know not, poor misguided souls,*
> *That they shall perish unconsoled.*
> *I am the batsman and the ball,*
> *I am the bowler and the ball,*
> *The umpire, the pavilion cat,*
> *The roller, pitch and stumps and all.*

LANGHOLM – an unpretentious Border League club who play at Castleholm. They were formed in 1856 and their one solitary success of note came in 1976 when they won the Border League. In their early days they owed much to the patronage of the Duke of Bucleuch who gave them the use of his Langholm Lodge.

LARGO – a recent arrival on the Fife cricket scene. They play at a lovely spot in East Fife near the home of Alexander Selkirk, who earned fame as Robinson Crusoe. Largo change in what used to be a private house and have tea in a Church Hall. They play in the Second Division of the East of Scotland League, but there is the possibility of expansion and improvement, given the enthusiasm of their committee, in particular their President Andrew Hutchison who is also an Umpire in the Scottish National Cricket League. Their first games were in 1983, their first full season 1984, but they did not join the League structure until 1989. Currently they have two full teams, an Under 15 XI , an Under 13 XI and a Sunday friendly team, which is not bad going for a Fife village.

There had been a Largo team from 1948 to 1953, playing on roughly the same site as they do now, but legend has it that they lost their ground following an unseemly dispute and lovers' tiff between the daughter of the Laird and the Minister of the local Church. Even after their re-formation in 1983 they did not get their ground back until 1986, being obliged to play at Waid Academy for a spell. The ground was re-opened with a game against Freuchie, then Village Trophy holders, and Mike Denness guested for Largo.

L.B.W. – the most contentious issue on any given Saturday. Was I (or he) really out? In club cricket where there are no neutral Umpires, one has to rely on the integrity of members of the batting side, but even with neutral Umpires in Scottish League games, there is much controversy. To give someone out l.b.w., an Umpire should be able to say yes to four questions;

    a. Was the point of impact between wicket and wicket? (If the batsman is not offering a stroke, he can be out if the point of impact is outside the line providing the Umpire thinks the ball would have hit the wicket.)

    b. Did the ball pitch between wicket and wicket or on the offside?

    c. Would the ball have hit the wicket?

    d. Did the ball hit the batsman's person (not the bat or the hand holding the bat) first?

No matter who is Umpiring, the Batsman will consider himself unlucky to have been given out, and the bowler will feel he has not been given justice by the Umpire who keeps his finger in his pocket. Fielders will often appeal from positions where they have no idea of whether the appeal is justified or not. The only person who can really decide is the Umpire.

It is often felt that this law would benefit from being made more simple. Why, for example, is a batsman not out if he hits the ball first with his bat? If a ball hits his bat, and then subsequently hits his stumps, he is out bowled. Why should he be given extra protection by his person? Why is a batsman not out if the ball pitches outside the leg stump, whereas a ball pitching outside the off stump provides no such guarantee of immunity? Is this not unfair to leg spinners? Does it not help left handers? One group of people who are penalised by the current Law are left arm over the wicket fast bowlers who aim the ball across the batsmen and towards the slips. It is extremely difficult for them to convince an Umpire that a ball did not pitch outside the leg stump.

What is the argument against the L.B.W. Law reading: "The batsman shall be given out L.B.W. if, in the opinion of the Umpire, the batsman while playing a ball, intercepts the ball with any part of his person, other than the hand holding the bat, and thus prevents the ball from hitting the wicket"?

LEG BYES – a little known (at least by spectators) rule is that leg byes are disallowed if the batsman is not offering a stroke. The Umpire must decide whether a stroke was offered or not. It does not mean that the batsman must get near to the ball. He can be playing a bad stroke, and still be allowed leg byes if the ball hits his person other than the hand holding the bat.

LEITCH, Neil – Scotland's scorer, historian and an assiduous and accurate keeper of records, following in the footsteps of the late Sandy Thorburn. His club was Royal High School F.P's, who have now of course merged with Stewart's Melville. Neil took up scoring in 1967 and was promoted to the Scotland job when Frank Smith of Forfarshire stood down. In the outside world he is a Personnel Manager with Scottish Widows.

LEITH – properly called Leith Franklin Accies, as they are an amalgam of Leith Franklin and Leith Accies. They play in the Second Division of the East of Scotland League at a public park called Leith Links. At one point there were many cricket teams in Leith e.g there was a Leith Caledonian and a Leith Albion, but Franklin, who were founded in 1852, managed to survive both of them, and have the distinction of having had a former chairman of Celtic F.C. (Tom Devlin) playing for them at one point. In the days when Leith was a hot-bed of Scottish cricket, one of the jobs of the youngsters before start of play was to put out the seats for the crowd. Sadly, nowadays, such a job is no longer necessary.

Leith Accies used to play at a ground called Hawkhill at the back of Easter Road. They had a struggle to survive thanks to vandalism and other problems, and their amalgamation with Leith Franklin was a sensible decision.

LIVINGSTON – formed in 1981, this team has had a somewhat nomadic existence. In 1982, they played at Deans Community High School in Livingston, then moved to Bankton Playing Fields in Murieston for 1983. From 1985 onwards, after a year in which they had to play all their games away from home, Livingston have played in the magnificent natural setting of the Bangour Hospital, a ground with a fine pavilion and which certainly looked the part. The only problem was that it was some distance away from Livingston, but from 1999 onwards the team will move back into the new town and play at an as yet unnamed ground in Murieston Valley Road. This ground will be one of the best in the East of Scotland League, with over £250,000 having been spent over the last three years.

Livingston have a proud record of constant progress in that they have never been relegated from any Division of the East League in which they have played. In 1982, they won Grade D, in 1983 were second in Grade C before gaining admission to Division 4 for the 1984 season. They played there for eight years before they won Division 4 in 1992, then Division 3 in 1993 and now play in Division 2 as it was until 1995, Division 1 as it became in 1996.

Jim Love lofts one to leg in a Benson & Hedges game against Essex in 1993 at Lochside Park, Forfar.

127

LOCKHART, Douglas

Establishing cricket in a new town is never easy, but Livingston are a real bunch of enthusiasts who are clearly hoping to become one of the great Scottish teams of the 21st Century. The awarding of a Scotland Under 16 Cap in 1998 to Craig Toms is perhaps an indication of things to come from this club.

LOCKHART, Douglas – (Glasgow Accies, Oxford University and Scotland) Douglas is a young batsman who also keeps wicket. He has now played 36 times for the Scotland side, and in 1998 played First Class Cricket for Oxford University

LOCKIE, Bryn – (Carlton and Scotland) Bryn is an attacking opening bat who has played for Clackmannan and RHSM before joining Carlton. He has played 26 times for Scotland (his top score for Scotland is 74), and in 1998 he was a consistent performer. He is a teacher at Daniel Stewart's & Melville College in Edinburgh.

LOVE, James D. (1955-) current manager of the Scotland team. Jim is not the first from the Broad Acres of Yorkshire to be connected with the Scottish team, for Brian Close was in charge for a spell before Jim. Jim has been with Scotland since 1992, since when there has been a slow and gradual development of the game, as evidenced in the qualification for the World Cup and the defeat of

Scotland coach Jim Love flanked by two pipers

Worcestershire in 1998's NatWest Trophy game. This is all a tribute to Jim's energy, enthusiasm and professionalism in managing the national squad, for whom he has played 15 times.

He played for Yorkshire from 1975 till 1989, a consistent performer with the bat, and some people think he was unlucky not to earn a Test Cap for England. He did however play in three One Day International against the Australians in 1981, managing to score 43 in one of them. After leaving Yorkshire, he played for Lincolnshire, then returned to Yorkshire to play for Harrogate before getting the Scotland job. In Scotland he has played for Grange and latterly Heriot's, but finds it difficult to get time to play, given all his other duties.

LOST BALL – Law 20 tells us that if the ball while in play cannot be found or recovered, any fielder can say "Lost Ball" when six runs shall be added to the score. This Law seems to be a relic from the old days before there were proper boundaries, and now it is difficult to imagine a ball being lost while on the field of play, no matter how negligent the groundsman has been in not mowing the outfield. Yet the Law was invoked once in the 1960s at one of the Dundee Corporation grounds, when the ball disappeared down a hole which had once been used for a rugby post, and had apparently been covered up. No fielder had an arm long enough to reach the ball, and "Lost Ball" had to be called when the batsmen had already run eight runs. Thus an edge through the slips, which was not strong enough to reach the boundary, earned the batsman 14 runs!

LUNCARTY – a village team who play at Langlands Park, Luncarty, just off the A9 to the north of Perth. Their exact date of founding is a matter of conjecture but there is certainly a photograph of Luncarty as early as 1891.

They play in the Perthshire League, which they have won on six occasions, including three years on the trot between 1984-86. Luncarty have also won the Perthshire Cup on six occasions. They have competed in the Village Trophy and won the Scottish section in 1975 in the era that one can call B.F. (Before Freuchie). They have also done well in the Small Clubs Cup, losing to Buckie in the Final of the latter tournament in 1997.

Two of their greatest characters are Ian Ferguson and Ron McIntosh. Ian was only 18 in 1968 when he set up the club and League record score of 199 in a game against Northern, and he was also a fine bowler as well. Ron "Rollo" McIntosh, who sadly passed away a few years ago while still in his 50s, took 1493 wickets for the club (approximately 70 per season) with his left arm medium pace deliveries until he retired in 1979.

M

MACGREGOR, Gregor (1869 – 1919) – a famous cricketing character who has the distinction of having played Test Cricket for England (capped 8 times) and

Rugby for Scotland. He was born in Edinburgh and played the odd game for Carlton as a wicketkeeper. It was when he went to Cambridge in the late 1880s that his talent behind the stumps was spotted and, after a glittering University career in which he teamed up with the famous fast bowler Sammy Woods who went on to play for Somerset, MacGregor went on to play for Middlesex until 1907. His first Test Match was in 1890 and his last in 1896, and he earned himself a tour of Australia in 1891-1892.

On a parallel with his cricket career was his rugby. He was a fine full back (although he could play as a three quarter as well) and played 12 times for Scotland, finishing his International career against England at Hampden Park (!) in 1896. He is probably the first Scotsman to play Test Cricket for England and also probably the only man to play Rugby for Scotland and Cricket for England.

He died suddenly in the summer of 1919, possibly as a result of the Spanish influenza which was still ravaging Europe after the First World War.

McGURK, Gordon – (Uddingston and Grange) a good batsman who earned 29 Scottish Caps between 1988 and 1996. He was also a fine fielder.

MAIDEN – a maiden is a completed over, from which no runs have been scored other than byes or leg byes. The symbolism is obvious. A maiden in which a wicket has been taken is called a "wicket maiden" or as they used to say in the 1960s, a "Christine Keeler", for she was indeed a wicked maiden. Perhaps in the 1990's, it could be called a "Monica Lewinsky"!

MAIDEN, Gregor – one of the rising stars of the Scottish firmament. He plays for West of Scotland, having previously played for Kelburne and has already earned 5 Scotland caps, although he has barely reached 20. He is a talented off spinner and can bat a bit as well. Much is expected of this young man in the future.

MANDERSTON – (not to be confused with Manderley of Daphne du Maurier's "Rebecca"!) are a team who play mainly friendlies on a lovely ground near Duns in Berwickshire. They were formed in 1899 by Sir James Miller. They are much associated with the Swan family, and their captain is Richard Swan who captained Scotland in the mid 1980s. The ground is fenced off from nearby cowfields, woods and the House grounds, and the wicket is as near level as it can be, given the distinctive slope of the ground. In 1991 they were awarded a £21,000 grant from the Scottish Sports Council to redevelop their Edwardian pavilion.

There is a very comprehensive account of the team's first 50 years in a pamphlet produced by Tom Heatlie of Duns. Famous players of that era included P.F.H. Wilson, a fine all-rounder who played in several trials for the Scottish International team but never quite managed to earn himself a cap, and J.B.D. Chapman, whose father was the famous Herbert Chapman, the legendary manager of the great Arsenal team of the 1930s and who presumably paid the occasional visit to see his son excel with bat and ball.

As well as friendlies, the club have also participated in the Small Clubs Cup, but with no great success. As yet they have not played League cricket. Cricket is played seriously enough, but there is a light-hearted side to it as well as can be seen in the amount of fines given for dropped catches, even though you subsequently run the batsman out!

1999 is their Centenary year, and it is hoped that Lord Colin Cowdrey will be able to attend at least some of the celebrations in the week from 12th to 19th June. The celebrations will include a Ladies game, a Boys game and a Veteran and Vintage game as well as a Dinner and a Ball.

"Last night I dreamt I went to Manderston again..."

MARCHMONT – an enthusiastic Edinburgh team who play in the East of Scotland League. Their ground, Cavalry Park, is a nice one with a lovely view of Arthur's Seat, and is situated near Duddingston Golf Course. In recent years they have done well in the Edinburgh Parks Trophy, winning it in 1993, 1994 and 1997. One of the few genuinely sporting teams, they have fine players in the Sardesai brothers and captain Stevie Mathers, who once gave an Umpire a hat to hold advertising the "Big Issue".

The Masterton Trophy Final 1985. Abdul Qadir injures his
ankle as Sandeep Patil of Kirkcaldy and his Stenhousemuir
colleague Ian Philip look on.

MASTERTON TROPHY – a trophy competed for annually by teams based in
the Edinburgh area. It is played in midweek, 25 overs a side (22 in the early
rounds) and no professionals are allowed to take part. It has been in existence
since 1964 – Grange, Carlton and Stenhousemuir have all won the trophy 6 times.
Current holders (1998) are Royal High Stewart's Melville.

Like quite a lot of midweek tournaments played in the early part of the
season, there are usually huge problems with the weather and often games are
played in circumstances where they wouldn't on a Saturday.

MEIGLE – a Perthshire team, formed in 1876 with a tremendous pedigree.
Probably their greatest ever players were the two Laings (J.R. and J.G.), who went
on to play for Perthshire and Scotland in the late 1960s and early 1970s.

They play at Victory Park (a public park dedicated in the aftermath of the
First World War). They won the Strathmore Union in 1954 and 1980 and have
been consistent performers in the Three Counties Cup, and have performed well
in the Village Trophy, on one occasion in 1988 getting the better of Freuchie in
the Final of the Scottish section. They are the current holders of the Three Counties
Cup and capped a fine season in 1998 by winning the Strathmore Union on the
last day, deservedly earning a commendation at the Famous Grouse "Team of the
Year" ceremony.

MELROSE – play at a ground called Huntlyburn, Darnick in Melrose. Founded in 1894, they have a sadly impoverished history, but in 1996 won the Border Knockout Cup.

MILNGAVIE AND BEARSDEN – a now defunct north Glasgow team who never survived the loss of their ground at Auchenhowie.

The club had played cricket since as far back as 1905, but latterly they were a multi-faceted sports club, and at a crucial meeting the cricketers were outvoted by the hockey section, who had obtained money to build an artificial hockey pitch over their wicket. The cricketers lacked the financial muscle to mount a legal action against this, and at the end of the 1994 season the club folded.

It was one of the tragedies of Scottish cricket, for this was a grand old club who in the 1970s under the name of Dumbartonshire had participated in the Scottish County Championship.

MISTAKEN IDENTITY – It is of course very easy to confuse someone with someone else in a cricketing context. Opponents we do not see very often – perhaps once or at the most twice in a season, then a long winter after which weight may have been put on, or taken off, beards sprouted or shed, hair removed or bleached. An additional problem is that with batsmen hiding under helmets these days, you never really get a good look at them.

Perhaps the best case of collective amnesia however occurred in early 1998 when Mitre 3rd XI turned up to their home ground of Inch Park (which they share with Kirk Brae) to play Leith 3rd. Smiles and nods were exchanged with the opposition, one or two of whom they vaguely recognised, although quite clearly there had been a few changes in personnel since last year. The captains tossed and the game was about to begin when suddenly several cars rolled up containing men who claimed to be the real Leith 3rd XI! The "imposters" were, in fact, Zeneca Grangemouth who had thought they were there to play Kirk Brae, but in fact, through a fixture mix-up, should have been at Dunfermline Carnegie! Confusing, wasn't it? But eventually everyone got to where they should have been, and the cricket commenced.

MITRE – their formation is usually dated to 1954 and they celebrated their 25th anniversary in 1979, dating their first game to May 4th 1954 when they defeated the Anglican Students' Union. But there is a certain amount of evidence in their Anniversary booklet in the shape of an article written by their Honorary vice President Douglas F. Mann to the effect that there was a Mitre team in about 1950.

Whether in 1950 or 1954 their origins are ecclesiastical and they owe their name to the headgear worn by clergymen of the Roman Catholic or Episcopal persuasion. The actual birth source is thought to be the Youth Fellowship of one of the Episcopal Churches in Edinburgh, perhaps Christ Church, Trinity or the Good Shepherd, Murrayfield, and their founding father was said to be a man called Eric Knott who played for Melville F.P. but was not good enough to displace men of the quality of Dougie Barr or Ronnie Chisholm.

From about 1960 the club tended to fizzle out but there was always an annual match played at the Episcopal Church's Youth House at Dalmahoy. In about 1967 the club resurrected itself (to use an appropriate term), again under ecclesiastical influence, with Canon McCutcheon being well to the fore. They played at The Meadows and in 1970 played competitive cricket as members of the Edinburgh Public Parks Association. It was some 11 years later in 1981 however before they won the Public Parks Trophy.

A new phase opened in the club's history in 1975 when the club moved to Inch Park, their current home near Cameron Toll, and also joined the East of Scotland League. They began in the Grades, but have since worked their way up so that in 1997 they won Division 2 and in 1998 competed honourably in Division 1, employing for the first time a professional in the shape of Soweto's Jacob Malao who averaged 42.07 with the bat and 8.61 with the ball. This team owes a lot to the wise guidance of Bill Polson and people like Jim Brimms in recent years and are now one of the better and more established teams in the East of Scotland League with a youth team who have done well, notably winning the East of Scotland Under 15 Cup in 1992.

They can claim to have had two Internationalists – R.H.E. Chisholm has guested for them and also Chris Ibenezim has played International cricket for Nigeria, although not during his time at Mitre. There are also a couple of connections, albeit tenuous ones, with Alex Tudor, the rising star of the English firmament. A former Mitre player called David Mann coached him at Primary School and Tudor was also on the Lord's ground staff at the same time as Jacob Malao.

MONKLANDS – formed in 1989, Monklands started life at Dunbeth Park, Coatbridge. They quite cheerfully describe their early years as being the worst team in Scotland playing on the worst park in existence. Seasons passed without a win but the move to Springburn Park in 1993 saw a turning point with the occasional game being won and the influx of new, mainly Asian players. They have played at Drumpellier's ground, Langloan, since 1995, taking part in various Sunday and midweek competitions, and normally doing well. They claim to have managed 10 League titles of varying descriptions and one Cup in the past 6 years and now play in Division 1 of both the Strathclyde League and the Glasgow and District Evening League.

Famous players include Johnny Grant, David Smith, Stuart Lang, Steve Slater, Shahed Shakoor, Irfan and Quyum. They are clearly a team with a certain amount of ambition and determination to do well.

MONTROSE – the Angus team have always suffered from having giants like Brechin, Strathmore and Arbroath near them, but have struggled on at Union Park, one of Scotland's colder grounds. They play in the Second Division of the Strathmore Union and in recent years have done well, particularly so in 1998 when they won the Second Division Championship and capped this by carrying off the Two Counties Cup, a 25 over midweek competition, (now called the Samuel Bruce Trophy), which they had also won in 1995. They were commended for their achievements at the Famous Grouse awards ceremony at Hughenden in Glasgow in October and it is to be hoped that this is only the start of a rebirth of Montrose cricket.

Their origins are obscure. There is certainly evidence to suggest that some sort of cricket was played in Montrose before the formation of Brechin in 1849, but their existence has not been continuous.

MOTHERWELL – founded in 1873, Motherwell play at a ground called Home Park, Dalzell Estate, Motherwell . They first moved to Home Park in 1890 and have been there ever since. Imaginatively, in 1990, to celebrate their centenary of being there, they held a Victorian style Gentlemen v. Players game and produced a programme to celebrate the event, describing the Players as "asylum attendant", "urchin" and even Barkatullah Khan earned the job as a "punka wallah". The Gentlemen were all Squires, Viscounts and Cardinals!

In 1873 they were formed as Motherwell Britannia and played at a place called the Meadows. In 1887 they were renamed Motherwell Trinity, then when they moved to Home Park in 1890, they became Motherwell Dalziel before in 1901 settling for Motherwell Cricket Club.

Great players who have played for Motherwell include Archie Black, who performed heroics both sides of the Second World War, and two R.K. Hinshelwoods (father and son) who flourished in the 1920s and 1950s respectively. Their most successful decade seems to have been the 1960s when they won the Glasgow and District League 4 times, and on one famous occasion in 1962 dismissed Cartha for 4 runs.

In the early days they managed to employ professionals, but for a long spell between 1936 and 1986 decided not to, presumably for financial reasons. Their pavilion which had stood since 1907 was torched by vandals in 1977, but the club rose again and in 1979 a new pavilion was opened by Ally McLeod of Argentina fame who was then manager of Motherwell F.C.

Their ground is a fine one and has been played upon in the past by greats of the game such as I.A.R. Peebles and Kim Hughes. Once or twice, the club have qualified for the Scottish Cup (in 1988 they managed to tie a match with Gala at 248 each!) and they have had their moments in the Glasgow and District League and in various cup competitions, but sadly any sustained success has eluded them. With the re-structuring of cricket in the West, there is always the possibility that they may one day reach the Scottish National Cricket League.

MURRAY, George

MURRAY, George – a great bowler for Aberdeenshire from the 1950s onwards. He became Captain, but remained mysteriously uncapped for Scotland in spite of years of prodigious performances for Aberdeenshire. In later days, he became Coach, earning a reputation for excellence and also fortitude for he held outdoor nets on wintry Sunday mornings at Mannofield for volunteers as brave as he!

MURRAYFIELD – a team with an interesting history. They play at Roseburn Park in the shadow of the Murrayfield Rugby Stadium. They were founded in 1909 as London Road Church when Reverend James Anderson and several of his Kirk Session decided to form a cricket club from among the number of his Bible Class. The historic decision was reached on May 25th 1909, but their first game was not played until a year later against the similarly ecclesiastical Central Wesleyans. Presumably these proponents of muscular Christianity saw cricket as a way of diverting wayward youth from the dangers of alcohol and other fleshy sins.

To survive, the club had to attract young men from outwith the Church, but the club continued to be part of the London Road Church until in 1952 when a little Presbyterian pressure over the vexed issue of Sunday cricket compelled the club to dissociate itself from the Church and to become merely London Road Cricket Club. After a nomadic existence over various of Edinburgh's parks, London Road settled in Roseburn Park in the 1950s, and in 1992 changed their name to Murrayfield to assume some local identity.

As a team they have had their moments, particularly in the Parks Trophy which they have won 16 times, totally dominating it in the 1960s and their latest victory being 1996. They joined the East of Scotland League round about the time that they severed their Church connection, and almost reached the Final of the Masterton Trophy in 1967, beating teams like Leith Franklin and Edinburgh Accies. They have played in every Division of the East League, and reached the First Division for season 1996. In 1998, however, they were relegated to Division 2 of the East of Scotland League, but not without beating St. Modans on the last day to give the title to Glenrothes.

They have produced some fine players, but quite a few of them move on to other Edinburgh teams – Billie Law, Alistair Swarbrick, David Fraser and Fraser Watts, for example, but they have also been well served by stalwarts like Phil Yelland, Dave Fisher and Murdo McLeod. They can also claim (something that few others can) that they had a player who has played in European football. Murray McDermott spent almost all his football career with Raith Rovers and is indeed still talked about in Kirkcaldy as Rovers' greatest ever keeper, but he spent some time with Hearts at the end of his career and on September 7th 1988 substituted for Henry Smith in a UEFA Cup tie against St. Patrick's of Dublin. Great cricketing moments have included the dismissing of Bangour Hospital for 7 runs in 1958, and Robin Ballantyne's taking of all 10 Leith Accies wickets for 35 runs in 1966.

A particularly sad occasion was the death of former player Chris Warne, one of the very few people in Britain to die of CJD. Yet there has been a happy side to this as well, for they were able to travel to Derby to play against St. Luke's and St. Michael's (another ecclesiastical connection!) for whom Chris also played and they hope to make this an annual affair.

London Road/Murrayfield have always been an enthusiastic bunch of cricketers, and have a good reputation for sporting behaviour. They try to field three teams every Saturday, but admit that this has been a struggle in recent years. Like many other Edinburgh teams who play on public parks, they have had cause to feel short changed by the Edinburgh Corporation whose fees rise and whose commitment diminishes.

MUSSELBURGH – a team who play at Lewisvale, Musselburgh and are in the lower reaches of the East of Scotland league.

N

NAIRN COUNTY – although cricket is mentioned in Nairn as early as 1843, the year normally given for the foundation of this club is 1856. Its first name was Nairn Union, but this was changed to Nairn County in 1874. They were founder members of the North of Scotland Cricket Association from 1893 onwards and first won the League in 1906. They have won it on 17 occasions, the last being in 1971.

They play on the Nairn Links which is claimed by some to be the most picturesque ground in Scotland. Leicestershire once played there in 1923. The pavilion was built in 1932 and a curiosity of Nairn is that their previous pavilion was not demolished, but sold and re-erected and still stands in Grant Street, Nairn.

NETS – any player, no matter how talented, must practice and this involves long stretches in the nets. Some great players, notably Tom Graveney of England fame in the 1950's and 1960's, question the value of net practice on the grounds that the batsman will feel inhibited if he is enclosed by nets and will find it difficult to transfer expertise learned in the nets to play on the open field.

The great advantage of course is that the ball is easily retrieved, and it is hard to see any other way of practising unless there is an army of fielders. A good team will insist on net practice at least once a week, and it is the captain's or the professional's job to make sure that net practice is well organized and constructive. It is too easy for practice to become a showing-off session with silly stunts like a pint of beer being placed on top of the stumps etc.

Great players like Geoff Boycott would practise in the nets at Headingley for hours and anyone who felt like it could bowl to the great man. This could be (and was) construed as selfishness, but it was also the mark of an enthusiastic professional who took a pride in his craft.

Net practice for youngsters should probably be held on a separate night, and this must be even more closely supervised. Apart from the obvious dangers of being hit on the head, it is very easy for a youngster to become discouraged when he sees others who are apparently far better than he is. Youngsters are the life blood of the game. They need to be cherished and valued and shown that someone from the club, preferably the captain, the professional or the Scotland star, is interested in them .

NEWBURGH – a team who had a brief existence from 1987 to 1998, participating latterly in the lower reaches of the East of Scotland League.

NEWSPAPERS – "The Scotsman" and "The Herald" on Mondays now do a better job than previously. With the advent of the Scottish National Cricket League, an effort has been made to provide comprehensive and accurate accounts of all these games. On the other hand, games in the Western Union and the East of Scotland League are sometimes ignored, or those that do reach the paper contain inaccuracies, sometimes blatant ones. Sunday papers generally leave a lot to be desired and it is obvious that many results reach the Sports Desk late and are "fielded" by someone who knows little about cricket.

During the week, with the exception of the "Courier" which does a good job for local teams with team selections etc., coverage is patchy and disorganized. There is noticeably less about cricket when the football and rugby seasons are on in the months of May and August, and often undue prominence is given to controversial incidents rather than the great deal of good cricket that is played. Unsavoury incidents like violent altercations (a rare event, thank goodness!) and suspensions are usually highlighted, and attempts at "character assassination" of individual Umpires are not unknown, and generally speaking, whenever Scottish cricket reaches the tabloids, it is usually for the wrong sort of reasons.

The bulk of the reporting of cricket matches in Scottish newspapers however is in the local Press. These worthy institutions will often carry quite lengthy reports of last Saturday and Sunday's games, and are great sources of information for anyone doing any research on the history of a particular club.

There are however drawbacks. Seldom is the report written by a trained journalist. This need not be a problem if the report is written by the enthusiastic scorer, for example, or even a committee member whose task it is to keep the local rag informed. The problem arises when the copy is badly written, is at odds with the scorecard or is partisan. One must for example be aware of statements like "the Umpire was prone to give lbw decisions" when in fact only one was given, and that against the writer of the passage! "Dropped catches cost Shire the match on Saturday" may mean that the writer's rival for a place in the team dropped a difficult one. "The team's miserable run under captain Smith continued" may well be a coded leadership bid by the writer of the passage.

Sometimes the problem with match reports is that they are just dull. "Shire went out to bat and lost their first wicket at 23. Then Brown came in and scored 8 before he too was out. The total mounted, but so did the tally of wickets" etc. Yet it is better for there to be some media coverage than for there to be none.

But so many teams miss the opportunity of building up interest in next week's encounter. It would not cost all that much to take out an advertisement and a relevant photograph of one or other of the team would help a great deal as well. The copy should read along the lines of "We have attractive visitors in Arbroath on Saturday. The Angus men come on the backs of three successive victories against Perthshire, Heriot's and Ferguslie. Much will be expected of in their star man Jim Smith whose encounters against our own Bill Brown will be much looked

NICHOL, Willie

forward to, as both are on the verge of a Scotland call-up. The forecast for Saturday is good, and a large turnout of spectators is expected" The last statement may well be euphoric moonshine, but it does no harm at all in building up morale.

NICHOL, Willie – (1912 –) a great player for Gala and Kelburne on either side of the Second World War. He played for Gala until 1931, then tried his luck as a professional football player with Sunderland, Aberdeen and St. Mirren. A nasty tackle in a game against Rangers in 1934 finished his football career, but by this time he had played for Scotland at cricket, something he would do 40 times in all until 1956. In his Scotland career he would score two centuries in 1951 against Warwickshire and Ireland, and in 1948 took figures of 7 for 39 and then 5 for 39 against Ireland. It was in September 1948 at Raeburn Place, bowling slow left arm, that he became one of the very few men who bowled Don Bradman.

His football travels which had taken him to St. Mirren meant that he played most of his cricket in Paisley for Kelburne, and he became so popular there that he became known as "Willie Kelburne". He was largely responsible for Kelburne winning the Western Union in 1947 and 1951 and the Rowan Cup on three occasions. Before a huge Derby crowd in 1951 he scored 133 not out against Ferguslie, arguably his best innings for the club.

His brothers David and Jack both played for Gala and Scotland, and his nephew Rae plays for Gala now.

NKOA – (North Kelvinside Old Aloysians) – this team had a strange time of it in the 1990s. The amalgamation did not go well, as old animosities and jealousies died hard. At one point some of them went off to join Kilmarnock, but the rump were doing well for a spell in the Glasgow and District League, playing at Millerston on the Cumbernauld Road, but then in 1997 they were expelled from that League because, we are told, other teams' patience with the vagaries of North Kelvinside ran out. This presumably refers to their inability to complete fixtures but there were other scandals involving this team, including allegations about illegal players and other irregularities.

NO BALL – a contentious Law. Most fast bowlers, when striving for some extra pace will be no-balled at one point or another in their careers, if no part of their front foot is behind the popping crease at the instant of delivery. Occasionally, a bowler will be no-balled for not having his back foot within the return crease. It is curious that some bowlers will argue with Umpires on this Law, when they are in no position to see exactly where their foot has landed at the instant of delivery.

The call of "No Ball" from square leg is unusual. Sometimes there will be illegal field placing, for example, more than two men behind square on the leg side or a wicket-keeper with his glove over the bowling crease line at the instant of delivery. Trouble really starts when a bowler is called for throwing i.e his arm not being straight at the instant of delivery. It is a brave Umpire who will do this, for it will almost certainly have serious repercussions on the bowler's future in the game. Yet there are one or two bowlers with "dodgy" actions who get off with it.

NOMPERE – a pretentious Old French word which appears on the tie and sweater of pretentious Umpires. The word Umpire is derived from it.

NORTH OF SCOTLAND CRICKET ASSOCIATION – formed in 1893, the same year as the Western Union, and thus pre-dates the Scottish County Championship by nine years. Northern Counties were the first winners of the League. In 1993 they produced an excellent Centenary booklet "The North's Cricket Century" by Patrick W. Scott.

NORTHERN – not to be confused with Northern Counties of Inverness, Northern play at Doo'cot Park, Perth (along with Mayfield and Strathearn) and participate in the Perthshire League.

NORTHERN COUNTIES – an Inverness team who play in the North of Scotland League. They were founded on August 26th 1864 at a meeting in Inverness Town Hall presided over by Bishop Eden. Most unusually for a club of over 130 years history, they have had but one ground, namely the Northern Meeting Park, Inverness, where they have entertained Dr. W.G. Grace's XI, Leicestershire, Kent and an Australian Forces XI.

They were founder members of the North of Scotland Cricket Association, being the first winners in 1893 and repeating that triumph in 1894 and 1895. They have won the League 20 times in all. It is only in recent seasons that they have struggled – in 1997 the season was a month advanced before they were able to field a team, and they "won" the wooden spoon for the first time in their history.

O

OLD GRAMMARIANS – founded in 1939 and since 1993 play at Birkmyre Park in Kilmacolm, having previously played at Blackhall in Paisley. They compete in the Glasgow and District League.

ORIGINS – it is almost impossible to trace the origins of the game of cricket in Scotland. It is probably true to say that the biggest single impetus was given by the Jacobite Rebellion of 1745. In the repression that went on for decades afterwards, some of the regiments would play cricket against each other and eventually against some of the locals, notably on the North Inch in Perth as early as 1750, a practice scurrilously denounced for some games were played on Sundays! The earliest recorded cricket match in Scotland is on 3rd September 1785 at Schaw Park, Alloa when the Duke of Atholl's XI played the Hon. Col. Talbot's XI. This game was commemorated at the Arns in 1985 on the bi-centenary of the event.

The Scottish club with the earliest recorded history is Kelso which is dated to 1820 or 1821, but cricket was clearly played before then, particularly in the garrison towns of Edinburgh, Stirling and Perth. The earliest recorded reference to cricket anywhere in the world is in 1300 at Newenden, Kent where in the wardrobe accounts of King Edward I, mention is made of the young Prince (who later became King Edward II) playing "creag". There is of course a Scottish connection here for Edward I was "The Hammer of the Scots", and Edward II was the one we sent home "to think again" as the song says. It would have been a lot better for all concerned in those bloodthirsty days if England and Scotland had played "creag" with each other, and if the "hammering" referred to a heavy defeat on a cricket field!

The game certainly developed very rapidly in Victorian Scotland, as indeed it did in England. No doubt the arrival of the railways had their impact in that it facilitated transport and meant that cricket needn't be entirely localised, but there are many clubs who flourished and developed miles away from any railway line. The biggest single influence was the giving of a half-holiday on a Saturday so that people could play and watch cricket in summer.

ORMEROD J.A. (1942 –) Alan Ormerod learned his cricket at Kirkcaldy before moving to Worcestershire in the mid 1960s. He played successfully for them for many seasons alongside men like Glenn Turner and Norman Gifford before he move to Lancashire where he played and eventually became Manager. In 1993 he became Coach of Notts, and then Cricket Manager in 1996, but was sacked at the end of the 1998 season when Notts failed to live up to the expectations of their supporters.

ORR, D.A. (Clydesdale and Scotland) has now played 16 times for Scotland. He is a competent wicket keeper, has been a reliable understudy for Alec Davies and is no mug with the bat either.

OUTFIELDS – there are some crackers of outfields in Scotland. Normally, the wicket is tolerable for the game of cricket, but the outfields are often sadly below par. In Lochee Park, Dundee for example, if several games are going on, the boundary of one pitch will often encroach deep into the outfield of another. Kirriemuir is notorious for rabbit holes and was once famously described by one of their players as "No matter what direction you run in, you always seem to be going up hill!" Falkland's fielder at long on can often be forgotten about by the batsman, for he is several feet below his level! All these things, however, merely add to the amiable diversity and idiosyncrasy that is Scottish cricket.

OVER – six balls in this, except eccentrically for one or two competitions like the Fife Cup which has 18 x 8 ball overs in an innings. The argument in its favour is that, given the limited time available in mid-week fixtures, it cuts down movement and therefore saves time. Until very recently, 8 balls in an Over were the accepted norm in Australia, including Test Matches played in Australia.

OVER RATE – the authorities in League matches are quite rightly strict about this. In the Scottish National Cricket League, for example, 18 Overs must be bowled in an hour, as long as 40 Overs are bowled in the Innings. Any side failing to keep up to this rate is liable to lose bonus points. Two minutes are allowed for each wicket that falls and the Umpires will allow time for Drinks, Lost Balls or any other reasonable interruption to play. The 40 Overs rule is in force because before 40 Overs, teams are less likely to have employed spinners, who generally get through their Overs more quickly.

The advantages in this rule are manifold. In the first place a slow over rate could be construed as cheating – the fielding team, for example, could be trying to delay things until the light gets bad or the rain comes on. In the second place, it gives every encouragement for spinners. Thirdly, a game like cricket must do all it can to attract casual spectators. This includes keeping them interested. Finally, it has long been your writer's belief, based on over two decades of watching and Umpiring, that a team with a fast Over rate bowls and fields better than they might do otherwise, simply because the fielders are perpetually on their toes and never fall asleep.

P

PAKISTAN – have played six times in Scotland, winning five and drawing the other. The only occasion when Scotland have looked remotely like beating them was in June 1954 at Grange. Willie Nichol's 93 enabled Scotland to declare at 353 for 7. Pakistan were then dismissed for 295, but Scotland then collapsed for 91 before the speed of Mahmood Hussain, who took 6 for 17, and the Pakistanis competently knocked off the 114 required for a 10 wicket victory. Later that summer Pakistan shocked the cricketing world by beating England at the Oval for the first time.

PAKISTAN ASSOCIATION – this club was founded in 1978, basically to allow the vast and expanding number of Asian minorities in Edinburgh and district to play the game. Originally they played only friendlies, usually on The Meadows, but very soon a midweek League was entered and the club itself also put up the M.A. Jinnah trophy, a six a side tournament which attracted great interest.

The club played on this basis until 1996, with most of the players playing for the Pakistan Association in midweek and one or other of the Edinburgh clubs on Saturday. Then the decision was taken to form a Saturday team and apply for membership of the East of Scotland League. Originally the application was turned down because the League had enough members, but then R.A.F. Leuchars withdrew and the Pakistan Association were admitted into Division 3. Their success has since been phenomenal, for in 1997 they won Division 3 and in 1998 Division 2, which means that in 1999 they play in Division 1 and may well reach the Scottish National Cricket League soon. In their two years so far in the East of Scotland League, the Pakistan Association have completed 25 matches and won 21 of them. They are very aware however that Division 1 will involve new challenges for this team.

In 1998, they enjoyed the services of a professional from Pakistan called Shahid Mansoor. He scored 751 runs and because of his ability to hold on to his wicket, he ended up with a staggering average of 187.75! He also took 31 wickets at an average of 9.19. Other players who have passed through the ranks of this club are Wasim Haider, Shahid Aslam and Asim Butt, all of whom have made their mark on Scottish cricket with other teams, and of course Asim Butt is a Scottish International.

This admirable club are very keen to integrate into the Scottish scene, encouraging youngsters to play the game at all levels. This can do nothing but good for the game, for youngsters so introduced will, of course, be very Scottish as well as being rightly proud of their ethnic origin. Further proof of their desire to integrate has come from their close links with the Lothian and Borders Police. Their Patron is Chief Constable Roy Cameron. Former patrons of the club have included chiefs of Police Sir John Orr and Sir William Sutherland.

This is quite clearly a team to watch for the future, and students of Scottish football will see a parallel with the rise of Glasgow Celtic over a century ago. Celtic were originally very much the representatives of an ethnic minority, and it was their inspiring early success that gave such a boost to the game in Scotland. Hopefully the Pakistan Association will perform a similar service for Scottish cricket.

PARSONS, R.A. (Prestwick and Scotland) – an accomplished all rounder who has played 21 times for Scotland.

PATTERSON, Bruce (Ayr and Scotland) a fine opening bat and off break bowler, who has opened the innings for Scotland for more than a decade with 99 appearances. His two fine innings include a spirited knock of 70 against the 1989 Australians and a praiseworthy innings of 71 in the memorable win over Worcestershire in the 1998 NatWest Trophy. He has been a professional with Edinburgh Accies and Clydesdale, but has now returned to his first team Ayr as an amateur.

PEEBLES COUNTY – a struggling East of Scotland League side. They have a long history, being formed in 1857, but since they won the Border League in 1909, success has been hard to come by. They play at Whitestone Park, and seem to retain their good humour in adversity. They have recently opened a nice new pavilion there.

The New Pavilion at Whitestone Park, Peebles

145

PEEBLES, I.A.R.

Their history in the 19th Century is chequered. They seem to have disappeared some time in the 1860s but were re-formed in 1870. They were officially dissolved in 1887 when their ground Kingsmeadows Park was given away by Sir John A. Hay Bart., but yet again they refused to disappear.

Their early history contains many times the name Thorburn. M.G. Thorburn was one of their founding fathers of 1870, W.H. Thorburn played 5 times for Scotland from 1909 until 1912, R.M. Thorburn once in 1924 and many others of that name have played for Peebles.

Other famous players are W. Eddie, who played for Scotland in 1913 and professional Fred Trott, who joined the club in 1906 to play a large part in the golden age of Peebles before the First World War. Fred's brother Alfred remains the only player to have cleared the pavilion at Lord's with a massive hit.

PEEBLES, I.A.R. – (1908 – 1980) Scottish born cricketer and later journalist who played 13 Test Matches for England, including two tours to South Africa. He also played for Oxford University and Middlesex, whom he captained in the years immediately before the Second World War. He was a great leg spin bowler, with a vicious googly called the "Peebles twister" and in the 1930 Test Match at Old Trafford had the great Don Bradman caught by Duleepsinhji in the slips for 14.

PENICUIK – an ambitious club who are currently experiencing the best phase of their history. They won the Border League in 1997 for the first time ever. Their ambition is proved by the employment in recent years of men like Alvin Greenidge and George Reifer as Professional/Coach. One of their better known players of recent vintage is Andy Goram, the famous Scotland goalkeeper. Their ground, Kirkhill, is increasingly used for representative fixtures.

The industrialization of Victorian Britain and the availability of railways probably helped to develop the game in Penicuik in the 1840s as Penicuik's paper mills opened and many English workers came to Scotland. The club was founded in 1844. Their first decade or so saw Penicuik with a nomadic existence, playing at places like Denholm's Park and Brown's Park, with unfortunate things happening like the tea being stolen on several occasions. Their first recorded game was at Prestonpans in 1848, and their move to Kirkhill was probably their first permanent home and followed a severe threat to the existence of the club as apathy and disillusion at not having a home of their own took over many of their players.

Having rented Kirkhill, however, the club settled for a spell. But so too in 1913 did the wicket! It had subsided to such an alarming degree compared with the rest of the pitch that a major effort was required to make things playable. In 1920 the club had another struggle to pay the rent, having lost so many players in the War, but thanks to a large extent to the Cowan family over the years, Penicuik have always survived.

146

They first joined the Border League in 1931, and have played successfully, if a little inconsistently, in that company ever since. In recent years, apart from the win in 1997, highlights have included the opening of a fine new pavilion in 1984, and a remarkable knock of 200 by Tony O'Hara, an Australian amateur, in a game against the Edinburgh Muslims in 1989.

Perth County Cricket Club, 1935.

PERTH COUNTY – formerly called Perthshire and nicknamed the "Big County" in the heyday of the Scottish County Championship. Cricket had been played on the North Inch in Perth as early as 1750, but as for when the club itself was founded there is no clear evidence until 1826. There is a reference in the "Perth Courier" to a game being played on the North Inch between the "Perth Cricket Club" and the 7th Hussars, which Perth won by two "notches". (The word "notch" refers to the primitive method of scoring by cutting a notch in a piece of wood for every run scored.) They still play on the North Inch, which, being so exposed, can be one of the coldest grounds in Scotland. There is also a major handicap in that, since the demolition of their venerable old pavilion (built after a fire destroyed a previous one in 1913), changing facilities are now somewhat distant in the Gannochy Sports Centre, and a marquee is usually erected for the more immediate needs of the players. Yet Scottish Internationals have played there on many occasions, notably the Benson and Hedges defeat of Lancashire in 1986.

Their first away game to be recorded in any detail was at Stirling against Glasgow University in 1829, and home games are mentioned against the 71st Regiment and the Edinburgh giants Brunswick and Grange from the 1830's onwards. In 1850 Grange refused a fixture with them, arguing that one of their men, Lawrence, was a professional. Perth saw this as cowardice and issued a public challenge in 1852 to dispute their contention that they were the Champions of Scotland. Edinburgh Caledonian accepted and failed, and then Perth beat the English tourists I Zingari.

PERTH COUNTY

In 1870 Perth changed their name to Perthshire. They beat the M.C.C. in 1876, were one of the founder members of the Scottish County Championship in 1902, and on August 1st 1903, an untoward event occurred. On the second day of the two innings game v. Forfarshire, with 10,000 reputedly on the North Inch, the grandstand, with 400 people in it, collapsed. Fortunately no-one was killed but many were injured. On another occasion at the North Inch in 1910 the game between the Scottish Counties and Yorkshire, scheduled for May 6th and 7th, had to be abandoned after one day because of the death of Edward VII.

Perthshire have always been lucky with their professionals, who have contributed hugely to sustained success of the club both by their own performances and by the development and encouragement of players around them. Their ranks have included Schofield Haigh, Bert Marshall, Wilfred Rhodes (admittedly long after his prime in 1937), Tom Lodge, and more recently Justin Langer, whose batting destroyed England in 1998. Perth people would like to think that he learned it all playing for Perthshire XI in the Strathmore Union in 1991.

Perth County, as they are now called, are currently in decline compared to the great days of the 1950s, 1960s and 1970s when they used to dominate the County Championship. But for West Lothian in 1965, Perthshire would have won the Championship 12 years in a row between 1961 and 1972. Players like Jimmy Brown, the wicket keeper/batsman (who was given the rare honour for a Scotsman of being invited to play for the Gentlemen i.e. amateurs against the Players at Scarborough in 1959 and 1960), and Len Dudman appeared to be almost fixtures in the Scottish side throughout the 1960s. Added to these were spin bowler Mike Kerrigan and a host of batting talent, notably the Laing brothers Ralph and Gordon from Meigle. Australian professional Alan Preen was a fine aggressive fast bowler as well, and it was not difficult to see how Perthshire dominated the Scottish scene in these days. They won the Scottish Cup in 1970 and 1976, and had the Scottish Cup been in existence earlier, it would almost certainly have been dominated by Perthshire.

Cricket on the North Inch in Perth, sometime before the First World War. The bowler is just a blur!

In the pre-war years, and the years immediately after, the derby between Perthshire and Forfarshire was always a great tourist attraction, on occasion bringing 4 figure crowds to the North Inch, but fortunately without any events like those of 1903. This is in stark contrast to the open, exposed and almost totally deserted North Inch that we are likely to see today. It remains a beautiful ground, however, and there is a tremendous sense of tradition of being where cricket has been played for almost two and a half centuries and possibly longer.

Currently, Perth County are in the Scottish National Cricket League, but as yet have had no great success. They play in Division 2 in 1999, thanks to a late rally in 1998 when it looked as if they were doomed to Division 3. A revival in the fortunes of the men from the Fair City is long overdue and one cannot help think that Scottish cricket is all the poorer for the decline of this great team.

PERTH MAYFIELD – a team who play in the Perthshire League, a competition which they have won six times, the last time being in 1998 when they defeated Luncarty and Rossie Priory failed to dismiss the last two batsmen of Northern. Along with two other Perthshire League teams, Strathearn and Northern, Mayfield play at a lovely ground on the east side of Perth called Doo'cot Park, so called because the pavilion does indeed resemble a dove cot. The pavilion has been recognised nationally and appears in books on the subject.

PINKIE – not to be confused with the pinkie on one's hand (where one can receive a horrific injury incidentally), Pinkie in Musselburgh where Loretto school play is one of the few cricket grounds where a battle has actually been fought. In 1547, in order to enforce the treaty of marriage between Edward VI and Mary, Queen of Scots, the English under the Protector, Somerset, defeated a numerically superior Scottish force. This battle, which has only recently been commemorated by the East Lothian Council, probably ranks third in the history of "Great Scottish Wellyings" behind Flodden and Culloden but ahead of Darien, Argentina, Wembley 9-3, 7-2 and 5-1 and too many cricketing and rugby humiliations to mention.

Cricketers from Musselburgh and Loretto School seem blissfully unaware that they are treading on the bones of their ancestors every time they play a game and the ghosts do not seem to mind.

PHILIP, Iain (Stenhousemuir and Scotland) – now in his fortieth year, Ian Philip is Scotland's most capped player with 129 appearances and has been the mainstay of the side since 1986. Highlights include 234 made against the MCC in 1991. He plays half the year in Australia and the other half for his native Stenhousemuir. He has also kept wicket and bowls slow left arm as well. Clearly a versatile cricketer who has also played for Poloc and Selkirk.

Iain Philip (Stenhousemuir and Scotland) tickles one round the corner.

POINTS – one of the things that is often adversely criticised by some is the complicated and cumbersome points system which obtains in League cricket in Scotland. It is too complex to be repeated here in its entirety (and indeed it is different in the various Leagues) but the main thing about it is that points are awarded for runs scored and wickets taken in drawn and lost games, but there is a set amount for a win and no additional bonus points can be scored in a game that is won.

The arguments in favour of this system is that it gives both teams something to play for in these games that seem, from an early stage, to be heading for a draw. This is particularly helpful in a climate like Scotland's where many games (or large chunks of them) are likely to be lost to the weather. The disadvantages are that they are difficult to work out and a calculator is indispensable when we come to the end of the season and have to work out the percentage success rate. In addition to this, it is not "user friendly" for people who have only a slight interest in cricket and might be deterred by this difficulty.

It might be an idea some time to try cricket points on the football line of three points for a win, and one for a draw or a postponement.

POLOC – a famous Glasgow team, founded in 1878, who play at Shawholm. Scottish Cup winners in 1984 and defeated finalists in 1994, they also won the Western Union 3 times in the 1980s. Keith Sheridan, Scotland International left arm spinner, plays for them.

Their first ground was at a place called Bangor Hill, but the same gale that destroyed the Tay Bridge in Dundee in December 1879 ravaged their pavilion in Glasgow, and the club were homeless until the 13 year old Sir John Stirling Maxwell allowed them to use Shawholm in 1880. The same gentleman was still to be seen watching Poloc as late as 1956, some 76 years later, even when he had to be pushed in his wheelchair.

Shawholm was a beautiful ground, particularly after a handsome pavilion was built in 1930, although problems arose in 1967 when the Maxwell family gave the surrounding area to Glasgow Corporation, so that Shawholm found itself surrounded by a public park. Poloc also, of course, played tennis and golf as well as cricket.

Poloc have never been one of the better Glasgow sides, although they did win the Western Union 8 times, the first time on their Golden Jubilee in 1928, two years after the first of their successes in the Rowan Cup. Games with Uddingston seem to have been close fought affairs, attracting a crowd of 2,000 apparently in 1907. 1891 saw controversy between the two teams when in early May with snow showers in the distance, the Uddingston umpire (perhaps because he was too cold) gave four dodgy lbw's against Poloc, and the game terminated abruptly.

Other interesting things about this unusual club are that in 1919 at Shawholm the Australian Imperial Forces XI made 733 for 6 than which there will have not been many larger scores in Scotland; in 1928, in the run-in for the

151

PRAYER

Western Union Championship, they advertised their fixtures on the local cinemas; Celtic player Gil Heron played for them for a spell in the early 1950's; and on May 7th 1955, Poloc v. West of Scotland became the first (and one of the very few) Scottish cricket games to be televised, BBC paying £75 for the privilege.

In 1999, Poloc play in the Scottish National Cricket League Division 3.

PRAYER – it is of course not unusual for prayers to be said as a nervous batsman walks out to face a fast bowler. Or if a skier of a catch is heading his way, the fielder will promise God that he will be in Church on Sunday, if the Almighty will make sure the catch isn't dropped. Moreover, many of the ecclesiastical profession, notably the Rev. J. Aitchison, for example, have played the game, and presumably prayers have been said by them at least in private.

With the arrival in Scotland of those of the Islamic persuasion, however, a new dimension has been added. On one occasion, an Umpire had to wait over half an hour to be paid by the devout Islamic Treasurer of one team, who clearly thought that Allah had to be attended to before Umpires. Then on another occasion, a player asked permission to leave the field to perform his devotions. Thinking that this was a euphemism for the toilet, the Umpire agreed and indeed the player made his way to a tree. The Umpire was however amazed to see a prolonged prayer taking place. Fortunately, however, he was back within 15 minutes and so was able to bowl if he wished to.

PRESTON VILLAGE – a recently formed team (1991) who now play in the lower reaches of the East of Scotland League. They are based at the Meadowhill Sports Centre in Prestonpans, a mining village in East Lothian. Some of their team were at the Gabba in Brisbane for the First Test Match between Australia and England in November 1998, for their banner was clearly picked up by the TV cameras.

PRESTWICK – formerly called Ayrshire and founded comparatively recently in 1955, (although there had been a Prestwick team from 1929 to 1939) they play at the Oval in Prestwick. As Ayrshire, they won the County Championship twice in the early 90s, but when they joined the Scottish League in 1995, they changed their name to Prestwick which had in fact been their original name until they joined the County Championship in 1984. In 1998 they reached the Final of the Scottish Cup but lost on the last ball to Grange in a nail-biting finale. There was some consolation when they won the Scottish Counties Cup, albeit on a bowl out against Aberdeenshire. Rain on the last Saturday of the season at Uddingston deprived them of a chance of reaching Division 1 of the 1999 Scottish National Cricket League, but with players like Haggo, Rigby, Parsons and Tennent around, they will be a strong team for some time.

One of their founder members and current Chairman is Henry Thow, a man of trenchant opinions but who believes in the traditional values of cricket. Henry, a war veteran whose experiences could themselves fill a book, has served the club as player, coach and every other capacity since the club's inception. In the 1960s and 1970s, one of Prestwick's players was the South African Johnnie Hubbard, more famous for his contribution as a winger for Rangers. When he failed to live up to the expectations of the more impatient of the Ibrox support, he earned the nickname "Old Mother" Hubbard. But the same Johnny Hubbard regards the winning of the Glasgow and District League Division One in 1972 as one of the greatest events of his sporting life. They also owed a great deal to the late Douglas Haggo, father of their current captain.

Their ground is an unusual one in that the pavilion and the bar are not in the same building, but the facilities are good. One of their number Paul Coffey writes for the Scottish Cricketer.

PROFESSIONAL – nearly all successful clubs employ one. They are not cheap to hire, and although wages vary and are naturally confidential, a figure of £20,000 is often quoted once extras such as air fares and the hire of a flat are taken into account. For a six month contract this seems excessive. Some clubs will never be able to afford one. Yet a good professional can be worth his weight in gold if he is prepared to take responsibility for coaching youngsters and helping the groundsman. It is not unknown for a professional to stay with the club as an amateur after his contract has expired.

The acquiring of a professional can be a hit or a miss basis. There are nowadays agencies like the Halcyon for example who have a list of people from Australia or the sub-continent who would be interested in coming to Scotland, or clubs can advertise in magazines like "The Cricketer" or "Wisden Cricket Monthly". But there is no guarantee that a player, however good he is in his own country, will play well in Scotland where he must adjust to the culture shock of the cold weather, loads of rain and a country which in many cases is vastly different to his own. It is not entirely surprising that New Zealanders tend to do well in Scotland, for conditions are similar in both countries.

There is also the visa problem. Sometimes a professional cannot be there at the start of the season because he has not yet received his work permit, and conversely, sometimes they have to leave early for similar reasons. In at least one instance in 1998, a professional simply disappeared and his club didn't hear from him until he telephoned from his home in Australia. Yet most professionals enjoy their time in Scotland and are an asset to their team. Quite a few Test cricketers have cut their teeth in Scottish conditions.

Other documented stories exist about "professionals" who never were, or who perhaps came to this country using the name of a bona fide cricketer. It is very easy to arrive in this country as a cricketer from the Asian sub-Continent and then gradually merge into the background of the ethnic minority. The big problem for illegal immigrants is actually getting into the country and passing passport control, customs etc. Once here it is very difficult for illegal immigration to be proved, and it is sadly true that some Scottish clubs have been used in this way

There are two problems on the cricket field associated with professionalism. Most competitions allow only one professional (some competitions are restricted to amateurs), and we often run into problems with the definition of a professional. Expenses are a particularly grey area, and allegations of clubs employing more than one professional are not uncommon. It is also difficult to prove that a team has not paid a player, or indeed that it has. It is the source of many undignified squabbles.

The other problem applies to the feeder Leagues of the Scottish National Cricket League. There the general standard of the amateurs is comparatively poor so that a good professional often plays a disproportionate role in the game. He also tends to bowl and bat in key positions, thus depriving aspiring young talent of the chance to shine. One game in particular springs to mind in the East of Scotland League in 1998. Clackmannan batted first and scored 183, of which their professional Ashok Malhotra scored 119. When St. Modan's batted, their Australian professional Cameron Coles hit 155 out of 184! It was electrifying stuff, but did it really do the game in Scotland at that level any good?

Freuchie have suffered in recent years from the fact that the Village Trophy competition, which they have cherished since their victory at Lords in 1985, actually debars professionals, and does not even allow an entrant to the Competition to employ a professional. This creates a dilemma for the club, because their efforts in the Scottish National Cricket League are much impaired by not having a professional.

The positive side of professionals is that youngsters can learn good habits from a good professional and one would not like to bar them altogether. Perhaps a solution might be to restrict their use to the Scottish National Cricket League where the standard is higher and the gap between amateur and professional is smaller. Certainly, one would not ever wish to see any more professionalism in Scottish cricket than there is at the moment. One just has to look at what has happened to Scottish rugby over the past few years, and the grotesque examples of the excesses of professionalism in Scottish football are incomprehensible at best and evil at worst.

PUBLIC PARKS – more than half of Scotland's cricket is played on public parks, often with rugby games, football games and children's play parks in close proximity. In these circumstances, it is difficult to shout about "no movement behind the bowler's arm" and other such niceties that private grounds can insist on.

Although many clubs have enjoyed a long existence entirely on public parks, often the loss of a private ground and the forced movement to a public park can be the catalyst for the dissolution of a club whose players have been used to luxuries like pavilions. Moreover, it becomes increasingly difficult to have any sort of control over the preparation of the wicket and often the players will arrive on a Saturday to find their wicket, if not deliberately vandalised, certainly damaged by the playing of golf or some other pursuit. Your writer recalls the occasion in Kirkcaldy's Beveridge Park in the dying years of Kirkcaldy C.C. when a horse and rider walked over the wicket one Sunday morning. Your writer remonstrated, but the reply was "public park"!

A particular problem seems to have developed in the Capital with Edinburgh Corporation who do not always prepare their wickets as well as they could, something which causes a great deal of embarrassment to the Edinburgh clubs but who find that there is little they can do about the subject.

Q

QUEEN, H.M. – although there is a team called Crathie who play on her grounds in Balmoral, and it is patronised by her husband Prince Philip, Her Majesty has no known connection with any Scottish cricket team and the sad conclusion must be reached that the good lady does not like the game. Even on occasions when she is presented to players at Lord's, body language seems to indicate a desire to be somewhere else, except perhaps the occasion when a famous Australian asked for her autograph and allegedly made another suggestion to her as well.

QUEEN'S CROSS – an Aberdeenshire Grades team who had to change their name because of religious bigotry! This team, calling itself Young Men's Christian Association, was formed in 1910, and played happily until the early 1970s, when they were told by the Y.M.C.A. establishment that they would have to stop playing on Sundays or change their name, and they chose the latter course. There had been an earlier team called Queen's Cross which had gone defunct.

QUEEN'S PARK – a Glasgow team who play at Victoria Park (not Hampden like their football counterparts!). In the 1990s they have done well in various Glasgow Parks and Evening League competitions and have been a strong force in the Small Clubs Cup, without however managing to lift the trophy although they were the beaten finalists in 1998. They are now mainly a team of players of Asian origin. Their problems lie in having to play on a public park, although they do have an adequate all weather pitch.

R

RACIALISM – Thankfully, instances of this are rare in Scottish cricket. Indeed it would be very difficult to find any evidence at all, given the fact that most teams in Scotland have or have had in the past a coloured man playing for them. Sometimes a good player will do a great deal to dampen racialism in the broader community – one thinks of Nigel Hazel in Forfar, for example, at a time when racialism was almost respectable and politicians like Enoch Powell were given more sympathy than they deserved.

At a game once on an Edinburgh public park, a youth decided to advertise the deficiencies of the comprehensive education system by shouting "sambo" at a bowler. A member of the batting side (white and waiting his turn to bat) grabbed the pitifully undernourished specimen of housing scheme humanity and dragged him into the pavilion to invite him to explain his remark to two other members of the batting side who were of Caribbean extraction, and one of whom possessed the physique of Joel Garner. The youth declined the opportunity and was never seen or heard again.

In Glasgow, there are one or two teams who are entirely made up of members of the ethnic communities. One thinks of Queen's Park, for example, who in 1998 reached the Final of the Small Clubs Cup. This is clearly to be welcomed and Scotland is a sufficiently tolerant and secure country to allow such diversification. Granted, the said Queen's Park did manage to get themselves into a little bother as well in 1998, but one hopes that this was not racially motivated.

Against this, there is of course the famous remark attributed to an Umpire in the West who was reputed to have said in answer to the question "When do you give an l.b.w.?" "It depends on whether the batsman is a Catholic, or not". This remark led to dark mutterings about aprons, flutes and the rolling up of trouser legs, until we were all assured that the remark was meant as a joke. As the Umpire concerned shares the surname of one of Jock Stein's Lisbon Lions, it is clearly nothing for us to be worried about.

R.A.F. – The existence of so many R.A.F./ R.N.A.S. bases in Scotland, particularly in the Cold War era, has encouraged the game and provided opposition for local teams. In particular, one thinks of Dalcross, Kinloss, Lossiemouth, Leuchars and Macrihanish and many other places. Often during the Second World War, the only cricket played in certain areas of both England and Scotland was by service teams. One recalls the film "Reach For The Sky" with Kenneth More, where the men were all playing cricket waiting for the "Scramble" call.

RENFREW – from 1998, Renfrew have played in the lower reaches of the Western Union. They play at a ground called Moorcroft in Renfrew, and their best success to date has been the winning of the Glasgow Evening League Knock Out Trophy in 1997.

RESERVE DAY – Such are the problems associated with the Scottish weather, that a reserve day often has to be allocated for important Cup ties, usually the Sunday immediately after the original date. The usual procedure is that if the away team has actually travelled to the original fixture, venues are reversed for the Reserve Day. If play is still not possible on the Reserve Day, and in the absence of any other mutually agreed arrangement, recourse is made to the dreaded "Bowl Out" – a Mickey Mouse way of deciding a cricket match, but surely preferable to the toss of a coin.

ROBERTSON'S FIELD – impressive new ground of Ayr, opened in the mid 1990s just across the road from their old ground at Cambusdoon and within half a mile of Burns' Cottage. It has already staged a Scottish International, and clearly the facilities are there for it to do so many times in the future.

ROSS COUNTY – playing at Castle Leod, Strathpeffer, Ross County are one of the outposts of Scottish cricket. But they have been in existence since 1902, and play in the North of Scotland League. Their ground at Castle Leod has always been their home, and we know that the first century scored there came from one Lieutenant Leggett in 1906 who, perhaps appropriately for a sailor, scored 111, the number commonly known as "Nelson", when playing for the Channel Fleet against Ross County.

Cricket was played in the area last century, and there was a Ross-shire County Cricket Club in 1879, which sadly did not last long. The present team was formed when Strathpeffer and Dingwall, who were both struggling, decided to amalgamate on 11th June 1902 and played games that first season against Tain St. Duthus, Clachnacuddin, Nairn County and Northern Counties. In their early years until the First World War they were able to pay a professional, the best being Leonard Tobbatt from Uxbridge in Middlesex, who once in 1905 took 8 for 10 in a game against Clachnacuddin. This was a club record until 1985 when George Mundell took 10 for 67 against RAF Kinloss.

The highest total ever made by Ross County is 304 against the Cameron Highlanders from Inverness. This enormous total was amassed in a match which does not seem to be able to be accurately dated, but we do know that the top scorer for Ross County was a Dr. Kaye, who scored 154, which is still a club record, although briefly threatened by G.P. Watson's 146 not out on August 3rd 1991 against Invergordon. The same G.P. Watson (nicknamed "Doctor" because of his initials?) hit 1,067 runs in 1998, which broke the League record and included 5 centuries. On the debit side, there was an occasion when Ross County were reputed to have been dismissed for 0 – but in mitigation, it must be said that on that occasion they only had 10 men!

The club's first major honour came in 1981 when they won the North of Scotland Cup, followed by the League in 1985 and 1990 and the Cup again in 1987. Since 1991, the club have had a reserve side who have done very well in the Reserve Competitions, proof of their flourishing youth policy.

ROSSIE PRIORY – one of Scottish Cricket's most venerable of clubs. They have played at their lovely ground at Inchture, near Dundee, since 1828 and claim to be the second oldest Scottish club after Kelso, although some historians would put Perthshire second. Their ground is difficult to find but well worth the effort, although there are the rural hazards of cow dung and midgies to be negotiated! The tea pavilion contains a small but excellent selection of cricket pictures and memorabilia, and there is the oddity that the away team changes in a separate pavilion half way up the hill.

The beautiful Rossie Priory ground outside Dundee. The opposition are Perth Mayfield and it is June 1996

Rossie Priory contain Hamish McAlpine (ex-goalkeeper of Dundee United) among their ex-players, and in recent years have done well in the Small Clubs Cup, reaching the Semi Final in 1998. They are a fine and hospitable club who have done much to keep the flag of cricket flying in what was traditionally a very strong cricketing area. Hamish McAlpine's brother Derek has been a consistent performer for the team for many years, and Derek's son Mark is beginning to do well for the club. They have a thriving junior section, and are to be commended for introducing the game to girls.

They were founded by Lord Kinnaird in 1828, and their connections with the Kinnaird family continue, as Diana, Lady Kinnaird is currently their patron, and two of her grandsons play as junior members. The original Lord Kinnaird brought in one John Broadley from Yorkshire to be the team's coach and professional. His son, also called John or Johnny, earned a reputation as a fine player and a prodigious hitter of a cricket ball. He had three bats, two of which are awarded as annual trophies and the third, which is called "Calamity Jane", is in the pavilion.

ROYAL HIGH STEWARTS MELVILLE

They play in the Perthshire League which they have won 6 times, the most recent time being 1996, and in 1998 they came within a whisker of doing it again but failed to dislodge the last two Northern batsmen. It was all the more exciting, for the game was played at Doo'cot Park, Perth, where on an adjoining park Mayfield beat Luncarty to win the title. Previously in the same summer, however, Rossie had won the Perthshire Knock Out Cup.

In 1978 they celebrated their sesquicentenary (150 years) with a game against the M.C.C. played in period costume appropriate to 1828, and it is a sign of this club's desire to move with the times that they would wish to celebrate their bicentenary in the year 2028 with another game against the M.C.C. but this time to include some of their female members.

Rossie Priory are a remarkable club!

ROYAL HIGH STEWARTS MELVILLE
– see STEWARTS MELVILLE F.P. and ROYAL HIGH

RUN OUT – without a shadow of a doubt, the most annoying way to get out. It is annoying because it is always somebody's fault. Being out to any of the ways that a bowler can collect a wicket is bad enough, but one can always shrug one's shoulder and say that it was a particularly good ball. Run out however is a different matter. There may have been some particularly good piece of fielding or wicket keeping, but the fact remains that it was an error of judgement that caused it.

The disconsolate batsman trooping off "Run Out 0" will of course curse everything in sight. There are two obvious targets. One is the Umpire who got it wrong and did not allow the benefit of the doubt, but a more likely one is the batting partner who called badly, or was too slow, or dithered. Friendships have been known to come to grief on these rocks, and woe betide anyone even vaguely responsible for running out the Captain, or worse still the Professional.

But run outs can be avoided usually if there is no hesitation or changing of mind. A good crisp call of "yes" instantly and unquestionably responded to will see the batsmen home more times than not. It is only when we get the Yes-No-Maybe that trouble arises.

From a fielding point of view, run outs are usually offered on an average of about two per innings. A good team, playing well, happy with their captain who has all his men in the right positions, will take advantage of the possibilities. They will also notice things like a batsman with a slight limp, an over weight batsman who might struggle for the quick singles, and any indication that communication between the two batsmen is not what it could be.

Run outs remain shockingly unworked upon in practice. They are one of the most appealing aspects of cricket and so often can swing a game. They are also very difficult for an Umpire (in Scotland sadly without any real prospect of an action replay) to judge.

S

ST. BOSWELLS – a Border League team, founded in their present form in 1895, who play at The Green, St. Boswells. There are accounts of cricket being played in the village as early as 1870, but the St. Boswells team of pre-1895 was a haphazard collection of whoever happened to be available. A fairly intense annalistic account of their first 50 years appears in the excellent publication "A Record of Cricket in St. Boswells 1895 -1945" by J.K. Ballantyne, containing *inter alia*, an account of how they dismissed Hawick for 5 in early 1928!

In recent years they have played competitive cricket in the Border League. They have always played respectably well, considering that they are a very small village, but their solitary triumph in the Border League was in 1983.

ST. MICHAELS – a Dumfries team who play on a public park called Kingholm Park. There was a team called St. Michael's Former Pupils formed in 1929 and this included a team called Nithsdale. This club never re-formed after the Second World War until 1952 when St. Michael's Cricket Club was formed, incorporating a team called the Dumfries Post Office.

From 1952 the team played in various local cup and league competitions, but the bulk of the weekend cricket was "friendlies". In 1985 the team joined the Glasgow and District League, gained rapid promotion from Division 4 to Division 1, and then joined the Border League in 1990. From the mid 1980s onwards the team had a second XI which has participated in the Glasgow and District League while the first XI have done well in the Border League, winning the competition in 1995 under the guidance of Australian Brad Spanner, whose batting average was a phenomenal 151.7! (Eat your heart out, Sir Donald Bradman – you ain't the best Australian after all!) They then rocked the Scottish cricketing world by reaching the Quarter Finals of the Scottish Cup in 1996, beating teams like Prestwick and Arbroath to do so. They have also played in the Small Clubs Cup, but like other teams in the South West have suffered from their own geographical isolation which has made it difficult for them to fulfil all their fixtures, particularly second XI ones.

St. Michael's have never had their own ground, but they have been based at Kingholm Park since 1961. This is a public park and has a peculiarity in that its pavilion has the river Nith running underneath it, a legacy from an occasion when the river burst its banks and re-routed itself in rather the same way that Hercules cleaned the Augean stables by re-routing a river!

The club has been indebted to several enthusiastic stalwarts like Davie Scott, Sandy McNay, Jim Scott and David Douglas, although their best player at the moment is Pat Druce, who has taken quite a few wickets for the South in District games. They have been blessed with many fine overseas players such as

ST. MODANS

Australians Brad Spanner (he of the phenomenal batting average) and Brian May, a fine fluent batsman, South African Hussain Manack, Indian Mac Spencer and West Indian Foster Lewis, who later went on to do great things for Ferguslie in the Western Union.

A peculiarity of this interesting club has been that they deserve a mention in any "cricket for the disabled" compendium for they have had a one armed player and a man called Jim Wylie who lost part of his leg in a sawmill accident and was wont to nonplus opponents by suddenly limping from the crease, saying things like "Excuse me, I've broken my leg. I'll be back in a minute!"

ST. MODANS – play at Bluebellwood Park, Bannockburn and are consistently good performers in the East of Scotland League, finishing up second in Division 1 in 1998 and losing it only because of an inexplicable last day loss to Murrayfield.

They were formed in 1950 by two young teachers at St. Modans High School – Alex Pollock and Davy Welsh. To a large extent they filled the void left by the loss of Bannockburn C.C., but the two men had to work hard to recruit local talent and eventually earn fixtures against local teams like Castings, Westquarter, Throsk and Alloa. The 1960s were the decade in which the Pollock family really began to make its mark on the club. In 1961, for example, Alex (who had already persuaded brothers Gerry and Jim to play the game) blooded his eight year old twins George and Alex junior into the team. These two have remained the mainstays of this team ever since. Alex's other son Eddie would also make his mark on the club. Eddie was a hard hitting, ebullient batsman who in 1983 earned a Scotland cap, although playing for Stenhousemuir at the time.

In 1966 Arthur McIvor joined the club. Arthur had played a few games in the early 1950's, but had then gone off to play professional football for Dundee. From 1966 until the present day, Arthur's batting and bowling have been of great service to St. Modans, and now, although in his early 60's, Arthur still turns out, often looking a great deal fitter than men half his age. This retired Primary School Headmaster now bowls a great deal slower than he once did, and bats a lot further down the order, but remains one of nature's gentlemen, and his contribution to the club has been profound.

In 1980 Alex Pollock senior managed to end a spell of homelessness by securing a lease for 21 years of Bluebellwood Park, and from that time the club has never looked back. Men like Terry Leahy, a fast bowler par excellence, and Willie Kelly, an effervescent character who keeps wicket and opens the batting, joined the club. In 1984, they joined the East of Scotland League and have steadily worked their way up to Division 1. Being an ambitious club, they intend to join the Scottish National Cricket League some day.

In July 1986 Alex Pollock senior died suddenly, depriving Scottish cricket of one of its great characters. The following day, St. Modans were due to play Mitre in a game which would have a vital bearing on relegation from Division 3. The club might have asked for a postponement, but the family's laudable decision was that the best way to show respect was to go ahead and play the game – something that Alex himself would surely have wished. Reward was granted when Alex junior took 5 for 38 and George scored 57 not out to win the game, and eventually save themselves from relegation.

The following year of 1987 brought the club's greatest success when they won the Small Clubs Cup, beating Rossie Priory in a tense Final at Lochside Park, Forfar. In 1991 they achieved promotion to the First Division of the East of Scotland League, and although they did not last long at this level (this Division then contained clubs like Grange and Heriots), this can be considered to be a remarkable achievement for the club.

Their professionals have included people like Robin Singh, who now plays One Day Cricket for India, and Raj Ganguly whose brother Shaurav the Test player once played a game for St. Modans as well, routing Kirkcaldy at Bennochy. In 1998 they had a remarkable Australian called Cameron Coles, who on one occasion scored 155 not out in a total of 184 to beat Clackmannan! What was really remarkable about that innings was that his number 11 batsman – Alex "Badger" Petrie (who heroically scored 7 not out) joined him when St. Modans were more than 110 short of the target!

ST. RONALD – an Aberdeenshire Grades team, founded in 1883 by shipyard workers from Hall Russells who were then building a steamship called St. Rognvald. They were founder members of the Aberdeenshire Cricket Association and have been one of the consistently strong teams in the city.

We've done it! George Salmond, captain of Scotland, receives the Invitation to join the World Cup after the defeat of Ireland in 1997, and (right) models Scotland's World Cup pyjamas – er, sorry, cricket costume.

SALMOND, George – Scotland's captain since 1995, and a fine ambassador for the Scottish game. George was brought up in Arbroath and his batting developed under the guidance of people like Omar Henry and Clarence Parfitt. He made his Scotland debut in 1990, has played 104 times for the national side and his best score so far is 181 against Ireland in 1996. After playing for his native Arbroath, George moved to Edinburgh where he now works as a Primary Teacher at George Watson's College. He has played for Carlton, but now plays for Grange, and deserves a great deal of credit for Scotland's performances in recent years.

SARACENS – an Aberdeenshire Grades team which sprung from Y.M.C.A. and were founded in 1959. Like Queen's Cross, they disagreed with the Y.M.C.A. line about playing sport on a Sunday, and had to change their name to the distinctly un-Christian name of the Saracens – men who fought against the Christians in the Crusades of the Middle Ages!

SCHOOLS CRICKET – sadly, cricket in Scottish schools has taken a severe dip over the past twenty years or so, at least in the local authority sector. It used to be no uncommon sight on a Saturday morning for at least three games to be in progress on the playing fields of schools, but several things have happened to militate against this. One is the emphasis in Physical Education Departments on the theoretical side of sport. There is for example a Standard Grade in P.E. which has tended to make P.E. teachers less enthusiastic about actually playing the sports, and cricket has been affected just like football and rugby. There are few signs of a backlash, and there is every reason to fear that this may be a permanent shift in emphasis.

Another factor was the teachers' industrial action of the mid 1980s which effectively stopped the playing of sports for many years, some of whom never re-started. In addition, there is the fact that given the massive intake of teachers in the 1970s, the profession is ageing, and the number of enthusiastic young men is few. When one adds other constant factors like the Scottish climate and the unhealthy obsession with a never-ending football season, it is hardly surprising that cricket in local authority schools is struggling, although a few outposts like Glenrothes High School, Dunfermline High School and Campbeltown Grammar School make a brave effort. In recent years a gallant attempt has been made in Edinburgh and District to recruit a Lothian Local Authority Schools XI to compete against some of the fee paying schools. One does not need to be a card-carrying member of the Socialist Workers Party to wish them every success, for cricket needs players and participants to come from every level of society.

In the private sector, the position is far rosier. There is the additional advantage of having fine facilities like rollers, scoreboards and so on, as well as a long tradition of expectation that there will be cricket. Among others, Dollar Academy, Dundee High School, Edinburgh Academy, Fettes, Glasgow Academy, Glasgow High School, Robert Gordon's, George Heriot's, Hutcheson's Grammar,

Scotland v Australia 1905

SCORER

Kelvinside Academy, Lomond, Loretto, Merchiston Castle, Morrison's Academy, Stewart's and Melville College, Strathallan, and George Watson's are active, and quite a few of them feed players into Former Pupils clubs, although most of these clubs are now "open" and no longer insist on the "old school tie" with all its quasi-Masonic implications.

SCORER – a good scorer is an asset to any team, yet some teams are surprisingly lax in this department, either relying on a member of their team to do it or leaving it to the other scorer and "getting a copy" later. In theory with two scorers there should be no problem with the scores, and, in truth, there seldom is. It is a job which demands concentration and accuracy, but is a magnificently rewarding one. The statistical side of the game is fascinating. It is often a fine way for a youngster to learn about the game, but if he is to remain a good scorer he must be able to resist all pressures to play when the "3rd XI are a man short". Many Scottish teams have fine scorers – one thinks of men like Neil Leitch, Allan Baxter, Joe Barrett and many others whose knowledge of the game and contribution thereto is immense, and occasionally taken for granted!

The statisticians! What they don't know about cricket is not worth knowing! Bill Frindall of Test Match Special with Allan Baxter (Scribe) of Cupar

SCOREBOARDS – vary throughout the country. It is very useful if the score is regularly updated, but very annoying when it isn't always done, or when the numbers blow over in the wind or get stuck. Sometimes scoreboards are very "busy" i.e. so full of information that it is difficult to see exactly what you are looking for. Some grounds have no board at all, and the information must be asked for. It is a shame for players and spectators have a right to be informed of what exactly the score is.

SCOTLAND – it is still the dream of every youngster to play for Scotland. Scotland now play a plethora of fixtures in the Benson and Hedges and NatWest Cups, as well as the Triple Crown Tournament, the Commonwealth Games and tours by teams like Bangladesh, South Africa "A" and Australia "A". There is also the traditional three day game against Ireland and other fixtures.

SCOTTISH COUNTIES CHALLENGE CUP – introduced in 1977 to spice up the old County Championship, but never a tournament which got off the ground, being increasingly used for pre-season practice matches and the final stages being played when the season is over. The 1998 competition, for example, was won on a rainy September day when Prestwick beat Aberdeenshire on a bowl out. It is now somewhat of an anachronism, but no-one has ever tried to get rid of it.

SCOTTISH COUNTY CHAMPIONSHIP – a now defunct competition which went by the boards when the Scottish Counties amalgamated with the East of Scotland League at the end of 1995 to form the Scottish League, which became the Scottish National Cricket League when they were joined by the Western Union teams at the start of 1998. At one point, the County Championship was considered to be the Championship of Scotland, but gradually fell by the wayside with the arrival of the various Cup competitions and the realisation, which dawned in the 1960s, that the Counties weren't necessarily any better than East of Scotland or Western Union sides.

Forfarshire were the first winners in 1902, and apart from the heyday of Fifeshire in the 1930's the honour tended to be shared between Aberdeenshire, Perthshire and Forfarshire. But Stirling and Clackmannan had their moments of glory, as did Arbroath and Strathmore when they joined in the 1980s. The last winners however in 1995 were West Lothian.

The benign Administrator – Alex Ritchie, General Manager of the Scottish Cricket Union.

SCOTTISH CRICKET UNION – formed in its present form in 1909, although there was such a body previously. They are now situated in Caledonia House in South Gyle under the wise administration of Alex Ritchie, who played for Clackmannan, Stirling County and Dumfries in his own cricketing career. They are the final court of appeal for disputes, of which there have been quite a few over the last few years. Much credit should be paid to the S.C.U. for the development of cricket in recent years.

They are not the first Scottish Cricket Union. The first was formed in 1879, but was forced to disband in 1882 after losing a financially ruinous lawsuit to a caterer who had been contracted to supply food for a game that was rained off. Between 1882 and the formation of the present Scottish Cricket Union in

SCOTTISH CRICKET UNION CUP

1909, the game was effectively run by the Grange Club in Edinburgh in rather the same way that the Marleybone Cricket Club ran the game south of the border until very recently.

SCOTTISH CRICKET UNION CUP – this is not to be confused with the Scottish Cup. It is a consolation prize for those teams who have not qualified for the Scottish Cup from the various Leagues that would allow such qualification. 1999 is its fifth year of existence, the previous winners being Arbroath, Ayr, Watsonians and Greenock.

It is run on a straight knock out basis, and comes from a laudable desire to give every team in Scotland a chance to play Cup cricket on a Sunday should they so wish. 1999's draw sees a Preliminary Round of three games on May 9th, followed by a 1st Round of 16 games on May 30th:

Preliminary Round	Stirling County	v.	Clackmannan County
	Arbroath United	v.	Pakistan Assoc
	Gala	v.	Uddingston
First Round	Falkland	v.	Edin Accies
	Corstorphine	v.	Helensburgh
	Weirs	v.	Cupar
	Huntly	v.	Penicuik
	Kelburne	v.	Selkirk
	Leith Frankin Accies	v.	Stirling/Clackmannan
	Poloc	v.	Gala/Uddingston
	Arbroath/Pakistan	v.	Stenhousemuir
	Dundee HSFP	v.	Perth County
	Kilmarnock	v.	Irvine
	Gordonians	v.	Clydesdale
	Holy Cross	v.	Glasgow High Kelvinside
	Brechin	v.	SMRH
	Inverurie	v.	Livingston
	Dunfermline	v.	Dumfries
	Kelso	v.	Forfarshire

SCOTTISH CRICKETER – a magazine, previously edited by Terry Brennan, but now edited by Mike McLean, 36 Marywood Square, Queens Park, Glasgow G41 2BJ. It appears three times per summer and does a brave job in trying to keep interest and information alive. It has a report on all Leagues, humorous articles, historical ones and personal anecdotes in the shape of a Diary written by Paul Coffey of Prestwick. It is well worth a subscription.

SCOTTISH CUP – this trophy has been run under various names, depending on the sponsor who has seldom really been interested in the game, since 1966. The first winners were Kelburne and the current holders are Grange who have now won it four times (plus once shared with Strathmore) in the 1990s.

Its format has been a bone of contention for several years, but most clubs seem happy with the way that it is at the moment. 24 clubs qualify in 1999 based on 1998s performances. These are the top 5 in Scottish National League Conference A and B, the top 6 in Conference C and the top 2 in each of the East of Scotland League, the Western Union, the Borders League and the Strathmore Union.

The 24 teams are then subdivided into 4 sections of 6. Each team plays every other in the section once, and two teams qualify for the Quarter Finals, the top team in each section being guaranteed a home draw. The draw for the 1999 Scottish Cup, in which there are 4 Scottish National Cricket League teams in each section came out as follows:

Section 1 –   West of Scotland, Prestwick, Strathmore, Watsonians,
               East Kilbride, Aberdeen Grammar School Former Pupils.

Section 2 –   Grange, West Lothian, Greenock, Freuchie, Berwick,
               Glasgow Academicals.

Section 3 –   Heriots, Carlton, Ayr, Hillhead, Glenrothes, St. Michael's.

Section 4 –   Ferguslie, Aberdeenshire, Stoneywood-Dyce, Drumpellier,
               Meigle, St. Modans.

Critics point out that the sectional format is unfair in that some teams have two away games and three home and vice versa. In addition, there are a great deal of meaningless games towards the end of the qualifying set-up if neither team can qualify. What is worse is that there are situations where one team can qualify and the other cannot and tries less energetically, using "fringe" players for example. In addition, there was the sad case in 1998 when Dumfries were unable to raise a team for a Scottish Cup tie – something that was clearly grossly unfair to all concerned.

Some people argue that it would be better to have a straight knock-out tournament, but it might not be so easy to arrange as what it seems, given the need for reserve dates and other Sunday commitments.

Yet, it is good that Scotland does have a Cup Final. It is just a shame that no television channel seems interested in covering at least the Final. It is important for historians to refer to this competition as "the Scottish Cup" no matter who it was sponsored by in any given year; otherwise the impression is given that it was a competition of less importance.

SCOTTISH NATIONAL CRICKET LEAGUE

SCOTTISH NATIONAL CRICKET LEAGUE – for many years, enlightened people argued in favour of a Scottish League so that, apart from anything else, someone could call themselves the Champions of Scotland. Football, Rugby and other sports all had a Scottish Championship, and although cricket had a long tradition of well established regional Championships as well as the County Championship (a competition that was rapidly beginning to lose credibility), a Scottish League was long overdue.

It could be argued that 1999 is the first real year of the Scottish League. It was formed in 1996 when the Scottish Counties joined forces with the East of Scotland League. Although feelers were sent out to the Western Union, they remained intransigent with the exception of Ayr, who broke ranks and joined for the 1997 season. In 1996 Aberdeenshire won, and in 1997 it was Grange, but they could not really call themselves the Champions of Scotland when the Western Union teams remained without.

In 1998, after protracted negotiations, the Western teams joined, but the price was the division of the 31 teams into 3 Conferences, basically to decide the League allocations for 1999.

Division One consists of:	**Division 2:**	**Division 3:**
Aberdeenshire	Arbroath	Corstorphine
Ayr	Clydesdale	Dunfermline
Carlton	Drumpellier	Edinburgh Accies
Ferguslie	Forfarshire	Falkland
Grange	Freuchie	GHK
Greenock	Hillhead	Kelburne
Heriots	Perthshire	Poloc
Stoneywood-Dyce	Prestwick	RHSM
West of Scotland	Strathmore	Stenhousemuir
West Lothian	Watsonians	Stirling Co.
		Uddingston

Two teams will be promoted and relegated from each Division. The two bottom teams in Division 3 will join a feeder League, whereas in 1999 a series of play offs will be held between the winners of the East of Scotland League, the Western Union, the Strathmore Union and the Border League to allow one team to join the Scottish National Cricket League. In 2000 therefore there will be three Divisions of 10. Thereafter two teams will be relegated from Division 3 and two promoted from the feeder Leagues.

SCOTTISH WIDOWS – based round the insurance company, they were formed in 1970 and play mainly midweek games at Inch Park, Cameron Toll, Edinburgh. They take part in the Edinburgh Parks Trophy, but sadly have yet to collect the trophy.

SELKIRK – founded in 1851, they play at Philiphaugh, Selkirk. They played originally on a public park near the River Ettrick, and moved to Philiphaugh in 1872, arranging a match against Grange to open the ground and another in 1886 against Edinburgh Accies to hansel the new pavilion. They were the first winners of the Border League in 1895 and have won the competition no less than 27 times.

Their heyday was the era immediately before the First World War when they produced five brothers called Grieve, three of whom, William, John and Walter, played for Scotland. The other two might have – James and George who both died young, but not before making their mark on Borders' cricket – James as captain and George as wicketkeeper. William and Walter, who played once and twice respectively for Scotland, were both killed in the First World War, two of 12 members of the club who did not return from the carnage.

Thus in 1919 the only remaining Grieve was John. It would be blasphemous to say that one brother could make up for another four whom illness and cannon fire removed prematurely, but John's performances speak for themselves and have earned him a niche in Scottish cricket history. Seven caps for Scotland, 30,000 runs at club level,

John Grieve of Selkirk, arguably the most famous souter of all.

including 1,000 runs in five separate seasons, 29 centuries, leader of the Scottish batting averages in 1934, a club record score of 160, which stood for 52 years. As well as that, he was an excellent spin bowler, and thoroughly deserved to be appointed President of the Scottish Cricket Union in 1935.

Other Selkirk Internationalists are T.W. Lang, who also played for Grange, Gloucestershire and Oxford University, D.S. Hiddleston, A. Blacklock, an outstanding wicketkeeper, D.W. Soga, A.W. Henderson and D.E.R. Stewart.

"The Souters", as people of Selkirk are nicknamed, have not yet had very much recent success, however, but they remain an interesting and enterprising club, doing things like going on tour to Barbados in autumn 1981. They had one statistical curiosity in 1996, when, in their game against Gala, the teams tied on 233 each.

The lovely ground at Philiphaugh has seen some fine players. Which other ground in Scotland could boast having witnessed Wilfred Rhodes, Frank Woolley, George Hirst, Archie McLaren, Ernest Tyldesley and Sir Arthur Conan-Doyle –

all of them bearing witness to the ambition of the club (and other Borders clubs), and its great success and popularity in the early years of this century?

Not the least of Selkirk's cricketing sons is Andrew Lang (q.v.) the Scottish literary figure and brother of T.W., A.C., and W.H. Lang, who all played for the club. Andrew Lang himself, although he wrote about the game (and many other things), did not play very well and is quite happy to describe himself as a "duffer".

SENDING OFF – there is of course no facility in the Laws of Cricket for a player to be sent off by the Umpires. Quite a few people regret this, for there can never be any excuse for the shows of tantrums and petulance that sometimes befoul the Scottish Cricket scene, as the toys are thrown out of the pram by an overgrown child having problems with insecurity and hormones. The Umpires have powers to discontinue someone's bowling if he infringes the laws about unfair play, intimidatory bowling or damaging the pitch, but the ultimate sanction of the red card is denied them. All they can do is submit a report to the appropriate authority.

Yet there is at least one documented occasion when a player was sent off by his own captain! This happened in a Brechin Second XI game in about 1963 or 1964. Ron Honeyman was less than happy with the captaincy of his team, particularly as Brechin were on the receiving end of a tanking. He showed his displeasure by allowing the ball to cross the boundary and ostentatiously signalling a 4. Captain Doddie Robb called him over and warned him, then when it happened again, sent him off! Mr. Honeyman's Brechin career came to an abrupt end, although he did make a re-appearance the following year for Montrose.

SHERIDAN, Keith – (Poloc and Scotland) – one of Scotland's better players of recent years. He has won 63 caps and his naggingly accurate slow left arm bowling has brought fine returns like 5 for 65 against Australia (including both Waughs) and 4 for 25 against Ireland in the game which qualified Scotland for the World Cup. He was one of the youngest ever Scottish caps when he was picked to play for Scotland against the MCC in 1989. In 1998 he deservedly won the Bowler of the Year award at the Famous Grouse awards, having been one of the few Scottish successes at the Commonwealth Games.

SHETLAND – a brave effort is made to keep the game alive in the most northerly outpost of the cricketing world. Appalling weather and sheer lack of population cause problems, but since the early 1980's there has been an Outdoor League and Knock-Out Cup, and also apparently an Indoor Competition held during the winter. The champions are usually a team called Knab. Occasionally fixtures are arranged against Orkney.

SHIP INN – in Elie, Fife the starting point for Elie Cricket Club. Like in Trinidad and Jamaica, they play on the beach. (See under Elie).

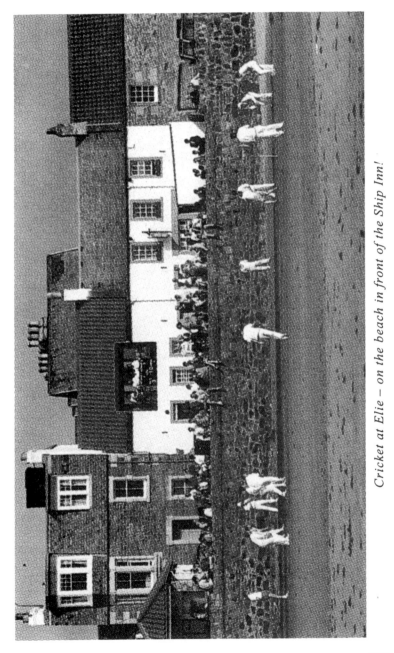

Cricket at Elie – on the beach in front of the Ship Inn!

A relaxed-looking Don Bradman, and a distracted Bob Sievwright before the Scotland v. Australia game in 1930.

SIEVWRIGHT, R.W. – (1882 – 1947) "Sivvy" was a famous Arbroath left arm spin bowler of the 1920s and 1930s who played 18 times for Scotland. He was born in 1882. In his first International season of 1912 he took 6 for 60 for Scotland against Australia at Raeburn Place, Edinburgh and one of his victims was the great C.G. Macartney. In 1921 against the same visitors he took seven wickets in two games, compelling the mighty Warren Bardsley to describe him as one of the greatest spin bowlers he had ever played against. For Arbroath, he bowled consistently well, notably in May 1936 when he was 54 years old, dismissing all the Aberdeenshire batsmen for 16 runs.

Reputed to be somewhat irascible on the field and capable, it was said, of more than a few bad words when the batsman seemed to be enjoying some luck, he was nevertheless a gentleman off it and a great ambassador for Arbroath and Scotland, becoming President of the Scottish Cricket Union in 1932. He met his death on 12th July 1947 in the way in which he would have wished. He was batting with his son Arthur at the other wicket in a game against Perthshire when he collapsed and died at the age of 65. Several of his family played for Arbroath in later years, notably his son R.G. Sievwright, and the family tradition still continues.

SIGHTSCREENS – can sometimes be a nuisance! It is better for a club to have no sightscreens at all rather than small flimsy ones which blow over in the wind or need to be shifted if a bowler changes to a "round the wicket" line of attack. If there are to be sightscreens, they should be fixtures and large enough so as not to need moved if a new bowler comes on. This can be very time consuming and infuriating!

SIGNALS – it is often a source of mirth in Umpires' households when he tries to explain to his wife and family the signals that he must employ to inform the scorers. A "wide" signal for example could be interchanged with that of an unlucky fisherman who tries to tell his wife the size of the one that got away. "Four byes" is not unlike that of a policeman directing the traffic, whereas the "Dead Ball" signal (at which some Umpires excel) could well be taken from the Charleston of the 1920s. Perhaps the most welcome signal however, and one which seldom meets with any dissent is the unofficial one from one Umpire to another of putting one finger horizontally on top of a vertical one to make the letter "T". It means "I am getting hungry".

SIMPSON R. B. – (1936 –) Bobby Simpson who played for Australia in the 1960s – a fine batsmen and certainly one of the best slip catchers of all time – is of Scottish descent. His mother and father came from Falkirk, and his father once played professional football for Stenhousemuir. There is however no record of his father having played cricket.

Wisden in 1965 lists Simpson as one of the five Cricketers of the Year following his leading of Australia to an Ashes victory in 1964 in a dull series. Simpson's 311 at Old Trafford had ensured a draw in that particularly tedious Test Match. Wisden says that Simpson's middle name Baddeley is "compounded from others in the family" implying that it is an ersatz, made-up name. Yet in the 1930's there was a Philip Baddeley who played for the now defunct Falkirk team Castings, and given the unusual name, he must be some relative of the illustrious Australian.

SIXES – Six-a-side cricket is usually played at the end of the season and looked upon by everyone as a piece of fun. Normally eight teams are invited to the Sixes, and with the players and camp-followers, the bar takings can expect to do well. On the field, one person is nominated as the wicket-keeper, and the other five all bowl one over each. Sometimes a four counts as a six, and a six as a ten, and a batsman has to retire on reaching 30. The cricket is often somewhat unsophisticated, but enjoyed none the less for that by players and spectators alike.

It is of course possible to play this sort of cricket indoors and various parts of the country have competitions like this in the dead of winter, but it seems difficult to sustain enthusiasm for this over any length of time.

SMALL CLUBS CUP

SMALL CLUBS CUP – an excellent competition which began in 1985. It is played on a Sunday on a straight knock-out basis, and it is for teams who either do not play in any League or play in a League like the Perthshire League, for example, which does not allow for qualification for the Scottish Cup. The benefit is that it allows smaller rural teams a chance to play out of their immediate environment. 1998's winners were Cults. Games are played at 45 Overs per side and the maximum number per bowler is 9.

The draw for the 1999 Small Clubs Cup is as follows:

Largo	v.	Ship Inn
RAF Leuchars	v.	Inverclyde
Ardrossan	v.	Edinburgh Beige
Kirk Brae	v.	Banchory
Boroughmuir	v.	Rouken Glen Young Men
Innellan	v.	Dunlop
Victoria	v.	Kinloch
Allan Glen's	v.	Renfrew
St. Andrew's University Staff	v.	Almond Valley
Huntly	v.	Luncarty
Kirriemuir	v.	Kingsway
Keith	v.	Dunnikier
Doune	v.	Monklands
Vale of Leven	v.	Trinity Accies
Manderston	v.	Highland
Cumbernauld	v.	Jerviswood
Dundee Asian	v.	,Montrose
Fauldhouse	v.	Old Contemptibles
Cramond	v.	Coupar Angus
Glendelvine	v.	Edinburgh University Staff

Byes   Buckie, Cults, Drummond, Ellon Gordon, Glasgow University Staff, Perth Mayfield, Queen's Park, Rossie Priory, Stonehaven Thistle, Strathearn, Townhill, Westquarter and Redding.

SMITH Alan – now an Umpire, Alan Smith of Stenhousemuir and St. Modan's has the record number of dismissals (1249) in Scottish club cricket. He first played for the club in 1961, and started to keep wicket in 1967 and did so until 1990 before playing one season with St. Modan's until his knees caused him problems. Keeping wicket to fine bowlers like Ronnie Melville, Stanley Bell, Clarence Parfitt and Abdul Qadir meant that he simply had to get dismissals, as Alan says, but in that he is being far too modest, for he was a fine performer and no mug with a bat either. It is a mystery why International honours eluded him.

SMITH, Mike – (Aberdeenshire and Scotland) a fine fluent batsman who has played almost 60 times for Scotland, scoring 100 not out against the MCC at Lord's in 1994.

SMITH, Roddy – (Grange and Scotland) brother of Mike, Roddy has surprisingly won only one cap and that as far back as 1994. A fluent left handed opening bat, Roddy's consistent form in 1998 with 931 runs at an average of 40.48 saw him win the Batsman of the Year award at the Famous Grouse awards ceremony in October and has led to renewed questions about why he has not been capped more often.

SOUTHERTON – a now defunct Kirkcaldy team who played at the Beveridge Park, and who have had at least two existences. One was in the early 1960s and another was for a brief spell in the early 1990s, the mainstay of both forays being Norman Halstead, son of Len, quondam professional for Strathmore and Kirkcaldy.

SPECTATORS – it is a sad fact, and much commented upon by overseas professionals, that cricket is no longer a spectator sport in Scotland. It is certainly true that the game does not do enough to market itself by advertising, for it is extremely rare to see more than 100 spectators at an ordinary game. Freuchie on a good run in the Village Cup can pull in the crowd, and several other occasions can be well supported, notably the Scotland v. West Indies game in 1995 at the Grange, but normally Internationals and Scottish Cup Finals are disappointingly ill-patronised.

And yet it was once different. Between 1880 and 1960, high crowds were reported at places like North Inch, Perth and four or even five figure crowds would attend events like Bradman's last innings at Mannofield in 1948. Often a young lad would have the job of setting out the seats and the benches for the spectators before play commenced at places like Leith Links in Edinburgh, and the Professional's Benefit in the 1950's at places like Strathmore and Stirling would be a great social occasion in the life of the town.

Sadly, from 1960 onwards, crowds dipped and then evaporated, possibly under the influence of television which similarly had a deleterious effect on institutions like football and the cinema.

SPONSORSHIP – a mixed blessing to Scottish cricket. Of course it is nice to receive the money for the game in this country is in need of any kind of financial support. It is not always very easy for Scottish cricket teams and associations to attract sponsorship, given the very low media attention that cricket receives.

The problem for a student of the game is that sponsors are usually able to dictate the name of tournaments. The Scottish Cup in the 1960s for example in its early years was known as the Rothman's Quaich. There are several problems about this. One is the ethics of tobacco sponsorship, another is that very few people

The days before whites! An early picture of a Stenhousemuir team, probably around 1876.

seem to know what a Quaich is (Strathmore's conscientious but crusty old groundsman, the late Bob Birse, for example persisted in calling it the Rothman Quelch) but a more serious objection lies in the fact that the winners find it difficult to convince people that what they won was in fact the Scottish Cup, not some Mickey Mouse pre-season six a side indoor tournament held by a curling club, who do indeed talk about quaichs.

The most serious objection of course is that sponsors suddenly up and leave, whenever they feel that it is no longer in their interests to pour money into the game. It would be a fine thing, one feels, if sport could learn to live without commercial sponsorship.

It is of course by no means new, particularly in Scottish cricket. Last century aristocratic patronage performed exactly the same function. Very often a Lord or an Earl would gift land, pay a professional's wages or provide transport and hospitality for visiting tourists.

STANGER, Ian – (Clydesdale and Scotland) an all rounder who has bowled and batted consistently well for both club and country, for whom he has played 57 times. Had a brief and unsuccessful foray with Leicestershire in the mid 1990's.

STEINDL, Peter – (Grange and Scotland) – an Australian all rounder from Queensland who has now settled in Scotland and is eligible to play for his adopted country which he has done on 23 occasions. He was at one point the professional for Cupar after a spell with Edinburgh Accies, but he now plays for Grange and has been a major factor in their success in recent years. He is also heavily involved in youth development.

STENHOUSEMUIR – founded in 1876, and one of the famous names in Scottish cricket. Their ground, The Tryst, is situated in the middle of a golf course and is close to Ochilview, the home of Stenhousemuir Football Club. Twice winners of the Scottish Cup (1973 and 1980) and many times winners of the East of Scotland League and the Masterton Trophy, they have always shown a tough competitive attitude which has not always endeared them to officialdom and Umpires. They owe their success to their well established and well organized coaching system, and the contribution to the club over many decades of Morrison Zuill, whose son Douglas is now the captain.

Over the years they have provided many Scottish caps, notably Iain Philip, who has played 129 times for his country. Another famous ex-player is Brian Hardie, who went on to play for Essex for many years. Wicket keeper Alan Smith holds the record for dismissals in club cricket. One of the more tragic stories connected with this club concerns a fine cricketer called Murray Peden who was capped 12 times for Scotland between 1973 and 1977, and died while at the height of his powers.

In the 1990s their form has shaded, and they play in Division 3 of the Scottish National Cricket League in 1999.

STEVENSON, DR. N. L. – one of the great characters of Scottish cricket. He played for Carlton for close on half a century, being appointed captain in 1902 for a season, then from 1911 until

Abdul Qadir as professional for Stenhousemuir in the mid 1980's

179

STEWARTS MELVILLE FP AND ROYAL HIGH CRICKET CLUB

1926 inclusively, then again in the mid 1930s and still was around for a few years after the Second World War.

Stevenson was probably a better captain than he was a player, for he was never considered for Scotland, although other Carlton players of the time like Sorrie and Jupp were. He was a great writer on the game as well, and his book "Play" (published 1946) is ostensibly a history on Carlton C.C. but in fact contains a lot more than that. To an extent it is autobiographical, but none the less interesting for all that. He tells us that in his first game for Blairlodge School, he took a hat-trick with his first three balls. *"And what a sensational debut I made as a senior cricketer!"* he tells us with a singular lack of modesty. He apparently made quite a habit of taking wickets with his first delivery, as he delights to inform us.

The eminent doctor wrote other smaller books on Carlton as well, telling of his Highland tours and other adventures, and of course eschewing stories that reflect less well on his good self. An indefatigable worker for cricket, he brought famous Test players to Scotland e.g. S.F. Barnes and J.W.H.T. Douglas, although Harold Larwood had to call off at the last minute.

STEWARTS MELVILLE FP AND ROYAL HIGH CRICKET CLUB – an amalgamation of a team which played together for the first time in 1997. The fact that they reached the Final of the Scottish Cup in 1997, then won the Masterton Trophy in 1998, proves that amalgamations can work, and often make sense. In 1997 they were known as RHSM, but now they are to be called SMRH.

The founding of Royal High School Cricket Club in 1861 is worthy of note, for it took place in a sentry box in Holyrood Park! Three men were present and they awarded each other the plum jobs in the new organization. A copy of the first ever minute of the club is in existence and hung for many years over the bar hatch of the Pavilion at Jock's Lodge, where Royal High played.

In 1996, Royal High Former Pupils had a good team, but a poor ground at Barnton (the grounds of the Royal High School) caused them problems with the wicket and accommodation. Stewart's Melville, who were themselves an amalgamation of Melville College and Daniel Stewart's (this happened in 1972), were to be relegated to the East League following an appalling season. It seemed a good idea to merge, and they did. The merger went ahead with very little blood spilt and with loads of goodwill on both sides. They now play at Inverleith, the original home of Stewart's Melville, and are potentially a strong team in the Scottish National Cricket League.

Under their various guises the combined club can list a very impressive list of Scottish internationalists, notably people like Ronnie Chisholm, Dougie Barr, Eric Thomson, and Bob Haywood from the Melville tradition, Bill Laidlaw, Charlie Scobie, A.V. Plowright and W.F. Turnbull from Stewarts and Gordon Haliday, Dougie Lawrence, Douglas Fraser, A.K. McTavish, Jim Roberts, Freddie Thomas and A.W. Wilson from Royal High.

1998 saw RHSM doing very well in the League, and looking likely to win a place in Division 1. Sadly a poor July and a catastrophic August saw them catapulted into 1999's Division 3!

STIRLING COUNTY – founded in 1862 in their present form, (although there was a team as early as 1827) and play at Williamfield in Stirling. Stirling's proximity to the Castle and the presence of Hannoverian soldiers probably meant that cricket has been played there since a lot earlier even than 1827. Previously they played at a ground called King's Park and Livilands, and moved to Williamfield in 1877, the ground being hanselled by a game against Aberdeenshire.

They seem to have been in abeyance between 1887 and 1892 because of a dearth of players, but started again enthusiastically and have taken part in Scottish cricket ever since, building a new clubhouse in 1902, the year in which they were one of the founder members of the Scottish County Championship along with Forfarshire, Fifeshire, Perthshire and Aberdeenshire. They were traditionally one of the weaker counties in the old Scottish Counties Championship, possibly because of the nature of the town of Stirling, which lacks any great manufacturing or industrial base. But they did have their moment of glory in 1952, when under the guidance of Willie Clark and with fine players like George Yorston and professional Irvin Iffla, they won the Championship for the first time. This feat was emulated only once in 1985, a success that owed a lot to the enthusiasm built up over many years by wicketkeeper batsman Neil Tranter.

Although not without some fine players like Willie Morton and Bruce Russell and professional Haravinder Sodhi, they have struggled in the 1990's, and now ply their trade in Division 3 of the Scottish National Cricket League. Former Rangers and England captain Terry Butcher has been known to play a game or two for Stirling County.

STONEHAVEN THISTLE – the first recorded game involving a Stonehaven team took place in 1858 when they are reported to have played against Laurencekirk. From 1872 (when they themselves date their founding) they played at Old Lodge Park, Ury (where Mackie Academy now stands), then in 1891 they moved to Cowie House. Raising over £500 (an incredible sum in those days) from a bazaar, Stonehaven Thistle were able to erect a handsome pavilion with changing rooms, spacious dining hall and verandah from which there was an excellent view of the town, the bay and Dunnottar Castle. Their facilities were officially opened in 1893 with a game against Aberdeenshire. Through aristocratic patronage Stonehaven Thistle were able to play against M.C.C. teams, notably in 1908 when M.C.C.'s captain Lionel Palairet, a stalwart of Somerset and England, remarked that Cowie House was the finest ground they had played on. In these halcyon days, Stonehaven could more than hold their own against the likes of Aberdeenshire and Brechin and one of their batsmen called Alfie Wood earned a few unofficial appearances for Scotland.

STONEYWOOD-DYCE

The club did not restart after the First World War (through loss of manpower and displacement from Cowie House) until 1929 and they joined the Aberdeenshire Grades in 1933, playing once again at Ury. Little is known about this period other than the names of players like Tony D'Agostino and Wallace Burness, and that having joined the Aberdeenshire Cricket Association Grade 2 in 1933, they won it in 1935 and 1938.

The Second World War then closed them down until 1955 when they were resurrected by the enthusiasm of men like Arthur Bisset, Willie Gall and Harry Allen. They won Grade 2 in 1971 and 1983 (the latter success under the guidance of Arthur Bissett's son Alan) but they had a somewhat nomadic existence and suffered because of it. They have now settled at Mineralwell Park (which has a certain notoriety for its lively bounce), where they built a new pavilion in 1994. Since then they have had a great deal of success in winning Grade 2 again in 1997 and more importantly in developing reserve and youth sections. They have yet to win Grade 1, but seem to be on the right lines to do so soon.

Clearly a team who enjoy their cricket, as evidenced in the story of their silly mid on saying to his bowler as he began his run up "Right Jim, remember what we talked about". From the slips came a chorus "Aye! Women!"

STONEYWOOD-DYCE – a remarkable club brought about by an amalgamation in 1991 of the two Aberdeenshire neighbours. Stoneywood were the older partners being formed in 1850, and Dyce almost a century later in 1948. Immediately after amalgamation they won the Small Clubs Cup that year (Dyce had won it previously in 1988), then joined the Strathmore Union in 1994 and won it twice in a row in 1996 and 1997. In 1996, they reached the Final of the second year of the Scottish Cricket Union Cup, but lost to Ayr. By defeating Cupar in a play-off at a wet Lochside Park, Forfar, in September 1997, they were entitled to enter the Scottish National Cricket League, where they have performed with distinction, so much so that they qualified to play in Division 1 in 1999. They have also had one or two reasonably successful forays into the Scottish Cup.

Their ground, People's Park Stoneywood, is a small, compact ground, where Stoneywood have played since 1880, but the most significant fact about it concerns the aeroplanes which land at adjacent Aberdeen airport with astonishing frequency and proximity. It makes for a noisy game of cricket! The clubhouse is somewhat spartan, but is one of Scottish cricket's longer lasting buildings. The club is friendly and is fairly obviously a family based club. The two brothers David and Robbie Lamb have a mother who lights a barbecue towards the end of the game, and the South African Peter Coetzer and his charming wife have three sons who are developing fast. Alan Barron is the enthusiastic Secretary, and in addition there is Andy Bee, ex-Aberdeenshire and Scotland, about whom many stories could be told for he is one of the game's characters.

Stoneywood-Dyce C.C. 1st XI – Strathmore Union Div. 1 Winners 1996

The history of the Stoneywood tradition of the club is well dealt with in their excellent Centenary booklet, and reveals how cricket developed in the Aberdeen area a good few years earlier than it did in other areas of the country. Stoneywood were founded in 1850 as a result of the influence of Mr. Pirie of Stoneywood Paper Mill. Their first two grounds were within the confines of the Paper Mill, and when they moved to the Market Stance (subsequently known as the People's Park) in 1880, they took with them their pavilion which has stood to this day. The game has continued to be strong in this area, and this phenomenon is confirmed by the astonishing progress of this team. It is confirmation that, where there is a will, amalgamations can work and prove a lasting success.

STRATHMORE – (sometimes called Strathmore County) a well established club, based in Forfar, where they play at Lochside Park, surely one of the most picturesque grounds in Scotland (it is also one of the coldest!). They have been there since 1873 and in recent years they have played host to many Scottish Internationals, and in particular seem to be asked to host the Small Clubs Cup Final on an almost permanent basis.

Formed in 1854, they are now members of the Scottish National Cricket League. They have a tremendous history and have over the years employed a fine litany of professionals – Len Halstead, Aston Powe and notably Nigel Hazel, under whose guidance the team were probably one of the best in Scotland throughout the 1960's. Only Blairgowrie in 1965 prevented them from winning 11 in a row Strathmore Union Championships. The club hotched with fine players like fast bowlers Neil Prophet and George Myles, spinner Gavin McKiddie and batsmen Don Crighton and David Patullo. From 1961 until 1965 they went 57 games without defeat.

They won the Scottish Cup in 1971 and 1992 (although the latter was shared with Grange simply because bad weather meant they ran out of dates for the much postponed Final), having reached the Final in 1969. They were one of the original members of the Strathmore Union, (which they won 21 times and the limited overs Three Counties Cup 10 times) but outgrew it by the 1980s when they and Arbroath left to join the County Championship in 1984, and won it a decade later in 1994. They joined the Scottish National Cricket League in 1996. Following a late rally in 1998 season, the club will play in Division 2 in 1999, not Division 3 as first feared. Their Second XI still plays in the Strathmore Union. Much of their sustained success over the years is due to their Chairman David McGregor, who was almost born into the club, for his father was a fine player for them in the 1930's.

Two Forfarians have won Scottish Caps – Gavin McKiddie and Mark Mudie, and it is a matter of dismay that several others of the team of all the talents in the 1960s did not do the same. Fast bowler George Myles, his partner Neil

David McGregor, Chairman of Strathmore.

Prophet, batsman Don Crighton and wicketkeeper Ian Ogilvie all had cause to feel neglected by the Scottish selectors, and their positions in the lists of great performers would indicate that they had a point.

They are renowned throughout the land for their hospitality and chivalry, possessing as they do a well-organized structure, and a playing surface second to none. There is a perpetual challenge of trying to hit the ball into the nearby Loch. There have been many claims that it has been done, but there has been no certain achievement of this feat!

Their name causes a little confusion with the Strathmore Union. It would be easier if they renamed themselves Forfar, but that would necessitate Forfarshire calling themselves Dundee. It would make life easier for the non-locals however!

STRATHMORE UNION – a tough League which now stretches far beyond the geographical term of Strathmore to Cupar in Fife and Inverurie and Huntly in Aberdeenshire. It was founded in 1929 and Brechin won it in the first five years. In 1949, there was a three-way split between Strathmore, Mannofield XI (Aberdeenshire reserves) and Perthshire XI (Perthshire reserves) for the title, but the 1960's saw almost total domination by Strathmore themselves. This League enjoys a reputation in the rest of Scotland for having good wickets.

For 1999 the Union has been revamped, and Huntly admitted for the first time into a First Division of 8 teams – Brechin, Cupar, Aberdeen Grammar School F.P., Dundee High School F.P., Gordonians, Meigle, Huntly and Inverurie. There is a Second Division of 8 and a Third Division of 10.

SUCH, Peter (1964 –) Peter who has played for Notts, Leicestershire and Essex is Scottish. He was born in Helensburgh in 1964, but unfortunately, the Scottish connections stop there for he was brought up almost entirely outside Scotland. He has played quite a few Test Matches for England, the first five in 1993 against Australia, and the latest being on the 1998-99 Ashes tour of Australia. In his debut game in 1993 he took 6 for 67 at Old Trafford, but thereafter throughout that difficult summer, he shaded. He never really bowled badly, but had the misfortune to be in an England side which was totally outplayed by the Australians.

He thus missed out on the trip to the Caribbean that winter but earned a place for the "A" tour of South Africa instead. In 1994, New Zealand were the first visitors. Such played in all three Tests but did not star, and dropped out of the Test team for some time. When recalled in the 1998-99 Ashes series, however, he did well and took 5-81 in the Fifth Test Match at Sydney. At county level he has proved himself to be a fine professional for all three counties that he has played for.

SUNDAY – wrongly called the Sabbath by religious zealots who managed for a long time to prevent games of cricket being played on that day. In the first place, anyone with an elementary knowledge of the Book of Genesis will know that the Sabbath or the "day of rest" is Saturday. The so-called Christian Sabbath does not exist. Nowhere in the New Testament are followers of Jesus Christ urged to keep a Sunday special, and certainly anyone attempting to ban cricket on a Sunday would be on distinctly unsound theological grounds.

Yet this was precisely what happened in Scotland until after the Second World War. Fixture cards for these days show that no cricket is ever scheduled for a Sunday. That this is deep and ingrained in the Scottish psyche is revealed in a Cameronian pamphlet of about 1750, quoted by Andrew Lang. Apparently some Hannoverian soldiers had been seen on the North Inch in Perth playing cricket on a Sunday. They are denounced as "the scarlet vermin of hell" and the complaint seems to be that they have removed the Stuarts and given us Sunday cricket instead.

For about two hundred years after this, we will look in vain for any enlightened attitude to cricket on a Sunday. Yet a close scrutiny of local papers will reveal that benefit and friendly games were beginning to be played even before the Second World War. After 1945, this trickle became a flood, and by the late 1950s, Sunday cricket was common practice, although some clubs suffered from quaint by-laws that prevented their grounds being used. The Aberdeenshire Cricket Association (the North East being a strongly religious area) held out until 1971 before sanctioning play on a Sunday. Nowadays, Saturday is the recognised day for League cricket, and Sunday for the various Cup competitions and representative matches.

SYMON, J.S. – (1911 – 1985). Scot Symon was a remarkable sportsman. He is of course better known for his football management career in which he managed East Fife (winning the League Cup twice), Preston North End (whom he took to Wembley to lose in the 1954 F.A. Cup Final) and Rangers (with whom he won countless trophies and must be unique in that he was sacked in November 1967 when Rangers were at the top of the League!) As a player he was a fine wing half, but was unlucky in that, just as he seemed to be getting to the top in 1939, winning a League winner's medal and a Scottish cap against Hungary, war broke out.

In cricket he was a fine all rounder for Perthshire and played 5 times for Scotland including twice against the 1938 Australians. On one occasion he took 5 for 33 for Scotland. He was the first man to represent Scotland at both cricket and football, a feat since emulated by Andy Goram.

T

TEA – Umpires are only half joking when they say that they judge a club, not by its performances on the field but by its teas. Some teams like Strathmore have a sit-down meal, but the majority provide sandwiches and cakes. Seldom can it be said that the tea is inadequate and Scottish cricket owes a great deal to the army of wives, girlfriends and mothers who do the needful.

Just occasionally, the system breaks down. Perhaps the player concerned forgot to tell the lady – sorry, to ask the lady to do the teas. Conceivably, the lady has taken umbrage, in extreme cases she has left him, because he takes her for granted going off to play cricket and expecting her to make teas for him. In these dire circumstances, as once happened at a Fife club, the players themselves must do the needful. It would not have been an insuperable problem if they had been batting, but as luck had it, they were fielding and after a pasting and leather chasing session, eleven tired men had to come off and slice and spread sandwiches.

This particular case was a merciful rarity.

TELEVISION – generally speaking, TV coverage of the Scottish game is virtually non-existent with even great events such as the NatWest defeat of Worcestershire in 1998 given less than one minute on BBC Scotland News and nothing at all on STV.

There has never been a Scottish game broadcast on terrestrial television in its entirety, although some overs of Poloc v. West of Scotland on 7th May 1955 were broadcast to the few people who had a television set in these days. Perhaps this was part of some kind of "anglification" policy of BBC Scotland, because it was only a couple of weeks previously that BBC Scotland showed for the first time the Scottish Cup Final between Celtic and Clyde – and had made the bizarre and, some thought, slightly offensive decision to send up Kenneth Wolstenholme to do the commentary, ignoring the talents of Scottish commentators like George Davidson and Peter Thomson.

In recent decades, Scottish cricket has been virtually ignored by all channels, although SKY has shown a little interest of late, notably Scotland v. Australia in 1997. It is hard to see why this is so, when sports like shinty and ice hockey have from time to time been shown in Scotland. It could hardly be imagined that cricket would be expensive to televise, given the grotesque amounts of money which is willingly spent on sometimes rather mediocre football. This will change to a certain extent with the 1999 World Cup, of course, which is already guaranteed huge television coverage. Much will depend on how the Scottish team does. A victory or two in front of a large TV audience would undoubtedly do something to regenerate interest in the domestic game.

The Tea Ladies

Mrs. Cissie Whitton

Mrs. Peggy Henderson

Mrs. Muriel McNab

Mrs. June Cowan

Watsonians' Tea Ladies, an indispensable part of the team, but woe betide any youth who forgets to remove his spikes, or spills tea on the floor!

On the other hand, there exists in Scotland a huge interest in BBC coverage of Test Matches with the expert commentary of Richie Benaud, in particular, highly rated. Admittedly, a large part of this audience did enjoy the spectacle of England being beaten and it has to be said that they have had more than their fair share of that in recent years. Occasionally BBC Scotland decided to anger more than half its viewing public by opting to show Ladies Golf from Gleneagles rather than a Test Match which is shown to the rest of the UK and seemed impervious to complaints about this issue, perhaps an indication of the undeniable complacency that has existed in Auntie's corridors for many years, and for which she is now suffering.

The awarding of the contract for Test Matches to Channel 4 and Sky TV in October 1998 has clouded the issue to a certain extent. It now seems inevitable that we will see advertisements between Overs and possibly even miss a few balls in the process, and the commitment of these channels to the long term cause of cricket is as yet questionable. On the other hand, BBC now has a great deal of money which it will not be using for Test Match cricket. Is there any hope that BBC Scotland might now be interested in the Scottish Cup Final, at least?

TENNANT, Andy – (Prestwick and Scotland) an all rounder who has deservedly been recognised by Scotland for his slow left arm bowling.

THOMSON, Kevin – (Aberdeenshire and Scotland) Kevin began life with Brechin, but has now moved to Aberdeenshire. He has been plagued with injuries but has still played for Scotland about 40 times and has attracted the interest of Durham County.

THORNLIEBANK – a Glasgow team who played at a ground called Muirend. They tended to play usually friendlies but also participated in the Glasgow Parks Cup, their last success being 1986. They changed their name to North Giffnock, but folded in 1993. One of their most famous players was Fraser Wishart, who distinguished himself on the football field as well, notably for Motherwell, Rangers and Clydebank.

THREE COUNTIES CUP – a well established and successful 25 Over Midweek competition. The three counties concerned are Aberdeenshire, Angus and Perthshire, but this is now somewhat vague because of local government re-organizations, and in any case, it includes Cupar, an undeniably Fife team. It was first played for in 1935 and its history contains a few oddities. They managed to play for it in 1940 (Forthill XI won it as Churchill became Prime Minister and the Luftwaffe flexed its muscles), yet not in 1946! The Cup was withheld in 1960 because of a dispute over dates. The Final was between Strathmore and Aberdeen University on July 6th. It was rained off, and as no date could be found to suit both teams as the Aberdeen students were dispersing and Strathmore's professional

TIMED OUT

Nigel Hazel would be touring with a Bermuda team in August, the Cup was withheld. It was a very unsatisfactory way of dealing with the situation. In recent years, the strength in depth of Aberdeenshire cricket has been proved by the amount of times that the Aberdeen Grade Select has won the trophy.

It is a tournament which specializes in close finishes, but none so odd as the one in the Final in July 1939. War was now more or less inevitable and imminent as Strathmore met Gordonians at Guthrie Park, Brechin. Strathmore scored 125 for 7. Gordonians batted bravely but could only reach 124 for 9 as the game ended. Stumps were pulled and congratulations exchanged. But then the Gordonians scorer claimed that the last over had been a five ball over, and managed to convince the Umpires that a mistake had been made.

Amazingly, the Umpires and both teams came out once again for one ball. George Youngson (who after the war would win 25 Scottish caps when with Aberdeenshire) hit the ball to leg. Strathmore fluffed a good run out attempt and Gordonians scrambled the two required to win!

TIMED OUT – Theoretically, according to Law 31, a batsman can be "timed out" if he takes longer than two minutes to enter the field of play from the fall of the previous wicket. As far as can be ascertained this form of dismissal has never happened in Scotland, nor one would imagine, any place else either. There have been occasions where such a dismissal could be justified, however, perhaps through some sort of internal dispute within the batting team of "who bats next", and then a desperate search for pads or other equipment. The Umpires are enjoined by the Laws to investigate the cause of any delay, and of course a wise Umpire will always bring into play the unwritten Law 43 (there are only 42!), which says that the Umpires should at all time use common sense. If ever a Timing Out does happen, one can be assured that it will hit the headlines.

TOWNHILL – a team from Dunfermline in the lower reaches of the East of Scotland League who face a continual struggle for survival in the face of apathy and poor facilities. They play at Recreation Park, Townhill and have played there since the ground and pavilion were donated by the Miners' Welfare in 1934. The origins are unclear but there was a Townhill Cricket Club in existence at the time of the General Strike in 1926.

Townhill play in the 3rd Division of the East of Scotland League in 1999, having been relegated from Division 2. They have however been in Division 1 in 1985, and for a couple of years in the mid 1990s.

TREES – a necessary phenomenon if a ground is to have any sort of charm. There can be fewer finer sights on Earth than trees blowing gently in the breeze on a fine summer's day on a lovely ground like Falkland, Strathmore or Carlton.

Sometimes there is a tree or two inside the boundary. There is of course the famous one at Canterbury in Kent, and on some Scottish grounds, notably Freuchie, there are several within the playing area. This normally presents no problem and a four is usually awarded if the tree is hit by the ball. Players can accept this apparent obstruction as long as the trees are near the boundary. A floodlight pylon, used by rugby players at Edinburgh Accies some 15 yards from the wicket, is a different matter, and in May 1998, a game was called off there on the grounds of safety, and jokes were made about appeals against the light etc.

TRIPLE CROWN TOURNAMENT – a competition of One Day Internationals which has taken place in the last six years in July between Scotland, Ireland, Wales and England Amateurs. Scotland have done very well in this tournament, winning it three times out of six. In 1997, mind you, a bowl out was necessary to give the trophy to Scotland, and the team disappointed in 1998, beating Ireland and Wales but losing to England. There were however mitigating circumstances in 1998, for at least two of the Scottish team were palpably unfit.

TURRIFF – joined the Aberdeenshire Grades in 1897 and have competed there ever since. In 1972, they received a legacy from a benefactor and offered the Turriff Cup, a competition to be played according to limited overs rules, along the lines of the then very popular John Player League in England of 40 Overs per side and 8 per bowler. The first winners were Kintore. Andy Bee, who went on to play for Aberdeenshire, Stoneywood-Dyce and Scotland, once played for Turriff.

U

UDDINGSTON – a town to the East of Glasgow famous for being the birthplace of Jimmy Johnstone and (less respectably) that of Peter Manuel, the mass murderer of the 1950's. The cricket team however was founded in 1883 (first game v. Tollcross on 18th August 1883) when Uddingston was a lovely village and before the Glasgow conurbation swallowed her up. Interestingly enough, their nickname in the early years was "The Villagers".

Uddingston 1933.

Their ground at Bothwell Castle Policies was officially opened in 1886 and it was obvious that Uddingston, largely through the influence of the Paterson family, were very ambitious, inviting teams like Grange and Edinburgh Australians to play (and defeating them). Founder members of the Western Union, Uddingston competed with conspicuous success in the early years, winning it 15 times up to the Second World War, doing particularly well at the turn of last century when they won six Championships in a row, although one was shared. In 1900, against Poloc at Shawholm, they hit a total of 347 for 8, a record for the Western Union. Something even more momentous happened a couple of years later in 1902. 1902 is the year always associated with Gilbert Jessop's 104 at the Oval for England v. Australia. Fewer people are aware that in that same year, the same Gilbert Jessop was in a full Gloucestershire team beaten by Uddingston by 55 runs. In 1925 I.A.R. Peebles who went on to play for Middlesex and England made his debut for Uddingston.

It can also be convincingly argued that Uddingston are the only Scottish team for whom a British Prime Minister played. This was Sir Alec Douglas-Home, who, as a young man and under the name of Lord Dunglass, was approached some time in the early 1920s and asked to play for Uddingston in a game against Greenock. Lord Dunglass, of course, was no mean cricketer, having played for Eton and the M.C.C and was delighted to oblige. Sadly, he chose this day to have a shocker. He dropped the great Greenock batsman John Kerr in the slips, and then was out for a duck. Uddingston players shook their head sadly and said "The Lord was not on our side" that day, and no further invitation was ever offered to the young aristocrat.

In recent times they have been less successful. The Western Union has not been won since 1933 and this in spite of fine players like Robin Prentice, who became an able administrator of the Scottish Cricket Union, and Scottish Internationalists like Bob McFarlane, Grant Johnston, Gordon McGurk and Sandy Brown (who was a professional with Uddingston – one of the few "Scottish" professionals)

Their closest brush with success recently came in 1967 when they lost in the Final of the Scottish Cup to West of Scotland, an innings of 93 by West's Pakistani professional Intikhab Alam winning the day for them. They joined the Scottish National Cricket League in 1998 but a poor season in the Conference season means that in 1999 they play in the Scottish National Cricket League Division 3.

UMPIRE – one of the most difficult jobs in cricket, requiring tremendous reserves of concentration, durability, equanimity and good humour allied to an ability to apply the unofficial Law 43 of the game, namely that "The Umpire will always act with common sense". The original Laws of Cricket define the Umpire's role as follows;

"Each Umpire is sole judge of all Nips and Catches, Ins and Outs, good or bad runs, at his own Wicket, and his determination will be absolute"

The use of the word "Nips" will raise a few eyebrows, as will the word "determination". Although in the 18th century sense of the word "determination" means "decision", there is also a strong case for expecting an Umpire to show a great deal of determination in the modern sense. He must be determined to do his job without fear or favour. He must not, in short, be bullied.

In Scotland, there are simply not enough neutral Umpires going round. The Scottish National Cricket League manages to provide Umpires every Saturday, but this is often at the expense of denuding the minor Leagues. This can mean, for example, that a very important East of Scotland League game in the month of August with a tremendous bearing on issues like promotion and relegation can be umpired by two members of the batting side. This can put a strain on relationships between teams, and sometimes the integrity of these "umpires" is called into question. Instructions from captains of batting sides to "umpires" have been overheard for example, along the lines of "They gave us nothing, so we give them nothing. Right?" or more brutally "No lbw's".

"She's my sugar candy
And she's awfae fond o' Sandy" (Harry Lauder)
Sandy Scotland, the erudite umpire.

There is nothing new about this, of course. In 1885 at Glenpark, Greenock, in reply to Drumpellier's 211, were taking quick singles and had one of their batsmen (Dan Kerr, the father of the legendary John Kerr) adjudged run out by the Drumpellier Umpire, one Mr. Sands. Greenock objected, demanded the removal of Mr. Sands and when Drumpellier turned down this inordinate request, refused to send out another batsman. The game was thus abandoned!

The solution to the problem lies, of course, in more neutral Umpires. Certainly, training courses are usually held every winter in Edinburgh and Glasgow, but still not enough people come forward. Any ex-player or even someone with an interest in the game will be welcomed. The fee is small – usually £10 or £12 plus travelling expenses plus tea, but it is a richly rewarding experience for anyone who loves the game.

Umpires are graded, with Grade 1 men able to Umpire Scotland Internationals and Scottish Cup Finals etc. There is an examination run by the Association of Cricket Umpires, which, though not compulsory, can help a man to improve his Grade. The important thing though is performance on the field. But how is this assessed? Mainly through Captains' Reports – a somewhat unsatisfactory way of judging an Umpire if, for example, both captains have been given out l.b.w.!

Some Leagues have "club Umpires" which means that each club provides an Umpire (not a player) for the game, so that, in theory, any bias would cancel itself out. A better idea might be if each club, as a condition of membership in a particular League, had to provide an Umpire to officiate at *another* game each Saturday. It need not be the same man every Saturday and would be a way of ensuring that fringe players and injured men were given something to do.

It is important that Umpires should be paid, even if a nominal amount, because otherwise there is the danger that the whole thing may be taken a lot less seriously than it ought to be. It must be seen as a job, not a recreation for a few hours or until the Umpire gets fed up and goes home. Situations can arise like the one in an S.C.U. Cup game between Weirs and Royal High in 1996. It was in the early rounds of the trophy, and each side was meant to provide its own Umpire. Both teams did so, but at the tea interval Royal High, suddenly and without warning, changed theirs, simply because the original one had gone home! Weirs rightly objected to this cavalier approach to a serious business in total contravention to Law 3.2

UNIVERSITIES – there is a Universities Championship competed for by the Universities of Edinburgh, Glasgow, St. Andrews, Aberdeen, Stirling, Heriot Watt, Napier, Dundee and Strathclyde and the winner plays in next season's BUSA competition.

As games have to be played in the early part of the season, this competition is more liable to be wrecked by the weather than others. There are also complications like exams and as students are, by their very nature, transient members of their community, continuity is difficult.

A strange thing happened in late 1998 when a trophy suddenly re-appeared at Napier University. This was called the McKerron Cup, in honour of a Professor of that name in the medical faculty of Aberdeen University. It was first awarded to Edinburgh in 1938, was competed for every year, even during the war (except 1942) and was last won by Dundee in 1982. They had won it four years in a row, but then the Cup seems to have disappeared and everyone had forgotten about it! It will now however be re-instated.

Not a man easily pushed around! Andrew Wood, man of Classics and Umpire extraordinaire.

V

VANITY – a phenomenon not unknown in Scottish cricket. Not to put too fine a point on it, one or two of Scotland's cricketers fancy themselves. One occasionally sees someone driving up loudly in a sports car (of course it has to be loud – no point in having a sports car otherwise) then stride out to the pavilion carrying a coffin of gear. On the field we then see him wearing a Harlequins' cap, possibly a cravat and certainly a multi-coloured tie to hold up the trousers. The sweater has funny colours round the fringes and he is dying to have a fielder ask what the colours represent, so that he can say in a loud voice "I Zingari" or "I'm not actually sure which Caribbean Island, but it was given to my father by a friend of Frank Worrell". We then get the pretentious twiddle of the bat and the long inter-over conferences with the batting partner. After all, cricket is an intense game, and there is every chance of a game for the First Eleven next week!

VALE OF LEVEN – a famous old club who play at Millburn Park, Alexandria. They have been in existence since 1852 when that area could rightly be considered the cradle of Scottish sport, considering how well football teams like Vale of Leven and Renton used to do in the early years of the Scottish Cup. They have performed meritoriously in the Glasgow Parks Cup, winning it six seasons in a row between 1989 and 1994. 1994 saw their greatest ever triumph when they won the Small Clubs Cup, beating near neighbours Helensburgh in a tense final at Lochside Park, Forfar.

VICTORIA – an enthusiastic bunch of Glasgow cricketers currently playing at Stepps Hockey Club because they lack a home since they moved from Richmond Park. They were formed in 1934 and have competed in the Small Clubs Cup and the Glasgow Parks Cup. They have won the latter trophy on two occasions, the last one being in 1980.

VIOLENCE – is fortunately not a phenomenon that one associates with Scottish cricket. Bust-ups within clubs are not unheard of, but actual violence on the field is rare. Yet two teams, Queen's Park and Renfrew, were temporarily suspended from the Strathclyde League following an alleged violent incident in 1998. They were re-instated at the AGM following profuse apologies, but relegated to a lower division. The Scottish Cup Final of 1995 between West of Scotland and Drumpellier at Hamilton Crescent was briefly disrupted by an outbreak of violence involving two sets of youths. It would have been grossly unfair however to associate either team with either of the sets of pea-brains. It also seems that violence is nothing new in Scottish cricket, for there is a report in the 1850's of a game between

VIOLENCE

Hurlford and Kilmarnock Portland being seriously disrupted because of the home crowd who "acted in an anything but gentlemanly fashion".

A pre season friendly in April 1997 was abandoned because of crowd disturbances. This happened at Lochee Park, Dundee on what should have been a peaceful Sunday afternoon. The game was proceeding pleasantly on the ground that Norwood used to play on, not far from the pavilion. A group of about a dozen youths had been confining themselves to the hurling of insults, but presumably fired up by drink or drugs, started to kick a football against a few cars in the car park. The police were summoned, or rather one policeman arrived. In spite of being seriously outnumbered, the gallant policeman managed to arrest the ringleader by putting his baton round his neck from behind and marching him off. The rest then, miffed at this, were then heard to say "Let's get the cricket" and invaded the field. Rather than let the incident get out of hand, the players agreed to up stumps and depart. It was possibly the best course of action, for what a burly fast bowler or two might have done to these under-nourished youths does not bear thinking about. Yet it was galling to think that the yobs were seen to have won.

A more serious incident occurred on the North Inch in Perth over 90 years earlier in 1905 in a game against Stirling County. Stirling had never defeated Perthshire, and on this occasion only did so by a single wicket after a confident lbw shout was turned down by the Umpire. The crowd, much fuelled by alcohol on a baking hot day, rioted. Some tried to attack the Umpire, but others were not so rational as that and tried to fight with anyone in sight. The constabulary made scores of arrests.

Barrachnie Park where Garrowhill used to play was by no means the most salubrious of spots and on one occasion, when Garrowhill played Weirs, a huge crowd of over 100 teenagers appeared. Sadly this was not to watch the cricket, but rather to see a fight between two girls. Appeals by the players for the young Amazons to ply their trade elsewhere were turned down in a torrent of unladylike language, but eventually the incident passed and play resumed.

A somewhat unsavoury incident reached the national press in July 1996 at a game between Penicuik and Gala. Gala had reached 130 all out, and having had to suffer some not particularly good natured sledging in their innings, decided to retaliate. David Simpson, Gala's New Zealand professional, exchanged a few pleasantries with a Penicuik batsman, who eventually snapped and marched down the wicket to join in the conversation, as it were. What happened next is in some doubt, depending who you listen to, but Simpson was quoted in the Press as saying "It was a little headbutt, nothing major. (sic!) He was waving his bat around a bit, so two of our side took it off him". At this point captains and Umpires intervened, and everyone agreed that the batsman should retire "hurt". He in fact came back but could do little to save his side who were dismissed for 90 runs. It was a rather unfortunate incident and reflected little credit on either club, both of whom have done a great deal for the cause of Scottish cricket.

W

WALMER – a team who played at Williamfield, the home of Stirling County, but only in midweek games and Sunday friendlies.

WATSONIANS – founded in 1875, Watsonians play at Myreside in Edinburgh, a ground which has hosted many Scotland Internationals and which has been their home since 1897. They started life at a ground called Bainfield off Dundee Street and then moved to First Myreside in 1879 before moving more or less across the road to their present site in 1897. Watsonians have tended to under-perform in comparison with other Edinburgh teams, but they have produced many fine players, notably T.D. Watt who was capped for Scotland 15 times on either side of the 1st World War and who was a fine batsman, a reliable bowler and an excellent captain. He later became Secretary of the Scottish Cricket Union. A.W. Angus and I.J.M. Lumsden are also worth a mention as fine players.

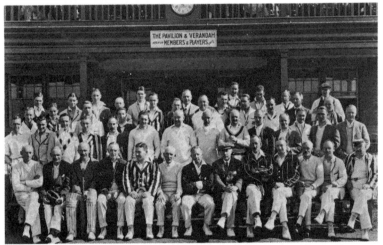

THE PAVILION & VERANDAH
MEMBERS & PLAYERS

Watsonians' Golden Jubilee – v "The Crocks" 1925

Bert Marshall, once professional at Perthshire, was groundsman and coach after the war until 1967, and arguably Watsonians' best ever year was 1976 when their captain was Brian Adair and their professional Kim Hughes who later went on to captain Australia. In that year they performed the double of the East of Scotland League and the Masterton Trophy. Other Australians who have played for Watsonians and have then gone on to play for Australia at Test level are Bob "Dutchy" Holland, a fine spinner of the ball, and Terry Alderman, who plagued England (and Graham Gooch in particular) in several Ashes series.

WATTS, Fraser

Watsonians enjoy a good reputation for fair play and for good teas in their impressive clubhouse and in recent years two of their members, Brian Adair and John Everett, have been Presidents of the Scottish Cricket Union. In 1999 Watsonians play in Division 2 of the Scottish National Cricket League. Their best recent performance has been the winning of the SCU Trophy in season 1997. They have a long tradition of touring in Ireland, going back to 1936, and a feature of their teams in the 1990s, since the club went "open", has been the number of Irishmen, as well as Antipodeans of all descriptions, who play for them. The school however remains their base and the club organize games for the boys when the school term finishes "just about managing", as they put it themselves, to field 3 teams every Saturday.

WATTS, Fraser (Carlton) – one of the rising hopes of Scottish cricket, Fraser, who has performed consistently well at youth cricket, was deservedly nominated as "Under 23 Player of the Year" at the Famous Grouse awards ceremony in October 1998. He has now made it into the Scotland team, and it seems that more caps will soon come his way.

WEATHER – usually a sore point with Scottish cricketers. Although statements like "we lost half our games to the weather this season" probably have a touch of hyperbole about them, there have been seasons when about a third of some teams' League fixtures were either cancelled or abandoned half way through because of rain. Other problems caused by weather in Scotland have included mist and the extreme cold that we are liable to suffer from in the early part of the season. Just occasionally, there has been snow on a pitch in April.

Cricket is often sneered at by devotees of other sports for being all too willing to cancel a fixture because of rain or a wet pitch, when other sports, notably football and rugby, persevere and even thrive in such conditions. It is true that there are many days when the playing of a fixture depends on the readiness and goodwill of the players, but the fact remains that on a wet pitch cricket can become a mockery because of a wet ball and an unpredictable bounce, and sometimes it can be quite dangerous. No real solution exists to this problem until such time as mankind can control and harness the weather!

Sometimes there can be a sinister *entente cordiale* hatched between captains who decide that they don't want to play. Imagine a situation in August in a League played under a percentage system. The team who are at the top of the League are playing the team who are just above the relegation zone at the bottom. Neither team wish to disturb their percentage. The conditions are verging on the playable, and the Umpires are willing to give it a go. But both captains insist that the conditions are dangerous to their players, and debating skills and dramatic performances are employed to this effect. What can the Umpires do?

Such scenarios can and indeed do happen. It is an utterly deplorable attitude in a country which suffers more from wet weather than any other. Yet it is a brave Umpire who invokes Law 3.8 saying, "Yes, the conditions are perfectly playable. Let's get on with it" when 22 players insist that they aren't.

WEIRS – founded in 1919, presumably by soldiers returning from the War, this Glasgow team play at Albert Park, Cathcart, Glasgow. They were 6th in the Western Union Division 1 in 1998. Their best moments have come in the Glasgow Evening Cricket League, a tournament that they have won three times in the last decade, as well as other successes. Until 1961 they played only friendly matches, but in 1962, they joined the Glasgow League and played in all four Divisions of it until 1996 when they joined the Western Union.

Throughout 80 years of existence, Weirs have had their fair share of ups and downs. They have tended to be overshadowed by near neighbours Poloc and Clydesdale in the south of the city, but in recent years have risen to a more prominent place in Scottish cricket, having now played first eleven fixtures against both the giants in their vicinity. Albert Park, their home since 1919, is a quiet, picturesque rural idyll in the midst of a highly populated urban area, although the ground has to be shared with other sports such as football, tennis and bowls.

On one occasion a Weirs batsman was doing rather well against the opposition, hitting the ball over the dyke into the neighbouring bowling green and threatening to disrupt their game as the cricket ball was seen to be lying "shot". An irate member of the bowling club returned the cricket ball with a few well chosen words and expletives not deleted. A fielder said to him "Just wait until one of your bowls lands over here!"

Much is owed to the Greenwood family of Bill and his two sons Neil and Craig, and to veteran Secretary Jim Clark. Craig Greenwood is undeniably the best player the club have had, although the two Shaw brothers, Alan with the bat and David with the ball, have done well in recent times. David has still some way to go, however, to catch up with Sid King, who accounted for 1400 wickets in a lengthy career.

WEST INDIES – one of the most encouraging days in Scottish cricket in recent times was the visit of the West Indies to Grange on 15th June 1995, an occasion blessed by lovely weather and a huge crowd. Although the result was somewhat predictable, Scotland did very well to get within 50 runs of the mighty men from the Caribbean who had topped the 300 mark.

Surprisingly, this was only the fourth visit of the West Indies to Scotland. The first time was in 1906 when Learie Constantine's father Lubrun was in the West Indies team and Scotland lost by 4 wickets in spite of fine performances by Maurice Dickson of Arbroath, Charles Mannes of Drumpellier and Harry Nixon of the West of Scotland. 60 years passed before the Windies returned, this time to Hamilton Crescent for an encounter that was sadly ruined by rain. In 1980 they

The West Indies touring squad of 1995 at Grange C.C.

came to Forthill once again to meet rain and the necessity of playing a one day game rather than the scheduled two. West Indies won, but Scotland emerged with some credit, particularly Willie Donald (4 for 78) and Chris Warner, who achieved an unbeaten half century.

Thanks to the quirky qualification rules of the Benson and Hedges Cup, Scotland can claim to have had at least three West Indian stars playing for them at one time or another, namely Gordon Greenidge, Desmond Haynes and Malcolm Marshall. Sadly, they have not been able to bring Scotland any sustained success.

WEST LOTHIAN – play at the strangely named Boghall in Linlithgow. It is a fine ground, however, and since 1996's Scotland v. Ireland fixture, it has joined the list of grounds which have hosted First Class Cricket. To approach it one must go underneath the Glasgow-Edinburgh railway line, which incidentally allows commuters to see some cricket.

They were founded comparatively late in 1928, building on a team called Linlithgow who played on a ground called Linlithgow Peel. The intention had been to play in Bathgate, but mining subsidence made this impossible and they chose Boghall. Since 1930 they have been good competitors in the Scottish County Championship, being the last winners in 1995 and having won it on two previous occasions in 1965 and 1984.

In 1965 they were involved in controversy at the North Inch when, in a time game, Perthshire supporters felt that they deliberately wasted time in order to gain the draw that they needed for the Championship and, in particular, bowler Peter Reid's massaging of his feet when apparently suffering from cramp did not endear him to the Perth supporters. 1984 was a far more comprehensive winning of the Championship, for West Lothian won 8 games and lost only one to Stirling County, but the 1995 triumph was not without its controversy when they were given 25 points for a game in which Aberdeenshire mysteriously did not turn up! West Lothian have won the Masterton Trophy on four occasions, the Scottish Counties Cup 3 times and twice have been beaten in the Final of the Scottish Cup. In 1999 they take their place in Division One of the Scottish National Cricket League.

Good players have included Fred Benham, who was capped for Scotland in 1949, and Malcolm Ford, who played 17 times in the early 1960's. He is not to be confused with his brother Donald, who also played football for Hearts and was capped for Scotland at football but not at cricket, although he was a squad member on a number of occasions. Peter Reid, that much travelled veteran of many a campaign and club, starred for West Lothian in the mid sixties as well, but in recent years they have had a sad inability to retain good players whom they have attracted. But players like Sandie Paris, Andrew Johnston, Ken Scott, David Fleming, Omar Henry, David Orr, Steve Crawley, Gavin Hamilton, Ian Bevan and wicket-keeper Alec Davies have played for West Lothian.

Boghall in summer during a Scotland v. Ireland game

203

WEST OF SCOTLAND

One of Scotland's strongest teams and a friendly bunch well organized by ex-player, the genial George Strachan, who also wore the Scotland sweater in 1965.

WEST OF SCOTLAND – in some ways the "establishment" team of Glasgow, playing at Hamilton Crescent, scene of many Scottish Internationals, Scottish Cup Finals and of course the world's first football International – Scotland v. England on November 30th 1872, ten years after the foundation of the cricket club in 1862. On the same ground in 1877 Vale of Leven beat Rangers 3-2 in the Final of the Scottish Cup.

Hamilton Crescent pre-dates the West of Scotland Cricket Club, for a team called Clutha played there before. Indeed West of Scotland were criticised by some for taking over Hamilton Crescent which was then in the village of Partick at some considerable distance from the centre of Glasgow.

Their playing record over the years has been patchy with the Western Union won in 1897, 1908, only once between the Wars in 1936, then 1968 and then four times in recent years. In 1997, they were the last ever winners before the amalgamation with the Scottish National Cricket League. Their greatest national success was winning the Scottish Cup in 1967 and 1989.

Currently however they are a fine side with good Scotland players like Craig Wright and Gregor Maiden. In 1998, they lived up to their potential by winning their Conference of the Scottish National Cricket League, and in 1999 they play in the First Division, and start as one of the favourites.

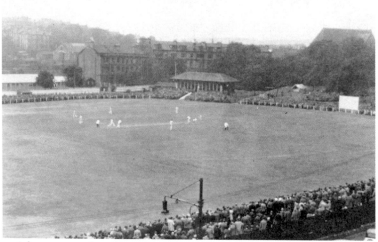

A huge crowd at Hamilton Crescent, Glasgow, in the 1930's.

Famous players have included David Snodgrass, who played 30 times for Scotland in the 1980s, and professionals Intikhab Alam, quondam player and Manager of Pakistan, and the colourful Salahuddin, who excelled with both bat and ball in the late 1960s and early 1970s.

It is probably true to say that their ground is more famous than the club. It became the natural "Hampden" of Scottish cricket at an early stage and although it faces strong competition from Grange nowadays, it is a fine setting for big games. In 1926 it saw the Australians Ponsford and Macartney score centuries, and in 1930 Bradman inevitably did likewise. During the War in the Clydebank blitz, it suffered some peripheral damage but recovered well and in 1941 staged the first ever Sunday game in Glasgow in which admission money was legally sanctioned. This was East v. West for the City of Glasgow War Relief Fund.

WESTBURN – an Aberdeenshire Grades team who may or may not be the "Westbourne" who were a founder member in 1884. They play at Westburn Park in the Rosemount area of the city and have had varying degrees of success in the Grades.

WESTERN UNION – Until 1997, this was the peak of ambition for any Scottish club west of Stirling. It was founded in 1893 with six member clubs viz. Clydesdale, Greenock, West of Scotland, Drumpellier, Poloc and Uddingston (the first winners were Greenock) and was played for every year apart from the war years. Curiously in 1914 when War was declared on August 4th, the Western Union continued its fixtures, Uddingston winning the title when the British Expeditionary Force was already in the field (and suffering casualties) at Mons, whereas in 1939 when one would have thought that everything would have been completed by September 3rd, the competition was scrapped.

It was often felt that the Western Union was a "closed shop" as far as the rest of Strathclyde was concerned, and their reluctance to allow other teams to join them was a source of resentment, but with the defection of the 10 top teams to join the Scottish National Cricket League in 1998, the Western Union has been much diminished, but has not disappeared altogether. In 1998, the Union was won by East Kilbride who led from a very early stage with Glasgow Accies coming second.

In view of the "Conference" structure of the Scottish National Cricket League in 1988, there was no promotion for East Kilbride, but it is envisaged that the Western Union will in future act as a "feeder" League with the top team entering a series of play-offs with the winner of the East League, the Border League and the Strathmore Union for a place in the Scottish National Cricket League.

WESTQUARTER (REDDING) – a team who play in the lower reaches of the East of Scotland League. Sadly they were relegated in 1998, so they are now in Division 3 in 1999. They used to play at a ground called Blairlodge until 1992, then they played at the BP Club in Grangemouth until 1997, but in 1998 they moved to Roughhaugh Farm, where they are currently involved in converting a barn into changing rooms with plans now to build a clubhouse.

Famous players in the past include Gary Gillespie, who played centre half for Liverpool, Celtic and Scotland, and their best personal achievement is that of Frank Riddoch, who took 10 for 44 in a match against Dunfermline Carnegie.

WIDE – an area of controversy, not helped by the fact that the rules are different in the various competitions. Law 25 enjoins the Umpire to call Wide if the ball "passes out of reach of the striker". Some competitions, notably the Scottish National Cricket League, have altered this so that a Wide should be given if the batsman is deprived of the chance to play "a normal cricketing stroke". This is done for the laudable motive of cutting down on negative bowling to prevent a batsman scoring boundaries.

This leads to all sorts of disputes, however, and tends to mean that most balls going down the leg side will be "wided". But not all Umpires are equally strict, and one does hear complaints about inconsistency. Quite a lot of this self-righteous twaddle ignores the simple fact that if the ball is bowled at the stumps and the batsman has to play the ball, a Wide cannot be given.

The Umpire must be the judge, and it is a very subjective judgement. One recalls the true story of a Scottish bowler being "wided" and doubting the Umpire's judgement, enquiring of the Umpire "Hoo's that a Wide?". The answer was instantaneous and honest "Cos I f—ing said it was a Wide!"

WILLIAMSON Greig (Clydesdale and Scotland) – a good all rounder who has played for Scotland off and on since 1989, winning a total of 77 caps. He was one of Scotland's "Players of the Year" in 1996, no doubt thanks to his fine aggressive innings of 57 against the West Indies at Grange the previous year.

WINTER – *"I've seen yon weary winter sun*
Twice forty times return
And every time has added proof
That Man Was Made To Mourn"

So says the "learned sage" in Robbie Burns' depressing dirge "Man Was Made To Mourn".

What do cricketers do in the winter in Scotland? The answer seems to be very little, as only the occasional AGM or meeting happens until the New Year. A few lucky ones can migrate to warmer climes, but most tend to forget all about the game, concentrating their energies on rugby, football, hockey or some other sport.

After the New Year, things begin to stir

And not through eastern windows only
When daylight comes, comes in the light.
In front, the sun climbs slow, how slowly
But westward, look, the land is bright!

The wonderfully evocative words of Arthur Clough, much loved by Winston Churchill during the dark days of World War 2, are very applicable to the gradual lengthening of the day, the looking out of kit, the practices (indoor at first perhaps if you play for an imaginative team then, by April, outdoors), the excitement generated by the thought of the first game and the realisation that the first love beckons once again. Like other kinds of love, however, the reality does not always match up to the promise, and the pain can overwhelm the pleasure. It usually rains early in the season in Scotland and it is not unknown for May to be well advanced before the first game can be completed!

WOMEN'S CRICKET – barely exists in Scotland, although it is not unknown for a brave virago to play in a men's team. Very few women's games have been played, although there is a tradition that Hillhead High School Former Pupils were originally a ladies cricket team in the days before the First World War. This may not be such a crazy idea after all, for the Edwardian era and the years immediately prior to the First World War saw women, particularly middle class women of the type that would have gone to Hillhead High School, agitating for the vote and even contraception! Perhaps their dear papas would feel that playing cricket would divert their minds from other more subversive and sinister activities. In modern times the exploits of girls like Lisa Batty of Helensburgh make one feel that this side of the game may yet be developed, and of course it is not entirely unknown for the occasional brave lady to play in the male game – one thinks of Nicola Hargreave of Gargunnock for example.

No domestic arguments here! Mr & Mrs Hargreave both play for Gargunnock against Crieff in 1994.

From the annals of Carlton Cricket Club comes a record of one of the first known ladies cricket matches to be played in Scotland. This occurred on 2nd July 1923 when the young ladies of Craigmount School played Carlton's men's team. The date of 1923 makes it hard not to see a connection with the female emancipation that had come about since the First World War with some women now allowed to vote since 1918, having spent the war years doing things like conducting trams, to the horror of the more traditionalist elements of British Society.

Dr. N.L. Stevenson, the chronicler of Carlton, is worried about this trend. "What of the Umpires, too?... Could any mere man be trusted to steel his heart and give impartial decisions? A winsome smile or an appealing look would bring about more bad l.b.w. decisions than the most frenzied "How's That" of today". Dr. Stevenson need not have worried. 11 men from Carlton batting left handed were more than a match for the 15 young ladies of the School, and it seems in any case to have been an experiment which was not repeated, or if it were, certainly not sustained.

From time to time teams like Berwick have had a Ladies' team, but the whole episode is usually treated with a certain amount of levity. Typically from Aberdeenshire, that hot bed of Scottish cricket, comes the Rosslyn Ladies C.C., who overcame a certain amount of male prejudice in the early 1980s to play a few friendlies against Reserve Grade teams. It would be nice to see a few more women's cricket teams. Perhaps they could bring their husbands along to make the teas.

Freuchie, the success story of village cricket, not surprisingly has on several occasions in the last 10 years arranged ladies fixtures. Equally unsurprisingly the Christie family has been involved with Aileen, wife of Brian and daughter-in-law of David, well to the fore. They have played games against St. Andrew's University, Dundee Ladies, Newburgh and an Edinburgh select team at Grange. It has been somewhat sporadic, but enthusiastic nevertheless.

For organized competitive women's cricket, we must cross the border and Grange Ladies have done just that. Not only have they competed in the Northumberland Ladies League, they actually, under the guidance of Linda Spence, won it in 1998, and some of the team are vying for selection for the Northumberland side to play against other English counties. On one occasion before a Scottish Cup match against Ayr, Grange Ladies took on Ayr Ladies, but, sadly, there does not seem to be any organized Women's League Cricket in Scotland.

WRIGHT, Craig – a fine young all rounder who captains West of Scotland and has now played 19 times for Scotland. His finest hour for Scotland without a doubt was his match winning 5-23 against Worcestershire in the victory in the NatWest trophy in June 1998. These included the prize scalps of Hick and Moody, both caught by Alec Davies behind the stumps, as indeed were two others. Such successes led to him being nominated the All Rounder of the Year at the Famous Grouse awards ceremony in October 1998.

Craig Wright receives his Man of the Match award after taking 5 for 23 in Scotland's defeat of Worcestershire in the Nat West Trophy in 1998.

X

X is the way that a wide is recorded in the scorebook. A wide is an extra, something that can easily be avoided by bowling straight!

XMAS DAY – some games on Xmas day have been arranged in the past, but only as a novelty.

Y

YARNOLD, Hugo – (1917 – 1974) the tragic death of Umpire Hugo Yarnold on August 13th 1974, when he was driving home after officiating at Northamptonshire v. Essex and his car collided with an eight wheel lorry in Leamington, did not seem at first sight to have much to do with Scotland. But thus perished the little man who seems to be the only person to have set up a world record at a Scottish ground.

The ground was Forthill, Broughty Ferry, the year was 1951 and the occasion was a friendly (although First Class) match between Scotland and Worcestershire. Wicket keeper Yarnold's haul of 7 dismissals is not a record (many people have emulated that including Scotland's Jimmy Brown in a game against Ireland in Dublin in 1957) but the fact that 6 of them were stumpings is. It is a record that is likely to stay for some considerable time, for the closest that anyone has come to that is 4 by three wicketkeepers, one of them the famous Australian Don Tallon for Queensland against Victoria in 1938-39. 6 stumpings in an innings possibly says a great deal about Roly Jenkins' leg breaks and googlies (4 of the stumpings were off Jenkins) and it may say a great deal about the lack of Scottish technique against such bowling, as well as the Forthill pitch, but nothing can be taken away from Hugo Yarnold.

The game began on Saturday 30th June 1951 with Scotland dismissed for only 114 with Jimmy Aitchison's 64 the only resistance to Jenkins 5-41. As an indication of things to come Yarnold took one stumping, that of Freddie Thomas. Worcestershire then went in on the Saturday afternoon and knocked Scotland all over Dundee for 351, with Outschoorn scoring 200 and Yarnold himself (no mean performer with the bat) 46. Scotland were glad of the obligatory Sabbath day of rest in these days and it was on the Monday with Scotland 237 runs behind that the fun started.

After a reasonable start with Aitchison getting 44 and Ian Anderson of Kelburne a respectable 40, Scotland collapsed before Jenkins and Yarnold, and the game did not reach the third of its scheduled three days. Jenkins took 5 for 69 with his venomous leg breaks delivered with a curious crab like action which some pundits questioned, and Yarnold's six stumpings and a catch were at the expense of 12 byes.

YOUNG MEN OF ROUKEN GLEN

Yet Yarnold had his bad luck as well. Both knee caps were removed before his career ended and, although he served Worcestershire well from 1938 until 1955, he never broke through to the England Test side. His career as an Umpire was more successful for he stood in three Test Matches in 1967 and 1968 before his fatal accident in 1974.

YOUNG MEN OF ROUKEN GLEN – a spirited bunch of enthusiastic cricketers who came together in 1991, and began playing in 1992, losing their first ever game off the last ball. In 1996 they competed in the Small Clubs Cup for the first time and in 1999 they will play for the first time in the Fifth Division of the Western Cricket Union.

Their fundamental and laudable philosophy, which they call Utilitarianism, is to "maximise the involvement of every participant in every game (not merely the most gifted) which should equal maximum entertainment" and thus to introduce the game to people who would not otherwise play it.

They tell for example with gusto of their game at Aberfeldy on the 10th of May 1998, the day after Celtic won the Premier League. A mixture of triumphant Tims, sulking Huns and one or two sad (as they themselves put it) cases who supported Partick Thistle, Aberdeen and Dundee United had all been drinking rather heavily to celebrate or forget as appropriate. The hung over Young Men were set 90 to win, and seemed to be struggling at 80 for 9, particularly as their last two had never played the game before, and had been bevvying rather heavily. Yet two heroes were born when "beautifully placed slip drives" brought home the bacon for the Young Men of Rouken Glen.

From such small acorns grow large oaks, and the Young Men are to be commended for introducing the game of cricket to other young men with perhaps no great tradition of the game.

YOUNGSON, G.W. – (1919 –) famous Aberdeenshire player who won 25 caps for Scotland between 1947 and 1955. He started off playing for Gordonians and was involved in the famous victory in 1939 against Strathmore in the Final of the Three Counties Cup when Strathmore had apparently won the Cup, but the Umpire had miscounted and they had to come back for the extra ball.

In 1947, Youngson achieved the remarkable feat for a Scotsman of topping the First Class Bowling Averages. In a season where Compton topped the batting averages, not many people would have guessed that Youngson would beat people like Johnnie Clay of Glamorgan, Bill Bowes of Yorkshire and Jim Laker of Surrey. Granted, he only bowled 58 Overs but his figures of 58 - 21 - 105 - 13 gave him an average of 8.07 and 6 of his wickets were against Warwickshire. It is hardly surprising that with a pace bowler like that in their line-up, Aberdeenshire also won the Scottish Counties Championship that year and in other years about that time, for Youngson played a great part in the post-war Mannofield glory years.

Z

ZENECA GRANGEMOUTH – a small team, based on the pharmaceutical firm, who have done well to keep the game going in such a heavily industrialised part of Scotland. In 1999 they play in Division 2 of the East League by virtue of their having been promoted from Division 3 in 1998.

Zeneca rose Phoenix like from the Ashes of an earlier club in the late 1980s. They were at one point called ICI and when they re-started they played only 20 Over slog matches in a midweek League before graduating firstly to the Grades and then to the League. The impetus for this improvement came from Paul Goerick, an Englishman who has now emigrated to Australia and will be sadly missed.

The team is about half Zeneca Works Personnel and draws its players from all nationalities. They play at the Zeneca Recreation Club Grounds in Earls Road, Grangemouth.

ZUILL, A.M. – (1937 –) famous batsman for Stenhousemuir who scored 27,588 runs in club cricket in a lengthy career which ran from 1955 to 1992. During his captaincy of Stenhousemuir, the team had a great run of success, due in no small measure to his knowledge of the game and the rigid discipline that he imposed on the field. He played 15 times for Scotland and his son Douglas now captains Stenhousemuir.

"My Dad plays for Scotland and my grandad takes photos. My name is Jamie Alexander Gavin."